WALKING HUMBLY WITH GOD

THE LIFE AND WRITINGS OF RABBI HERSHEL JONAH MATT

WALKING HUMBLY WITH GOD

THE LIFE AND WRITINGS OF
RABBI HERSHEL JONAH MATT

Edited by

Daniel C. Matt

KTAV Publishing House, Inc.
Hoboken, N.J. 07030

Copyright © 1993
Daniel C. Matt
Library of Congress Cataloging-in-Publication Data

Matt, Hershel Jonah, d. 1987.
    Walking humbly with God : the life and writings of Rabbi Hershel
Jonah Matt / edited by Daniel C. Matt.
        p. cm.
    "Bibliography of the writings of Rabbi Hershel Jonah Matt": p.
    ISBN 0-88125-430-4
    1. Judaism. 2. Matt, Hershel Jonah, d. 1987. I. Matt, Daniel
Chanan. II. Title.
BM45.M34 1992
296--dc20   92-26969
                                                                  CIP
        Manufactured in the United States of America

Photograph of Rabbi Hershel J. Matt kindly provided by John Hincks.

For Hershel's grandchildren:

Adina, Aliza, Elah, Elizabeth,

Gavriel, Leora, Michaella, Shira...

CONTENTS

Preface   ix

Part 1   The Life of a Rabbi   1
Part 2   Theological Essays   53
         Introduction   53

         1) Believing in God Today
              What I Believe   65
              Human Choice and God's Design   73
              What Does It Mean to Believe in God?   85
              Dogmas in Judaism   95
              An Outline of Jewish Eschatology   100
              Talking with Our Children about God   112
              Taking the First Step of *Teshuvah*   125
              Not Every Mysticism Is a Jewish Mysticism   128
              Fading Image of God?   131

         2) Prayer and *Mitzvot*
              Miracle and *Berakhah*   141
              Acknowledging the King:
                   The You and He, the They and We, of *Aleinu*   148
              The Goals of Teaching Jewish Prayer   159
              Kashrut in Conservative Judaism   167
              Covering My Jewish Head   173

         3) Judaism and Christianity
              Synagogue and Covenant People   178
              Principles and Policies for the Ideal Congregation   190
              How Shall a Believing Jew View Christianity?   195
              Should Christmas Mean Anything to Jews?   211

         4) Judaism and Sexuality
              A Jewish Approach to Sex Education   213

Sin, Crime, Sickness, or Alternative Life Style?
A Jewish Approach to Homosexuality   223
A Call for Compassion   236
Homosexual Rabbis?   239

Part 3   *Kavvanot* and Prayers   245

Bibliography of the Writings of Rabbi Hershel Jonah Matt   297

PREFACE

It is bittersweet to edit a book by and about one's father who has passed away. When he departed from the world in December 1987, Hershel Matt had accomplished an immense amount and touched countless people. He still had plans and dreams and ideas: articles to write, prayers to compose, budding rabbis to inspire, strangers to befriend, friends to counsel, souls to heal.

Since my father's passing, I have wandered through mourning over his death to celebrating the gift of his life. The pages that follow tell his story and preserve his writings. I have woven the first part of the book, "The Life of a Rabbi," from Hershel's diaries and files, and from the memories of his family, friends and colleagues. I am grateful to all those who have written to us since his passing and, knowingly or unknowingly, contributed to this biographical section. The bulk of the book consists of Hershel's essays and articles on God, prayer, *mitzvot,* the synagogue, Judaism and Christianity, and sexuality. Most of these originally appeared in various religious journals, and I am grateful for the permission granted to reprint them here. There are twenty-two in all, like the number of letters in the Hebrew alphabet; together they spell out a theology of creation-in-the-divine-image. To this section I have provided an introduction that identifies and discusses the salient features of his unique theological approach. The last section contains Hershel's *kavvanot* (his "bridges to prayer") and several prayers he created.

It is common to add the phrase *zikhrono li-verakhah,* "May his memory be a blessing," to the name of one who has passed away. If the person was especially worthy, the phrase becomes *zekher tzaddik li-verakhah.* With Hershel Jonah Matt, the formula regains its power. He incarnated the divine words of Micah: "Do justice, love kindness and walk humbly with your God." He is still affecting those who knew him and those now learning about him. Just thinking of his life is uplifting; remembering him yields a blessing.

WALKING HUMBLY WITH GOD

THE LIFE OF A RABBI

1

My father, *Ha-Rav Zvi Yonah ha-Levi*, Rabbi Hershel Jonah Matt, was a believer, in a very traditional sense. He believed in God, Revelation, the Messiah and life-after-death. Yet he was innovative, bold and progressive, fighting for women's equality back in the fifties, for civil rights in the sixties and for gay rights in the seventies. Devout and passionate in his observance of *mitzvot*, he wasn't satisfied with merely fulfilling the requirements. For him, religion was a full-time affair. Hershel Matt was a living embodiment of spirituality. He devoted himself to the love of God and the love of his fellow human beings, and he inspired others to do the same. Not for the sake of reward, but rather, to become attuned to the divine will. He sensed that he was involved in an intense personal relationship with the *Kadosh barukh hu*, the Blessed Holy One, and he tried to live each moment as a faithful, intimate partner in that relationship. The most mundane activity was an opportunity for holiness or a test of moral judgment. Every April, for example, he used to give extra money to *tzedakah*. This had nothing to do with the approach of Passover. Rather, Hershel was concerned that, in paying his income taxes, he might have taken unfair advantage of some provision in the tax code. His extra generosity was intended to make up for this.

But we are jumping ahead of ourselves. Hershel was born in Minneapolis, Minnesota on July 11, 1922. His father, Calman David Matt, was the rabbi of Congregation Adath Jeshurun, and a poet. C. David Matt's family had come to the United States from Kovno, Lithuania when he was three. The Matt family settled in Philadelphia, where C. David's father, Isaac Matt, served as aide to Bernard Levinthal, dean of the Philadelphia Orthodox Rabbinate.[1] C. David Matt attended the Jewish Theological Seminary in New York, graduating in 1913. Later that year in Minneapolis he married Lena Friedman, whose family had also emigrated from Kovno. In Minneapolis they began to raise a family. Hershel had two older brothers, Leonard and Joseph, and later, twin sisters, Beulah and Zeldah.

---

1. For a sketch of Isaac Matt, see Israel H. Levinthal, *The Message of Israel: Sermons, Addresses, Memoirs* (New York: Lex Printing Company, 1973), pp. 182-84.

In 1927, when Hershel was five years old, the family moved to Buffalo, and in 1929 they settled in Philadelphia, where C. David Matt served as rabbi of the West Philadelphia Jewish Community Center for over twenty years until his death in 1951. The family's move back East was not the only momentous thing to happen to Hershel at age five. It was then too, he always claimed, that he decided to become a rabbi. "That was the time when I stopped wanting to be a shoeshine boy. Once the shoeshine phase was behind me, I wanted to become a rabbi. And I never wavered."

Hershel was studious as a teenager. One sultry Philadelphia summer, at age sixteen or seventeen, he volunteered along with his close friend Max Ticktin to catalog the un-air-conditioned library at Gratz College, a Jewish teachers training school. Throughout the year, he used to help his father at the synagogue by chanting the Torah at the *Shabbat minhah* service. But he was a fairly good softball player too. Perhaps this explains why later, as our father, he let us divide *Shabbat* afternoon between playing touch football in the backyard and studying the weekly Torah portion at his side.

Hershel attended the University of Pennsylvania, majoring in philosophy. He received his Bachelor's Degree in 1943, graduating Phi Beta Kappa. A year earlier he had received a degree from Gratz College. Hershel kept a diary while he was at the University; the part that is extant covers the months September through December 1941. The following selections reveal a nineteen-year-old college junior struggling with religious and ethical issues that remained central and troubling throughout his entire life, in particular, the inherent contradictions of the American synagogue, the sad state of Jewish education, the questions of how to believe and how to pray in the modern world. We discover Hershel the pacifist as he responds to World War II and Pearl Harbor. (He was one of the founders of the Jewish Peace Fellowship and served as its National Secretary from 1944 to 1947, also editing its journal, *Tidings*.) As we learn in the diary, the war also brought a blessing to Hershel: a German Jewish refugee, Gustine Kanarek. They were married after the war, on March 10, 1946.

September 21, 1941
I think I'll gain from teaching Sunday School a sense of constructive accomplishment. I'll have a chance to influence for good a number of youngsters; and without exaggerating the amount of influence, I will be having a share in molding their character and Jewish knowledge. Not to mention the value of the teaching experience itself, let alone what I fortunately can still consider the relatively unimportant factor of income.

September 22, 1941
Rosh ha-Shanah. I find that as long as the service remains reasonably unfamiliar [in comparison with the daily and Sabbath liturgy], I can be sufficiently preoccupied with the mere reading that I need not worry about the meaningfulness of the prayers or the absence thereof—hardly a comforting thought!... As is obvious, I am quite discouraged.

September 23, 1941
Whether the sermons are good or bad, forceful or weak, provocative or stale, clever or obvious, new or old, they are not helpful. Granted that at certain times the only source of strength is faith, even an apparently unjustified faith, in a happy outcome—still those times are limited in number; the call to blind faith should be the last resort. Yet, once and again, unceasingly—"Believe and you will be saved"—I'd almost call it un-Jewish!

September 26, 1941
Ellis said to me that, frankly, he feels that my views on war, on dancing, etc. are prompted by a desire to be outstanding by being different. I felt neither insulted nor angry nor even surprised—at being thus misunderstood. I understand that Ellis can't believe I honestly entertain some of the views that I claim—he credits me with too much intelligence. And so he seeks a reason for my assuming these views. Oh dear!

September 29, 1941
I mentioned to Dad and Mother recently that I wouldn't be willing to be deferred on grounds of studying for the ministry, that I considered it cowardly. Asked by Dad why I shouldn't be willing if the government is, I replied that that's how the government makes sure of the clergy's support. I got a dirty look. Whether or not the reason I gave is true, I feel that under no circumstances would I try to avoid a uniform by covering myself with the cloth.

October 1, 1941
Yom Kippur. I took the fast rather easily this time, until five o'clock when I grew weak. It is indicative that a group of the Board went outside in the afternoon, sat in an auto and listened to the World Series game. And from my point of view it is indicative not only ... of the fault or wrong attitude of those who did it—not nearly so much as of the whole system.

October 7, 1941
I've met a young refugee, Gustine Kanarek, who has had a full life in her short sixteen years. She's pretty, smart, serious, observant, interested enthusiastically in her Judaism; she speaks seven languages including Hebrew and French. Mathematically all these qualities add up to the right kind for me; but I must wait and see whether in other respects and in the intangibles she's alright for me, and I for her.

[A further note on Gustine and Hershel's first meeting: My mother's family attended High Holiday services that year at my grandfather's synagogue in Philadelphia. After services, Hershel approached Gustine and said, "You might as well tell me your name; I've been staring at you all day!" We used to joke about this and say to him: "Dad, if your *kavvanah* had been better, you and mom might never have met!"]

October 21, 1941
As I'm writing to Stan, I think I am these days suffering the consequences of ultrabroadmindedness. I condemn no tolerance except of intolerance. I try to understand and sympathize with every point of view; and so I tend to hold no fixed view of my own. Some problems remain as baffling as ever: war and peace, for instance. But some, thank goodness, are gradually being solved by my adoption of certain premises and elimination of others. Yet I rejoice: though some see weakness, I see strength in having constantly to think.

October 30, 1941
This year, more than any other thus far in my life, I am interested in girls and it's not merely that I've grown so much during this twelvemonth. It's rather that for the first time I have, or am allowing myself, the leisure for them. I'm searching for a girl with whom I might see Shakespeare, talk religion, speak Hebrew, and be affectionate—perhaps all in the same evening—and who would enjoy all four ardently and do them well!

November 4, 1941
Handed in today a paper on "My Religion" for the Religious Orientation course with Mr. Kolb. "My views on religion are constantly fluctuating, constantly dissolving and re-forming. Partly because of my immaturity and partly because of the essential intangibleness of the subject, I find great difficulty in framing my thoughts in words. It is with trepidation, therefore—yet with a deep earnestness—that I record herein an account of my religion." Conclusion: the God of my religion is impersonal.

November 10, 1941
Though Dad does not approve—he fears it might be Communist-tinged—I attended a meeting tonight of the Youth Committee Against War. But I wish I could find someone to help me solve some of the basic war-peace problems that bother me. I'm searching for a convincing argument for pacifism, or at least nonintervention, an argument that I could present to those who say: Are you going to do nothing to stop Hitler? And I seek religious sanctions for peace.

November 26, 1941
Max [Ticktin], Stan Ulick, and I met tonight to try once again to clarify our beliefs. Two discoveries emerged, for me at least: 1) I cannot decide whether I am unqualifiedly opposed to all and every war, or whether there

might conceivably be a situation when I would approve of war. 2) In seeking support in Jewish tradition for the pacifist position, I must be willing to cast overboard as of inferior ethical quality those elements in Jewish tradition which condone war.

December 6, 1941
Seymour Harris was *bar mitzvah* today—the first of this year's crop. He did well, considering the quality of his singing voice. But it pains my heart to realize that we are not taking advantage of his closeness at this minute to the synagogue. The negligence is criminal; yet my hands are tied. Or are they? Perhaps I should insist on being allowed to give a *bar mitzvah* course.

December 7, 1941
The United States was attacked today by Japan in Hawaii—and the long-expected war has come. At present I am still a firm pacifist on grounds partly moral and humanitarian (I cannot sanction mass killing) and partly practical (I can see no likelihood of any gain whatsoever from a war).

December 8, 1941
The United States today declared war on Japan. I have not yet been able to decide upon a course of action, to decide how far I shall go in refusing to cooperate in a war that I cannot approve. Perhaps I shall come to feel that it is the government's duty to punish me for dissenting, and that it is my duty nonetheless to continue to dissent. At present I am pondering the matter.

December 9, 1941
As I listened to the President this evening, I felt that his voice, his delivery, his message indicate an assurance, a cleverness, and, yes, a greatness—all this though I disagree heartily with his foreign policy of the last eight or six years. I am trying to be broadminded; I am trying to admit quality where I discern it; yet I am trying likewise to discover truth.

December 14, 1941
Went to the Race Street Forum tonight, and heard Villard on planning for postbellum world. He wasn't very enlightening, and I seem only to have been confirmed in my conviction that war, exploiting as it does man's lower emotions, delays all the more, and militates against, a just order and a vengeless, righteous peace.

2

After graduating from the University of Pennsylvania, Hershel followed in his father's footsteps and entered the Jewish Theological Seminary, beginning his studies in January 1943. Two of his roommates at JTS, Max Ticktin and Monford Harris, remained his lifelong friends. Max and

Hershel had known each other since age fifteen in Philadelphia, and together they had helped found the Jewish Peace Fellowship. Monford Harris recalls being struck by Hershel's piety and by his unselfconscious intimacy with his father, C. David Matt:

> We became fast friends almost immediately. Some few weeks later, Hershel invited me to his parental home in Philadelphia. It was a delightful weekend. One incident in particular made a deep and lasting impression on me. On our walk to the synagogue with his father that Sabbath morning, Hershel held his father's hand during the entire walk. There was nothing infantile about this, nor was there a need for physical support. It was an act of communion and fellowship. It struck me ... as a remarkable piety that I had never encountered (and would never encounter again)....

> This is what startled me at the very beginning of our friendship. The phenomenon of personal piety I had always associated with the East European immigrants in my family and in the synagogue. Hershel was the first adult American Jew that I met who was a profoundly pious person.

Hershel's piety did not render him timid. Returning to the Seminary late one Saturday night, or rather, very early Sunday morning, he found himself locked out. Undaunted, he scaled the twenty-foot-high gates, adroitly avoiding the spiked tops.

Together with his roommates, Max and Monnie, Hershel challenged the style and substance of rabbinic education at JTS, criticizing the lack of spirituality. One night in December 1944 the three comrades decided to write a letter to the Chancellor Louis Finkelstein. They typed it up and slid it under his door.

> Dear Dr. Finkelstein,

> We are wondering whether, in this large and expanding Seminary, it is possible for some of your students to talk with you, at least in writing, as man to man about conditions in the Seminary which have been disturbing us.

> The Seminary is now embarked on its expansion program: it will soon be engaged in a five-million-dollar campaign; it has a new home for its museum and Institute of Religious Studies; it sponsors a national radio program that is attracting widespread attention; it has enlarged its administrative and publicity staff. But in spite of all this external development and growth, the inner spirit of the Seminary is being progressively dulled and stifled.

> These are our criticisms: First, in the minds of many informed laymen and almost all of the students, the Seminary administration is character-

ized by a secular and materialistic attitude. We are now a big business. Many of us are deeply ashamed, for instance, that our arrival on a High Holy Day position is signalized by the receipt in that community of a request for money—as if prayers on the holidays must be backed up by a money guarantee! And in innumerable instances—almost every student can mention one or two—the Field Office has engaged in practices and displayed an attitude that are in complete contradiction to religious idealism.

Secondly, though the students are asked to share at all times in the concern for the Seminary's prestige, influence, and power, who is concerning himself with the spiritual growth of the students? Our teachers are professors: they turn out books and achieve worldwide fame; but do they have the unique quality of the *rebbe* of old: do they think about molding the character and personality of their students? Accepting the curriculum as it is, almost every one of our courses fails to talk in terms of the spiritual life. The deep piety that we know characterized the creation of the Bible, the Talmud, and the Codes is all but ignored in our classes. The spiritual struggle in Jewish history is obscured. In terms of the spirit, our curriculum has been a failure.

Finally, in its efforts to achieve its larger aims, the Seminary seems to have forgotten that there are some very ordinary people in one or two branches of the maintenance staff who are obliged to work such long hours that they are denied any possibility of spiritual growth. Any institution, even a Seminary, which obliges a man to spend *seventy* hours a week in order to earn a living wage is sinning. Even if the man receives a union wage, a religious institution must not look to statistical, minimum formulas for determining the needs of a man's soul.

We realize that you are a man with many duties and responsibilities. But we earnestly believe that none of them takes precedence over those we have all too briefly outlined. The Seminary is on trial: not so much before the world as before God.

Sincerely yours,

Monford Harris
Hershel Matt
Max Ticktin

The chancellor called in his three rabbinical students the next morning and also responded in writing, but nothing much changed. Still, Hershel found intellectual and spiritual mentors at the Seminary. At first, he was attracted to the founder of Reconstructionism, Mordecai Kaplan (1881-1983), who had previously taught C. David Matt at JTS. Max Ticktin and Hershel had originally sought out Kaplan when, as nineteen-year-olds, they decided one day that they were Reconstructionists. Later, Hershel credited Kaplan with making it possible for him to come to JTS. While at the University of Pennsylvania, he began to have doubts about many aspects of Jewish belief: God, prayer, creation, the idea of the chosen people, and life after death. Could he attend rabbinical school with integrity? When he expressed his doubts to a young JTS graduate, the latter said, "Have you heard of Kaplan? If he teaches there, you could certainly be a student there!"

Hershel was deeply impressed by Kaplan's intellectual honesty and his boldness in confronting the challenges to tradition posed by modern thought. Kaplan replaced classical Judaism's doctrine of supernatural revelation with reason, intuition and experience. God was envisioned not as a personal being but rather, as the power that makes for salvation. Divine power is expressed when we learn to cultivate physical and human nature, when we find strength to overcome despair.

Kaplan rejected the idea of the chosenness of Israel. In the past, he argued, the notion of divine election compensated for the Jewish people's sense of isolation and persecution. Such divine favoritism, however, tends to inflame rivalry among sibling religions, each asserting superiority. Kaplan replaced the notion of a chosen people with "vocation," the calling to serve God that religious civilizations rightfully claim. No religion is precluded from serving God according to its own concept of salvation.

Kaplan preached a social existentialism: the existence of the Jewish people is prior to any attempt to define its essence. Judaism is not a set of dogmas, doctrines or ritual prescriptions. It is a civilization, the creative expression of a people's instinctual will to live. This will constantly manifests itself in fresh ways. Kaplan had a deep understanding of, and respect for, what he termed the *sancta* of Judaism: heroes, events, places, celebrations and holidays that function as unifying factors in Judaism. But in the modern world, he contended, Jews should not be unduly bound to traditional formulations. Kaplan offered a genuine alternative for Jews who could no longer accept the presuppositions and authority of supernaturalism. He sought to integrate naturalism and tradition. The new is no less sacred than the old. "The past has a vote but no veto."

In 1945, while Hershel was in his second academic year at JTS, the first Reconstructionist prayer book appeared. It substituted prayers in praise of Jewish uniqueness for those proclaiming the exclusive chosenness of Israel. It omitted prayers for the restoration of the Temple and animal sacrifices. It deleted references to the physical resurrection of the dead and to superstitious notions, e.g., that rainfall was given by God as a reward and withheld as a punishment. Prayers that discriminated against women, slaves and gentiles were replaced by positive affirmations of freedom and the celebration of the divine image in all human beings. A group of Orthodox rabbis issued a *herem* (a ban of excommunication) against Kaplan, and a copy of the prayer book was burned publicly in New York. Hershel published a positive review of the new *siddur* in Hebrew.[2]

For a time, Hershel shared Kaplan's idea of a nonpersonal God, but "after a year or two I couldn't take him theologically." As Monford Harris puts it, Hershel's "piety was too profound, virile and personal. It could not be corroded by historicism. God, Hershel well knew, is not only Power ... but also Presence." Still, elements of Kaplan's thought were an enduring influence on Hershel, for example, the voluntaristic approach to *halakhah*.

Kaplan realized that his potential disciple had drifted away. He was surprised to learn that Hershel retained an appreciation of Reconstructionism. This is reflected in an anecdote from Hershel's first rabbinical position in Nashua, New Hampshire. In his original salary negotiations with the congregation, the young Rabbi Matt had requested $4500. The Board agreed to pay him $4000. In responding, Hershel wrote, "As a rabbi, I cannot refuse to serve you just because you cannot pay what I ask, even though I am asking only for what I feel are legitimate needs." Hershel took the position. After the first High Holy Days, the Board sent him a $500 bonus in appreciation of how moving the prayers had been. Hershel told them that he couldn't accept the check, that he didn't believe in taking money for individual services rendered. As Will Herberg wrote him at the time: "It is just the difference between the proper 'practical' thing to do and a counsel of perfection." Hershel suggested that the congregation divide the money between two worthy causes: the Jewish Theological Seminary and the Reconstructionist Foundation. When the $250 arrived at the Reconstructionist office, Kaplan was dumbfounded: "Matt? Matt recommended giving it to me? I thought he was one of my enemies."

If Kaplan had been his only inspiring teacher, Hershel might have left rabbinical studies, but two new mentors came into his life during his third year in rabbinical school: Will Herberg (1902-1977) and Abraham Joshua Heschel (1907-1972). In 1945-46 each made his first public appearance at JTS. Heschel joined the faculty that fall as Professor of Jewish Ethics and Mysticism, while Herberg came as a lecturer in a series on "My Faith as a Jew." Heschel remained at JTS until his death in 1972; Herberg, though

2. Zvi Matt, *"Siddur Hadash,"* Niv 7:4 (May-June 1945): 15-16.

never a regular faculty member, taught and lectured occasionally and met with students.

The two teachers differed in many ways. Herberg grew up in New York City; his background was Marxism and atheism. He could study Jewish sources only in translation. Heschel was born and raised in Poland, descended from Hasidic masters and steeped in Torah, Talmud and mysticism. Having fled from the Nazis in the late 1930s, he taught at Hebrew Union College from 1940 until 1945 before coming to JTS. Herberg was cold, rational and dogmatic; Heschel was warm, charismatic, poetic and mystical. Herberg became an outspoken conservative, while Heschel opposed the war in Vietnam and espoused other progressive causes such as civil rights. Yet both were religious existentialists and, in a sense, neo-orthodox. On many issues they stood together against the prevailing religious liberalism of modern Judaism. Hershel discovered in their thinking a cogent alternative to Kaplan's naturalism.

It is worthwhile to explore briefly several of Herberg's and Heschel's key teachings, since these had such an impact on Hershel's own thinking, writing and living.[3] Herberg, an ardent Marxist, came to see Marxism as a "god that failed." As he writes, "Sacrificial dedication to the welfare of humanity had given way to narrow, ruthless, self-defeating power politics.... It seemed to me that ... Marxism went far toward destroying the very objectives it was presumably out to achieve." Having rejected this "bankrupt religion," he sought a new commitment. "I felt intensely the need for a faith that would better square with my ideal, which in tenor, doctrine, and spirit could give impulse and direction to the radical reconstruction of society which I so deeply desired."

Herberg sought out Reinhold Niebuhr and declared to him his intention to embrace Christianity. Instead of receiving him as a convert, Niebuhr directed him to seek his own roots in Judaism and recommended

---

3. I am drawing here on certain passages from Herberg and Heschel assembled by Hershel Matt, as well as: Seymour Siegel, "Will Herberg (1902-1977): A *Ba'al Teshuvah* Who Became Theologian, Sociologist, Teacher," *American Jewish Year Book: 1978*, ed. Morris Fine and Milton Himmelfarb (New York and Philadelphia: American Jewish Committee and Jewish Publication Society, 1977), pp. 529-37; and Fritz A. Rothschild's introduction to his anthology of Heschel's writings: *Between God and Man: An Interpretation of Judaism* (New York: Free Press, 1959). For a valuable study of Heschel's thought, see John C. Merkle, *The Genesis of Faith: The Depth Theology of Abraham Joshua Heschel* (New York: Macmillan, 1985). Hershel published excerpts from Herberg's letters to him in "Will Herberg: A Tribute," *Conservative Judaism* 31:2 (1977): 5-14.

that he go to JTS. There he had his first contact with the Jewish spiritual tradition. Though guided by both professors and students, he learned mostly on his own. He was particularly impressed by the writings of Martin Buber and Franz Rosenzweig.

Herberg's mission became expounding Judaism. He was probably the only Jewish ex-Marxist to embrace theology as a vocation. As opposed to Kaplan's naturalistic theology, Herberg espoused orthodox ideas of a supernatural God, Messiah and Torah, though interpreting each in a new way. He was the first American Jew to teach a Jewish religious existentialism. Faith, for Herberg, was not the result of intellectual reasoning but rather, a basic orientation of life.

> He understood from his own experience that a human being cannot live without placing his faith in *something* as the source of the meaning and value of his existence, in something that for him is absolute, ultimate.... Whatever we say, there is something that we take as our absolute, as our anchorage in reality, as our "god." The only question—but it is as great, decisive, shattering question—is: *What* shall we acknowledge as absolute—some man-made god, in fact ourselves writ large, or the God beyond the abyss, the God who is Lord of all? This is the decision which each of us must make every moment of our lives.

Ascribing value to something that is not ultimate, such as things of this world, is idolatry. Substitute faiths, such as science, Communism, nationalism and money, have led to disaster and unhappiness. The alternative is to anchor one's faith beyond oneself, in God. Though he recognized the need for government, Herberg was skeptical of it. "Earthly government still remains a kind of usurpation of the divine prerogative, even though it may be necessary for social existence."

Herberg was both theologian and sociologist. In rejecting Marxism, he did not surrender his political sophistication or his critical social awareness. His critique of American religion was trenchant.

> The religiousness characteristic of America today is very often a religiousness ... with almost any kind of content or none, a way of sociability or "belonging" rather than a way of reorienting life to God. It is thus frequently a religiousness without serious commitment, without real inner conviction, without genuine existential decision.... The new religiosity pervading America seems to be very largely the religious validation of the social patterns and cultural values associated with the American Way of Life.... In this kind of religion it is not [the human being] who serves God, but God who is mobilized and made to serve [the human being] and his purposes.

There is a danger that religion can become "an exalted public utility, a mere instrument of the social order." Robbed of its transcendence, of its prophetic protest against the existing power structures, religion becomes "merely an idolatrous cult sustaining society." Authentic religion "sustains the social order to the degree that it is worth sustaining, but at the same time subjects it to a radical, and what must sometimes seem shattering, criticism. Its standpoint can never be simply that of society itself."

Religion, Herberg claims, should not validate one's goals and ideals but call them into question, not enhance one's self-regard but challenge it. Rather than offering salvation on easy terms, religion must demand repentance and a "broken heart." It is characteristic of Herberg that he insists on the traditional category of sin while investing it with contemporary meaning. "I know that the very mention of sin is offensive to the modern mind," he wrote, but "we can no longer do without the concept of sin." Human sinfulness "is rooted in egotism and self-centeredness." These traits prevent us from loving our neighbor as we love ourselves. "The universal tendency to exalt the self and subject others to its will is the radical violation of the moral law and hence the source of all moral evil in individual and social life." But the human being is not left stranded in sinfulness. God provides the gift of *teshuvah*, which Herberg defines as "the fusion of repentance and grace." Through *teshuvah* one gains "the power to break through the vicious cycle of egocentricity and return to the divine center of our being."

As opposed to Kaplan's impersonal "power that makes for salvation," Herberg, drawing on Buber, speaks of God as "a dynamic power that is *personal*."

> What do we mean when we speak of God as a Person? We mean that we meet God in life and history, not as an object, not as a thing, not as an *It* ... but as a *Thou,* with whom we can enter into genuine person-to-person relations. Indeed, it is this I-Thou encounter with God that constitutes the primary life-giving experience of faith.

Herberg's theology was traditional, but he was too modern to be a fundamentalist. The Bible contains God's word but "only as it has passed through the medium of the human heart and mind." Since it is recorded by human beings, Torah is "subject to all the relativities and contingencies of human experience." Yet it is still Torah, a "teaching about the ultimate truth.... An adequate understanding of revelation must take into account what both [fundamentalism and modernism] have to say and combine them into a higher and more pregnant synthesis."

Herberg advanced a dialectical understanding of Israel's role as the chosen people. It is through Israel that God's covenant is destined for the entire world.

> When the vocation of Israel is finally and completely fulfilled in the Kingdom of God at the "end," Israel will lose its reason for existence and [humankind] will again be one. The election of Israel was never meant to be a thing in itself, but as a first step toward the realization of the Kingdom of God on this earth.

The justification of Jewish existence "derives from the never-ceasing work of preparation for *malkhut shamayim*, the Kingdom of Heaven." Israel's vocation is to live a holy life, to bring others to the awareness of the divine, "to stand witness to the Living God amidst the idolatries of the world."

In the fulfillment of its mission, Judaism has a special relationship with its daughter religion, Christianity. Drawing on Rosenzweig, Herberg taught that "Judaism and Christianity represent one religious reality, Judaism facing *inward* to the Jews and Christianity facing *outward* to the gentiles." He quoted Rosenzweig's provocative lines: "The two religions are equal representations of the truth—equal before God." As history has unfolded, wrote Rosenzweig, "Israel can bring the world to God only through Christianity."

Abraham Joshua Heschel offered Hershel another interpretation of Judaism, one tinged with mysticism. Heschel tried to synthesize Western thought and the traditional learning and piety of Eastern Europe. Not content with advocating a theology, Heschel created and lyrically described "depth theology." "The theme of theology is the content of believing; the theme of depth theology is the act of believing." For Heschel, awareness of the divine begins with wonder. "Wonder or radical amazement is the chief characteristic of the religious attitude." The experience of radical amazement is not limited to a spiritual elite; all human beings are endowed with a sense of the ineffable. To be fully human is to be open to this perspective on reality. Herberg had underscored selfishness as the root of sin. For Heschel, "indifference to the sublime wonder of living is the root of sin."

Heschel and Herberg shared much common ground. As opposed to Kaplan, both spoke of God as a personal Being. According to Heschel, to be a person is to have concern for the other, and God overflows with such concern. "He is encountered not as universal, general, pure Being, but always in a particular mode of being, as personal God to personal man, in a specific *pathos* that comes with a demand in a concrete situation." Personal concern is perhaps the key concept in Heschel's philosophy. Religion originates in our awareness of being the object of God's concern. Since we are created in the divine image, we can share this divine concern for others.

God is passionately involved with human beings and is intimately affected by them. God is not the Aristotelian Unmoved Mover but the Most Moved Mover. Here Heschel reflects the Kabbalistic notion of *tzorekh gavoha*, "the need on high." God needs our participation and searches for us. The goal of the spiritual life is not mystical union but sympathetic union. A feeling of complete solidarity with God engenders a divine-human partnership in which the attainment of God's aims depends on our cooperation and effort. This is the significance of the covenant. Religion enables the human being to identify with God's ends and serve them. "Our ultimate commitment is our ultimate privilege."

The Sabbath, in particular, offers an opportunity for the Jew to harmonize herself with God. This day is, in Heschel's famous phrase, a palace in time. It is a time to pause and celebrate creation. "We abstain primarily from any activity that aims at remaking or reshaping the things of space." For Heschel, *Shabbat* is also a denial of the false god of materialism: "a day on which handling money is considered a desecration, on which man avows his independence of that which is the world's chief idol." On this day "the goal is not to have but to be." The spiritual richness of the Sabbath overflows and affects the weekdays as well. "All days of the week must be spiritually consistent with the Day of Days."

Heschel was observant in his religious practice but sensitive to the dangers of formalism. He describes the tension between *keva* (fixed form) and *kavvanah* (intention, feeling). If one limits oneself to the prescribed patterns, *keva* will gain the upper hand. There must be room for spontaneous response to the divine reality. The wonder of existence must not be forfeited. "Just to live is a blessing; just to be is holy."

Both Herberg and Heschel had a lasting impact on Hershel; he maintained contact with each of them and cherished whatever they wrote. Near the end of his life, he was working on an article comparing his two teachers. Here he wrote, "Heschel and Herberg both came into my life during that year of 1945-46. My thought and my faith have remained under their joint influence ever since." He once remarked that Heschel was the only person he could honestly call his *rebbe*.

Hershel received his rabbinical ordination and Masters of Hebrew Literature from the Jewish Theological Seminary in 1947. To celebrate Hershel's installation as rabbi in Nashua, New Hampshire, C. David Matt wrote a poem entitled "A Rabbi to His Rabbi Son."[4] Two of the verses read:

> Precepts well-conned in parental abode
> Let guide thee and guard thee through life—
> Patient, consid'rate, forgetful of self,
> Eschewing ambition and strife.
>
> Meager emolument, recompense scant—
> As deemed by the trafficking mart—
> Thine the reward be of duty fulfilled,
> The tribute that swells from the heart.

3

Over the next twenty-eight years Hershel (who preferred to be called by his first name rather than by his rabbinic title) served four congregations: Beth Abraham Congregation in Nashua, New Hampshire (1947-1950); Temple Beth El in Troy, New York (1950-1959); Temple Neve Shalom in Metuchen, New Jersey (1959-1970); and The Jewish Center in Princeton, New Jersey (1970-1975). He was active in the Rabbinical Assembly, serving on its Executive Council and on its Prayer Book, Ethics and Convention committees, and as chairman of its Committee on Home and Synagogue Practice. Throughout his career he worked for interreligious dialogue and improved race relations.

He taught at a number of schools and seminaries: Akiba Academy (1963-64), the Jewish Theological Seminary (1974), Georgian Court College (1976), the Reconstructionist Rabbinical College (1983-1987), and the Academy for Jewish Religion (1984-1987). He had a profound impact on students and colleagues.[5] He also taught frequently at National

4. *The Collected Poems of Rabbi C. David Matt*, ed. Milton Nevins (Philadelphia: The West Philadelphia Jewish Community Center, 1953), p. 107.

5. See Nancy Fuchs-Kreimer, ed., *Perpetuating the Memory of Hershel Jonah Matt*, *Raayonot* 6:2 (Spring 1988): 4-21.

Havurah Institutes. He lectured widely on college campuses and in congregations on various aspects of Jewish faith, thought and practice, and on the relationship between Judaism and Christianity. He was present at the founding conference of New Jewish Agenda, and was elected to its first board. He later served on its task force for theology. The chairman of NJA noted: "In his quiet way he was the moral leader of our group."

In Nashua, Gustine and Hershel had their first child, Jonathan, in 1949. Their three other children (Daniel, David and Deborah) were born in Troy in the 1950s. The children gradually spread out over a wide territory, each one carrying on the spiritual tradition in a unique way. Jonathan became a rabbi, graduating from the Jewish Theological Seminary and then making *aliyah* to Israel, where he lives on Kibbutz Malkiyah in the Galil. Daniel teaches Jewish mysticism at the Graduate Theological Union in Berkeley, California. David lives in Iowa, where he divides his time between meditating and marketing. Deborah lives near Gustine in Highland Park, New Jersey, where she is raising a family and teaching at a local synagogue.

In his various congregations, Rabbi Matt avoided multi-year contracts. He saw no point in committing himself and the congregation to each other for an extended period of time. He wouldn't have wished to stay as rabbi if he were not wanted or if it would have caused a conflict in the congregation. Hershel simply remained in each community until he decided to leave. He attempted to instill a love of Judaism in his congregants and urged them to involve themselves in the essential *mitzvot:* prayer, study of Torah, genuine interpersonal relations, ethical behavior, celebration of *Shabbat* and the holidays. He worked himself too hard. On one so-called summer vacation, he received a mild admonishment in a letter from Will Herberg: "It looks as if your 'vacation' is running true to form, Hershey-form. Some people are accident-prone; Hershey is work- and responsibility-prone. It must be something you ate when you were small."

Hershel expected too much and cultivated a kind of holy stubbornness. Though he was very effective, though services were well attended (compared to many other synagogues), he never felt satisfied with the degree of commitment on the part of his congregants. As we will see, he went so far as to ask them for written pledges of commitment to various *mitzvot.* He dared both himself and his flock to engage in Jewish spiritual discipline. This was very unrealistic, as he knew. Finally, in each case, convinced that he was not succeeding, he moved on to a new locale and started all over again. But here too his hope withered and disillusionment came on more quickly. Each community mourned when he left. As his lifelong friend, Max Ticktin, noted: "That restlessness was the man and part of his greatness."

To give some idea of the kind of rabbi Hershel Matt was, I have selected passages from another diary, which he kept over the course of a year in Metuchen, New Jersey.[6] Here we see the highs and lows of the congregational rabbinate, its frustrations and holy opportunities. Hershel bares himself here, and we are confronted with the depth of his self-awareness and the unrelenting precision of his ethical lens.

February 27, 1969
Milt Spiegel had sudden heart attack, 4th, died. Went over to home. Leaves 5-year-old son, 83-year-old father, besides wife and 2 girls.... 5-year-old Danny full of questions: "Where is Daddy? If God took him because He liked him, why not take others He likes? When will he come back? Will he die again? Will God punish him (throw him down) if he's bad?"

March 7, 1969
Snow today; when I called mother of tonight's *bat mitzvah* to commiserate with her, she said, "Even if some guests aren't able to come, isn't the main thing the service itself?" Stayed in because of sore throat—except for *shul,* which I went to because of *bat mitzvah.*

October 1, 1969
Went to say goodbye to Goldbergs, going on *aliyah*—and brought them Heschel's book on Israel as farewell gift. Jack, in saying goodbye, said: "I'm not crying or embracing you on leaving, as I've done with some. You haven't been able to find time to spend with me (and some others?) or get close to me. I've been close to other rabbis. I don't know whether you dislike me or Bnai Brith or what; thought I should tell you," etc. Thanked him for his honesty, told him some feel I've been close to them; each rabbi has his own way, strengths and weaknesses. His honesty was courageous but also cruel since it wasn't really an appropriate farewell or necessary.

October 2, 1969
Good session in high school class on Judaism and Christianity. A few new things became clearer to me about meaning of Christian affirmation (and comparable Jewish affirmation). For example, when a Christian says "Christ died for my sin," if he says it with genuine *kavvanah,* he means

6. In the following selections several names have been changed to protect the innocent and the remiss.

seriously not only "Christ died" but also "my" and "sin"!—and therefore must be engaging in true confession and true repentance!

October 6, 1969
Call from Sprintz. Telephone previously shut off, electricity today unless gets $20 for deposit. Usual frustration (what can I do, will anything help, am I being taken, what will really help, who should be helping her, will she accept referral?) Anyhow, called electric company manager and [city of] Perth Amboy, got one day's extension, sent $20 check.

October 12, 1969
Double unveiling out in Brooklyn. Can't escape some feeling of resentment since a) unveiling not necessary altogether, b) why not rabbi who knew the deceased as well and/or closer geographically, but "couldn't" say no to this family (nor about November 2, for another unveiling in same family, where I knew deceased much less). Hate to admit that $50 fee made me feel less resentful.[7]

October 14, 1969
New York City to see Heschel, home from hospital. He's so weak; said and appeared glad to see me. When I told him about irreverence of *Simhat Torah* morning here, he quoted Hasidic sources: a) that sadness is work of *sitra ahra* [the demonic], and b) that even lowest level *simhah* is a *kiddush ha-shem* [sanctification of God]! Wow!

October 23, 1969
Bar and *bat mitzvah* parents meeting for next year, as always quite well attended. Someone suggested switch [meeting] to Youth Lounge to allow for smoking. Told them I had ethical compunctions about being party to suicide!

October 24, 1969
Call from mother of a girl in my high school class. What was this I had told her daughter about each one must decide for self what is right and wrong? Daughter wanted to go to Europe with new boy friend. She [the mother] had tried to instill very strict standards of right and wrong.

November 19, 1969
Cooper and brother at morning *minyan.* Turns out that though he never comes weekdays or *Shabbat,* puts on *tefillin* daily! (Brother also "except when on vacation.") Who'd ever guess?...
Was raining when I got gas at night. Saw attendant without raincoat, and gave him mine that I had in car. Told him I'd pick up next day. His mouth gaped but he took it.

---

7. It was not until 1967, the onset of his four children's college tuition payments, that Hershel agreed to accept fees for services rendered at funerals, weddings, etc.

December 3, 1969

First election campaign for student council in Temple school. Cute and good training in participatory democracy, but does it encourage hollowly aping the forms of adult society and "is it really at all necessary"?! Is there real power and responsibility to be shared?...

Interviews with this week's *bar* and *bat mitzvah*. Former said: A number of people who'll be at evening affair will not be at service in morning: men have to work, women have to have hair done.

December 5, 1969

Hanukkah. Bat mitzvah today—all seems so silly. Preached on need to safeguard against assimilation by observing the distinctive elements in Judaism, in addition to affirmation and values that are shared in common. Hope it was not taken as slam against *bat mitzvah's* family and friends— and yet hope it had some effect, which no doubt it didn't.

December 10, 1969

Call from a colleague in connection with auto accident involving death of mother and a child, one or two more injured. What can we honestly say theologically? Is everything that happens God's will? Discussed for while. Don't claim anything more than fragmentary answers, but he feels I've faced and wrestled with [the questions]. Decided to give him outline on Issues in Contemporary Jewish Faith—and received new stimulus to write my article....

In class kids had great difficulty in understanding that holy living possible or even appropriate in sports. "Supposed to hurt, if want to win. Not for babies!"

December 19, 1969

It's understandable, even if troubling, that my own kids don't find services satisfying. But for D. to have M. come to our house Friday evening instead of to Temple is harder to take—even though, I gather, they had spirited discussion on God.

January 17, 1970

Non-kosher meal at restaurant to follow *bar mitzvah* service—and yet father can say, on presenting *tallit:* "Fulfill the Commandments." The whole institution of *bar mitzvah* is so empty!

February 9, 1970

L.L. told me how moved and impressed he was, while attending *bar mitzvah* recently elsewhere, at announcement of Israeli casualties of week by name. Recommends same here. I'd hesitate, at least on regular basis: a) may be melodramatic; b) unless includes victims also among Arabs, and both sides in Vietnam—and what about other types of victims?

February 14, 1970

Can it really be that nothing worth recording occurred today???!

March 8, 1970
M.S. unveiling.... Very cold at cemetery. Father said *kaddish;* said to me, "I'm a pretty good actor, don't you think?" Pathetic.

March 11, 1970
UJA buffet supper. Initial Gifts, speaker chauvinistic, extremist, insulting—effective! $70,000 pledged.

March 17, 1970
Wrote Blumsteins on marriage of son to Christian girl—sharing in their joy, tinged with pain; admiring their wisdom and courage in accepting Marc's decision and in accepting his wife; praying for wisdom and strength to find happiness in spite of obstacles; asking for address so that I can write couple greeting and blessing.

4

One of Hershel Matt's greatest strengths was his personal approach, his genuine concern for his congregants and for everyone around him. He used to send anniversary notes, birthday notes and graduation notes to members of the congregation, often accompanied by a *kavvanah,* a short prayer.[8] He would write or type these himself, never dictating them to his secretary. This was a human gesture, not a perfunctory, professional duty.

When Rabbi Matt spoke to the congregation, he would often come down from the *bimah* instead of sermonizing from on high. Yet he did not hold back from expressing his criticism. As Will Herberg wrote to him at his first congregation in Nashua: "Perhaps what I find most striking in all the sermons is the direct and unequivocal manner in which you castigate the sins that are actually committed by the people sitting before you in a way that makes it impossible for them to miss the point." Herberg was glad that his disciple was fulfilling the essential function of religion: "to afflict the comfortable and comfort the afflicted."

A congregant recalls one of Rabbi Matt's sermons that had a personal message for her.

> I used to take Fresh Air kids from New York City. One year I took two Jewish girls.... The girls had lice in their hair. My own girls got it as did some of the neighbors. I cried on your father's shoulder. And he lit into me and asked me what I expected. The sermon that week was: It's easy to love your neighbor as yourself, especially if he is clean and dresses well; the test is to love the one who is lying in the gutter. I've never forgotten that sermon.

8. Some samples appear below, in the section *"Kavvanot* and Prayers."

Rabbi Matt knew how to criticize and admonish lovingly. He took people seriously, but always tried to help them penetrate their own false images. One congregant, who grew up with Hershel as her rabbi, put it this way:

> He had a way of making an innocent comment that managed to deflate my ego without humiliating me or making me defensive. I've never met anyone who so consistently saw through pretense but never took advantage of that talent to belittle a person. He held a mirror up to a person, and then respectfully looked away as they blushed.

Rabbi Matt was effective because he practiced what he preached. The triteness of this phrase dissolves for those who knew him. In the words of one congregant, "He was the only rabbi I ever met who lived up to my idea of what a rabbi is." Another congregant and friend, Shirley Segal, writes:

> The most important thing he taught us as our rabbi and friend was to live life according to the highest standards, morally and ethically. Our relationship to family and friends had to be understanding and filled with love. It wasn't hard because one only had to emulate him and his feelings for others and his code of ethics.

But to emulate Hershel Matt was no easy task! His ethical standards were excruciatingly high. When confronted with a situation, the first questions he posed were: "Is it ethically based? Is this the right thing to do?" As he once wrote, "If to be truly human is to be concerned with issues of right and wrong, to be truly Jewish is to be preoccupied with them."[9] His uncompromising sense of justice was not a lofty ideal but an immediate demand informing his relations with everyone and everything. Stanley Messer recalls one revealing example:

> He once asked me if I had a certain book, which I didn't, but I said that he could borrow my university library card and search it out. His response was that he would then be passing himself off as me, which he felt wasn't right. I had never before given any thought to lending my library card to someone in need, but, upon reflection, I recognized the level of moral sensitivity involved in his response. In addition, he expressed it in a way, so very characteristic of Hershel, which was not disparaging or guilt-inducing. It also conveyed how the details in life matter as much as the big issues.

9. "Human Choice and God's Design." (Unless otherwise noted, all essays cited are reprinted in this volume. The Bibliography lists the original sources of all of Hershel Matt's writings.)

In Troy, New York the congregation offered Rabbi Matt a free trip to Israel. Amazingly, he declined the offer, writing to the delegation of three who had approached him:

Dear Friends,

I can't hope to put into words how deeply I have been moved by your wonderful and generous offer. It was so completely unexpected and unanticipated—and it is so beautiful and gratifying an expression of friendship and appreciation—that I have been completely overwhelmed. I find it really difficult to know how to thank you and express my sense of gratitude.

You can imagine, therefore, how close to impossible it is to explain why I cannot accept your offer of a trip to Israel.... There are a number of reasons, to be sure: my concern about my health, my reluctance to leave Gustine alone with the four children, my hesitation about not sharing such an experience as this with her (she cannot leave them this year), my uncomfortableness about accepting gifts in general, etc. But for all of these questions, there were answers—and you supplied them.

But the one real reason, the valid reason, the one I could not articulate till today, is compelling—and is related to the very reason why you and Gustine and I were excited about the idea: namely, the fact that this act of visiting the Land of Israel is a very special *mitzvah,* one of the greatest *mitzvot* a Jew can perform. Because of that very fact, I feel that a Jew who performs it must do it on his own; he cannot have it done for him by others. Just as someone else's going for him is no substitute for his going, so too someone else's paying for him is no substitute for his paying. I feel this about other *mitzvot,* but especially about this one. This is a *mitzvah* a Jew must save for, sacrifice for and pay for.

I know that this line of reasoning may sound strange and unacceptable; I know that at first it may seem to make no sense at all. But I hope that you will try to respect and accept it as my deep conviction.

Your kind offer itself I simply cannot accept. But the *kindness* of your offer I do accept and I will cherish always—as the precious sign of real friendship.

May we continue to encourage and help and love one another in the future, as in the past—and may I be forgiven for any hurt that this ungraciousness may cause you.

Warmly,

Hershel

At Hershel's funeral, his friend Joe Rosenstein made note of his ethical nature.

Many of us try to act ethically, and sometimes we succeed. But what we are supposed to strive toward as an ideal, Hershel Matt seemed to do so naturally. He had a gift for goodness. He somehow embodied each of the ethical teachings of our tradition. One example. Many of us try to avoid *leshon ha-ra*—destructive speech—and through effort we learn to catch ourselves just before, or sometimes just after, we have begun to say what we shouldn't. But Hershel seemed to avoid *leshon ha-ra* naturally—he could not speak ill of people because he recognized the humanity—and the divinity—of each person.... Each person before God was his equal, and so he spoke to each person without pretentiousness, without arrogance, without condescension. He would never flaunt his learning or his piety.

Shulamit Magnes, a colleague at the Reconstructionist Rabbinical College, recalls what it was like to be on the faculty with someone so ethical.

I remember Hershel being concerned about personal ethical behavior almost to the point of obsession. We would smile at it, sometimes, so exaggerated it seemed to be on occasion, but when he was gone, we knew our moral "insurance policy" was gone too. Hershel had a veritable allergy to anything that smelled, even before anyone else got a whiff of it, and so his presence elevated the moral level of everything that went on around him.

Hershel had a wonderful sense of humor, but he never understood how people could laugh at pratfalls. He was kind to others because he genuinely believed that each person was created in the divine image. Nothing made him happier than helping someone out. A friend of his noted that Hershel "always seemed to live on a plane that was above the pettiness that consumes much of our lives; yet he also was always a presence when someone needed support and encouragement."

When a poor, hungry man came to the synagogue in Troy one day, Rabbi Matt took him to the local Jewish delicatessen and asked the owner to provide the man whatever he wanted, for as long as he wanted. Hershel assured the owner that he himself would pay the bill. Typically, he never mentioned this incident to anyone. It was only after Hershel left Troy that the owner shared the secret with members of the congregation.

On the eve of *Rosh ha-Shanah,* perhaps the busiest day in the always hectic rabbinical calendar, Hershel would spend hours driving all over town bringing apples and honey to those who were sick or disabled or in mourning, so that they too could celebrate a sweet new year. On the eve of Passover he would deliver bottles of wine. As one congregant expressed it, Rabbi Matt "had a love of humanity that I have never seen equaled in anyone I have ever met, and I will always feel blessed by having known him."

Of course, as his son, I must admit that there were times in our childhood when we wished that our father was a bit less ethical. He would never let us sneak into a movie theater on a lower-priced ticket by pretending to be under age twelve. One year on Halloween, he insisted that we combine our trick-and-treating with a collection for UNICEF. We used to tease him about his ethical standards, which seemed to us a bit extreme. My brother David recalls how when Hershel would find a dime in a public telephone, he would debate with himself whether or not to send it back to the phone company, since the postage cost more than what he would be returning! My sister Debbie remembers another example of telephone ethics. Among our friends it was customary to call one's parents back at home after arriving at some out-of-town destination. Rather than paying for the phone call, the teenager would let the phone ring just once and then hang up. Hershel did not approve, reasoning that this was a minor type of stealing from the phone company.

But he was no stick in the mud. One autumn he took us to a Yankees' World Series game on a school day. Not that he was a great baseball fan; I remember him sitting in the bleachers reading *Commentary* magazine. He just understood how important it was for American kids to do things like this with their dad, and he wrote a letter to our teacher in the Hebrew Day School explaining his reasoning. She was not particularly impressed, but we sure were. A friend named Roy came along with us, skipping classes in public school for the occasion. His father's note to the school principal read something like: "Please excuse Roy's absence yesterday. He had to go to New York with his rabbi."

The day-to-day functioning of the synagogue exercised Rabbi Matt's ethical muscles. He insisted that financial considerations should not outweigh ethical ones. Every issue had to be scrutinized. For example, it is common practice for congregations to acknowledge donations publicly, either in the bulletin or from the pulpit. One reason generally given is that it is proper to give credit, though another consideration is that public mention will spur others to donate. With Rabbi Matt's urging, the Board of Directors of Temple Beth El, Troy discussed this issue and came to the conclusion that neither reason was valid, and that therefore they would no longer acknowledge donations publicly. Their statement read as follows:

As a synagogue we must teach and preach that gifts are properly given out of thanksgiving, or as a private personal tribute to the living or in memory of the dead, or out of desire to help in holy work. In none of these cases should we encourage the cheapening of a precious *mitzvah* by holding out the incentive of attaining glory, credit or publicity.

From then on, each donor was thanked in writing by the rabbi or by an officer. The Board was convinced by Hershel that "deep in their hearts our members will agree that it is a higher form of giving to give without seeking public thanks or credit."

Fund raising was always a target for Hershel's ethical scrutiny. He disliked fund raising altogether and eventually proposed in his "Principles and Policies for the Ideal Congregation" that synagogues engage in no fund raising at all![10] At Temple Neve Shalom in Metuchen, New Jersey, he only opposed certain events, such as a proposed raffle, concerning which he quickly issued the following list of objections:

Gambling is morally objectionable because it encourages the unworthy desire of obtaining something without earning or paying fair value for it. If the item to be raffled is a luxury item, the raffle encourages luxury and ostentation, which violate the Jewish standard of modest living.

It cheapens the *mitzvah* of supporting a synagogue, by implying that Jews will not adequately and directly support it for its own sake but only for ulterior gain.

If the raffle is publicized and tickets are sold in the general community, there will be the additional factor of *hillul ha-shem*—the desecration of God's name (and of the Jewish good name) by publicly indicating that Jews are not willing to support their own institutions adequately.

The way the synagogue spent its money was also an ethical issue. Once Rabbi Matt tried unsuccessfully to get his Temple Board to grant raises to the couple who served as caretakers of the synagogue. The Board said no; so Hershel quietly began giving the couple extra money out of his own pocket.

The conspicuous consumption of congregants upset Rabbi Matt's moral equilibrium. He was disgusted by the ostentatious displays that accompanied, or rather overwhelmed, *bar* and *bat mitzvah* celebrations. So he convinced the Board of Temple Beth El in Troy to pass a "Resolution on Moderation in Serving *Kiddush* at *Bar* and *Bat Mitzvahs*":

10. Reprinted below.

Whereas the act of becoming *bar mitzvah* is a sacred act in the life of a Jew, marking the recognition on his part of the covenant between God and Israel; and

Whereas any lavishness in food and drink in conjunction with a *bar mitzvah* tends to detract from its significance as a religious act; and

Whereas such lavishness encourages irreligious display of wealth on the part of some, imposes a financial burden upon others who are pressured to follow suit, and furthers a spirit of vain competition that is particularly out of place on a religious occasion;

Be it therefore resolved that the membership of Temple Beth El in Troy, New York, at its annual meeting on the fifth night of *Hanukkah* 5711 [December 7, 1950], urges upon its members henceforth to limit their *bar mitzvah* celebration on Temple premises following Sabbath services to a modest repast, which will be free from any lavishness or sumptuousness and which will rather be in the traditional spirit of a *se'udah shel mitzvah,* a meal appropriate to a religious moment.

His ethical standards were matched by an extraordinary humility. Many people considered him a *tzaddik,* a truly righteous person, even a *lamed vavnik,* one of the thirty-six hidden, unacknowledged righteous upon whom the world depends, according to tradition. We often heard this about our father as we were growing up. His colleague, Cantor Benjamin Stein, reflected on Hershel and wondered, "How does a *tzaddik* relate to himself and think of himself? How does he maintain his humility? Can one be aware of one's own humility?" Rabbi Matt was certainly aware that people thought of him as a *tzaddik.* He even joked about it. Once he said to Ben, "People tell me it so often that soon I may start believing it!" But if he did believe it, it didn't show. He guarded vigilantly against the temptation of self-importance, never allowing himself to remain inflated.

In 1967 Temple Neve Shalom planned to honor Rabbi Matt for his twenty years of service in the pulpit. One member of the synagogue recalls: "We knew he would veto the whole idea if he knew; so we didn't let him find out until after the invitations were sent out." When Hershel was interviewed in the local press, he gave this reaction to the event:

You know how these things are. People feel obliged to say nice things. And really I don't quite understand why a person should be honored for twenty years of rabbinical service. It's a reason for me to be thankful, but other people shouldn't feel they have to celebrate.

When one of Rabbi Matt's articles was accepted by *Conservative Judaism,* the editor, Samuel Dresner, had to contend with the author's humble opinion of himself. Dresner wrote:

Your [article is] already in galleys and will appear I hope in the next issue. [It is] a superb contribution to the problems of the American synagogue and will be read with great appreciation by layman, rabbi, teacher, theologian and philosopher alike. We are indebted to you for this work. And even though you consider it "unfinished, incomplete, poor, insignificant, and unimpressive," I consider it just the opposite and I am sure that many of our [readers] will. Therefore, until the Messiah arrives, I shall be forced to use such "poor" materials as you provide me.

His humility did not connote grimness. In certain situations it was even jocular. Monford Harris recalls one instance of Hershel's "merry humility." In his first congregation, in Nashua, Rabbi Matt intentionally neglected to inform people that he was a *levi* who merited being called upon to chant the blessings over the Torah immediately after the *kohen*. When his father, C. David Matt, visited Nashua and was called to the Torah, Rabbi Matt, Sr. pointed out that he was a *levi*. "The congregation was astounded at this revelation. And Hershel enjoyed many a chuckle."

Monnie Harris remembers another example of Hershel's humility, during their third year at JTS:

I did not know of Hershel's earlier accomplishments. One day I learned about one. He was at home in Philadelphia when he called me in New York. He asked me to please open the top drawer of his dresser, in the corner of which I would find a little box containing his Phi Beta Kappa key which I might be kind enough to send him in Philadelphia. He was to be engaged and he wanted to give this to Gustine. I was most happy about the engagement but also shocked by the discovery that he never let on that he had made Phi Beta Kappa.

Humility wasn't an abstract ideal for Rabbi Matt. He practiced it constantly; it was central to his *yiddishkeit*. On the eve of *Yom Kippur* he used to ask forgiveness from anyone he might have wronged, including each one of us in his family. In Nashua, he sent this letter to each member of his congregation:

October 10, 1948

Dear _____ ,

As you may know, our tradition teaches that *Yom Kippur* can bring atonement only for sins between a human being and God. For sins committed against one's fellow, *Yom Kippur* cannot bring atonement unless people have first been forgiven by each other. And so the beautiful custom has arisen of asking the pardon, before *Yom Kippur*, of all we have sinned against.

I wish I could come to you personally to ask your forgiveness, or at least write to you a letter that is not mimeographed. I cannot do that. But I am personally writing your name at the top of the page—and am thinking of how much of what I have to say in the next paragraph applies to the relationship between YOU and me.

Some of you I have neglected to visit or to talk with at length—to get to know you better and learn what is in your heart. To some of you I have spoken harshly or meanly, and have hurt you by word or deed. When I have at times felt compelled to disagree with you and have not accepted your advice, I have not always been kind enough in explaining why I did what I did. Some of you I have thought about in my heart uncharitably and unlovingly. For all these wrongs that I have committed against you intentionally and with full knowledge or unintentionally through negligence, and for any other wrongs I am not aware of, I ask your forgiveness on this *Erev Yom Kippur*.

And I hope that if you have wronged any of your neighbors, Jew or non-Jew, you will approach them and ask their forgiveness. Only then will God allow Himself to grant atonement for our sins.

Sincerely,

Hershel Matt

As we have seen, Rabbi Matt's humility did not make him shy or hesitant when a vital issue was at stake. As one of his colleagues, Neil Gillman, wrote,

> He was one of the most courageous men I have ever known. He knew his own mind. He knew what he believed. He had his values—and he stood up for them unflinchingly despite all of the repercussions. The mild manner was deceptive. There was iron in the man—and it was that, not the mildness, that made him so intimidating to me.

Rabbi Matt spoke out and published on controversial issues that he easily could have avoided. In the 1950s he pioneered in the field of equal rights for women, calling them up to the Torah at Temple Beth El in Troy, New York. Later he was among the first to support women in their struggle to be accepted for rabbinical studies at the Jewish Theological Seminary. He championed the cause of those being treated unfairly, making their troubles and concerns his own. He constantly made the effort to see and respect the uniqueness of each person: homosexual and heterosexual, male and female, black and white, Jew and non-Jew. He was a Zionist from childhood, but on his joyous visits to Israel he felt a deep concern for the rights of the Palestinians. As his son Rabbi Jonathan Matt noted at Hershel's funeral, his life was a modern midrash on the creation of each human being in the divine image.

He created a great stir when he wrote on homosexuality, adopting a compassionate and tolerant tone. In one interview he stated: "Homosexuality is not an illness.... [As we go through life] we discover who we are and what we are.... Their way of life is the only way for them to live with integrity." When he was challenged by someone who insisted that the Torah condemns homosexuality, he responded as follows:

> As opposed to the Torah being strictly God's word, we should look upon it as "containing" God's word.... This allows for a human element, subject to growth, error and interpretation. We must remember that the idea of hearing God's word includes the idea of "mis-hearing" God's word, that the recording of God's word can also mean the "mis-recording" of God's word.[11]

Despite his striking, unconventional views, Rabbi Matt was, on the whole, a traditional believer. He was certain that God has a plan for the world, and that this plan will ultimately be revealed. He could speak sincerely about sin or even Satan, without sounding dismal. As he once wrote, "[Our] greatest glory lies in ... being able to sin but choosing not to."[12] He believed in miracles, the Messiah, the world-to-come, life-after-death and bodily resurrection. Hershel admitted that he had an odd reputation at the Jewish Theological Seminary: "They say I'm the only one who's ever graduated from there who *believes* in the resurrection of the dead!" Yet his focus was on the here-and-now. In his sermons he often spoke of holding "the Torah in one hand and the newspaper in the other." Religious sensitivity makes it possible to have a taste of paradise here on earth.

> Whenever we are truly aware that we stand in God's holy presence, we can catch from within time a glimpse of eternity.... The reality of heavenly paradise is known in the moment of radical amazement at the grandeur

11. *The American Jewish World*, Minneapolis, Minnesota, October 30, 1987, p. 1. Cf. the essays reprinted below: "Sin, Crime, Sickness, or Alternative Life Style?: A Jewish Approach to Homosexuality," "A Call for Compassion," "Homosexual Rabbis?"
12. "Human Choice and God's Design."

> of God's creation,... at the moment of perfectly unselfish love for a fellow human being in need or in distress,... at the moment of true joy in the performance of any *mitzvah*. [13]

He believed not only in traditional formulations but in the reality of God. And since God was a reality for him, he wasn't frightened of new approaches to the divine. For example, he welcomed the opportunity to balance the masculine references to God with the feminine. As Joe Rosenstein said in his eulogy, "Even God will miss the natural and unchallenging way in which Hershel spoke of Him and Her interchangeably. God lost a friend. And we did too."

In his observance, Rabbi Matt was also quite traditional, and he took special delight in performing and promoting ritual practices that were widely neglected, such as wearing a *tallit katan* (a fringed undershirt), reciting *kiddush levanah* (the blessing over the new moon), *tashlikh* (casting one's sins into the water on *Rosh ha-Shanah*) and *dukhen*ing (the public blessing offered by the priests). Yet he could be very flexible, even with major elements of the tradition. After a number of years in the pulpit, he realized that it was unrealistic to expect the congregation to listen intently to the full Torah reading. As he later explained to a group of colleagues, "Too often the period of the Torah reading has, in most of our synagogues, been a period for physical exit and recess or physical presence and inner recess!" So Rabbi Matt printed up pamphlets for each weekly Torah portion containing selections in Hebrew accompanied by a modern English translation. This turned the Torah service into a dramatic part of the *Shabbat daven*ing, with the congregation listening to the Hebrew chant of the biblical text and then joining in to read the English translation together aloud. Hershel didn't mind when someone joked that he was turning the Jews into "the people of the pamphlet."

Faith and openness often seem mutually exclusive, but with Hershel Matt they went hand in hand. He had a great willingness, an eagerness to learn and evolve, to reinvigorate the tradition, to participate in unfolding the infinite meaning of the Torah. The progressive views he adopted were not, for him, alien imports; they were *mitzvot*. He confronted the real and difficult questions that face Jews in the modern world, including questions stemming from doubt and skepticism. As he once wrote, "The greatest indictment against religion is when it's guilty of irrelevance." By wrestling

---

13. "An Outline of Jewish Eschatology."

with issues of belief and practice, by fighting against social injustice, he served as a model of how a mature religious thinker can continue to grow.

With his gentle courage, Rabbi Matt was somehow able to affirm and explore unpopular ideas without alienating people. In the words of Yitzhak Greenberg, a prominent religious thinker,

> He challenged, he deepened, he forced us to consider new possibilities without betraying the tradition or the seriousness of the past. This is one of the extraordinary things about Hershel. He was so kind and his spirit so touching that he was able to say radical things that nobody else could say and yet get people to open their minds. They would not have done this for someone else.

At the Reconstructionist Rabbinical College, where Rabbi Matt taught for the last several years of his life, he helped lead the fight for the acceptance of gay and lesbian Jews. Yet, as his colleague Arthur Waskow remarked, "He was able to create around himself a zone of gentleness, even when he was exploring intensely controversial questions."

He never claimed to know all the answers. Even when he articulated courageous positions, he always remained aware of the ambiguities. At home we used to tease him about one of his favorite expressions: "On the other hand...." At synagogue board meetings, he would often expend great effort in convincing the members of the importance of a certain program he wanted to push through. Then, once he had made his point and the opposition was nearly overcome, he would say, "On the other hand, I can see your side." As his son Jonathan put it, "I have never met a better listener."

Hershel was genuine through and through, *the* authentic person," in the words of Monnie Harris. Shulamit Magnes recalls that when Hershel said "How are you?" it "was not a formulaic way to begin a conversation. He remembered what you told him the last time he asked." Everything he did came from the heart; he made himself totally available to people. Every detail of daily living, every encounter with another human being he infused with a sense of holiness. Perhaps one of his faults was that he didn't set priorities. But this was also an aspect of his greatness: the particular human demand of the moment was what mattered most to him. He was *tam ve-yashar,* pure and upright. Amazingly, he was as good as he seemed. In the Talmudic idiom, *tokho ke-varo:* his inner self matched his outward appearance. A colleague at the Reconstructionist Rabbinical College, Jacob Staub, put it this way:

> When I spoke with him for any length of time, I was acutely aware of being
> in the presence of someone who had made his way through life with his
> convictions and principles intact, someone who had refused to allow the
> difficulties of his life to impede him in his pursuit of the most exalted
> things.

It was this purity and simplicity that had such an impact on the people he met. He really didn't have to preach. People sensed, "If this is what Judaism can do to one person, then maybe it can do something for me."

Rabbi Matt was not naive, but in a way, as his friend Reena Bernards remarked: "He was childlike. He approached the world with a sense of wonder and wide eyes, as if the whole thing was one big, terrifying and wonderful mystery, which he felt himself supremely lucky to be able to observe and experience." A friend and colleague, Edward Feld, notes how Hershel's sense of wonder extended to the interpersonal realm:

> He was forever hopeful. As each new person met him, as each new
> situation came upon him, he always sensed the almost messianic possibili-
> ties of the moment. Each person was a special messenger with a divine and
> unique message to deliver. And Hershel moved himself to attend to what
> was extraordinary in this otherwise ordinary encounter.

Hershel yearned to be a *pashuter yid,* a simple Jew. He wanted people to think of him as someone who happened to have studied a little more Torah than they had. He loved to attend a *minyan* and just *daven* instead of serving as the leader. His longtime friend and colleague, Solomon Bernards, recalls:

> He had a passion to hurry and be present at the announced time of the
> beginning of the service. He wanted to fulfill with relish the command of
> the Almighty, in the spirit of the Codes of Law, which ordain that a person
> should "ever hurry to fulfill the bidding of his Creator."

After he left the congregational rabbinate and they moved to Highland Park, New Jersey, Hershel and Gustine were members of the Highland Park Conservative Temple and also of a small, intimate *havurah*-style *minyan.* For this *minyan,* Hershel sometimes led *daven*ing and read from the Torah, but he would also attend the meetings, make telephone calls, write letters and prepare lists. Nothing seemed too mundane, if he was helping the group arrange its *daven*ing. He wasn't the kind of person to delegate jobs to others. Here especially he didn't want to be referred to as Rabbi Matt, just Hershel.

But anyone who heard him *daven* knew at once that here was a unique, high soul, a master of prayer. Monnie Harris remarked, "He was the first modern American that I knew who took prayer seriously." Rabbi Matt composed an entire series of *kavvanot,* "directions" for the heart to follow, or "bridges to prayer," to help people focus on the inner meaning of the words in the *siddur,* to bring the prayers alive.[14] He would often chant part of a prayer in English translation or introduce a new melody. Though he loved the *siddur,* or perhaps because he loved it, he was flexible and an advocate of change. As he once wrote,

> The traditional Jewish concern for the anguish of others, and for the needs and well-being of others; the traditional awareness of the ... fellowship of all human beings ...—these need to be given fuller, more detailed and more powerful expression [in the *siddur*].[15]

One memory I have of my father is of *daven*ing with him early *Shabbat* morning when there were still only a handful of people in the synagogue. We would be sitting together, chanting softly, while someone else led the early part of the service. I remember, in particular, how he used to rejoice in the lines of Psalm 19: *Ha-Shamayim mesapperim kevod el u-ma'aseh yadav maggid ha-raki'a.... Torat adonai temimah meshivat nafesh.... Yiheyu le-ratzon imrei fi ve-hegyon libbi le-fanekha adonai tzuri ve-go'ali.* "The heavens declare the glory of God and the sky tells of His handiwork.... The Torah of *YHVH* is pure, restoring the soul.... May the words of my mouth and the meditation of my heart find favor before You, O *YHVH,* my rock and my redeemer." I learned, week by week, how to rejoice in this psalm too.

Sol Bernards describes Rabbi Matt's *daven*ing in these words:

> Whether leading the congregation, or being seated in the pew, he showed a singular joy in being involved in prayer. His face glowed with a sense of privilege and an almost uncontainable sense of peace and pleasure at being part of the public praise of God. He would not allow himself to be distracted by the slightest bit of conversation. He concentrated totally on the content of the worship, singing the antiphonal responses with the freshness of a new discovery, a new insight which had occurred to him at that particular moment.

Two people whom Rabbi Matt influenced deeply, Rabbi Daniel Siegel

---

14. Many of these are printed below, in the section "*Kavvanot* and Prayers."
15. "The People Israel and the Peoples of the World as Reflected in the Jewish Prayer Book" (see Bibliography).

and Ellen Frankel, offered these accounts of him leading a *Shabbat* service:

> A memory of a *shul* full of *bar mitzvah* and silence, of only two rows of people singing. Of Hershel chanting *yotzer or u-voreh hoshekh* ["who forms light and creates darkness"] as though he had seen the sunrise for the first time that morning, as though he had only that second connected morning with God. He was quietly breathless with wonder. I felt sadness for a community that didn't know the value of such an awareness and an equally strong desire to achieve that level of awareness in myself.

> I have a clear memory of [Rabbi Matt] reading the English translations of [the] Silverman [prayer book]—some of the least inspiring prose ever written!—but with such *kavvanah* that the prayers worked: "True and certain it is," "On that day the Lord will be one and His name one," "Who is like You, O God?" Today, as my feminist contemporaries wrestle so passionately with God-language, especially in English, I am amazed by how *untroubled* I am by the awkward gender problems of language, largely because [Rabbi Matt] helped me see beyond the words to the spirit beneath.

A congregant recalls how, when Rabbi Matt recited the blessings upon being called to the Torah, "The words came alive with the quiet fervor that he brought to them." Zalman Schachter, a leader of contemporary Jewish spiritual renewal, used to come from New York City to Metuchen, New Jersey just to hear Hershel *daven*. Another rabbi, Orthodox and nonmystical, recalls: "His *daven*ing was a genuine dialogue between man and God.... Whenever he was at our synagogue, I was always mesmerized."

Rabbi Matt was a Conservative rabbi whose spirituality and personality had an impact on Orthodox, Reform and Reconstructionist Jews and on non-Jews. As Yitzhak Greenberg remarks,

> He was one of those non-Orthodox rabbis whose spiritual power and intellectual and human integrity were so extraordinary that they broke me out of my complacency as one who could live comfortably and exclusively within the categories of one denomination. My only regret is that every Orthodox rabbi and rabbinical student did not meet Hershel, since no one could resist the magnetism of his kindness and spiritual search.

Rabbi Matt was a rabbi's rabbi, a moral and spiritual influence on those whose job it was to inspire others. Zalman Schachter put it this way in a letter to Hershel in 1967:

> I suppose you'll never know in this world (and, since you don't buy a

discarnate existence in *olam ha-ba,* you may have to wait until the resurrection to find out) what your contribution was to friends and *haverim,* and how often you entered into their consideration and decision making.... From time to time, when I'm faced with an ethical decision, I ask myself, "What would Hershel do?"

For his lifelong friend and colleague Monford Harris,

> Hershel was my anchorage in the world of the personal. Or perhaps I should say he was the personal world for me. He was the *Thou.* Characteristic of Hershel was his being present, to God and to neighbor.... Hershel was always with the one whom he faced. The one he faced was always to him a significant other.

A cantor who studied with Hershel recalls that she once asked a friend: "Who is your favorite rabbi?" The response was: "For what? If you mean for *mentshlekhkeit,* it would be Rabbi Matt."

Perhaps Rabbi Matt should have had a position as a *mashpi'a ruhani,* "a spiritual guide," at one of the seminaries. He certainly had such an effect at the Reconstructionist Rabbinical College and the Academy for Jewish Religion. But Hershel was not so presumptuous as to claim that he could guide others. His guidance came naturally and spontaneously, through baring his self. Ellen Frankel recalls how one day, as a beginning graduate student, she confided in Rabbi Matt: "I don't know if I'm doing the right thing, going to graduate school. I don't know if it's the right decision for me."

> He smiled in that serene way of his and said quietly: "I've been a congregational rabbi for twenty-five years, and I still don't know if it's the right thing for me!" He chuckled and I joined in, although I was shocked.... But that was Hershel. A *tzaddik* who, by definition, could not advertise, maybe even appreciate, his own special status.

Part of his beauty was his self-effacement. At one of his early congregations he composed a prayer that read:

> O Lord, teach us, as members of a holy congregation, what we should seek for in a rabbi, as well as what we should not seek. Teach us, as rabbis in the Congregation of Israel, how to lead our people, as well as how not to lead. And speed the day when we shall no longer have any need for rabbis, when we shall indeed be what we are called to be: a kingdom of priests to You and a holy nation. Amen.

Rabbi Matt may have wished, as Moses did, that all of Israel could have tasted the gift of inspiration, but he knew that, in fact, there was a deep need for rabbis. He constantly urged his congregants to deepen their understanding of Torah and their commitment to observance; yet he also encouraged them to adopt their own approach. As one person put it simply, "He showed me a way to worship God in my own way that was meaningful." One of his greatest satisfactions was when someone experimented with a new *mitzvah;* his greatest disappointment was that most Jews did not even try.

A congregant in Troy recalls:

> He inspired all of us to lead more Jewishly committed lives and yet he felt that he wasn't successful. He invited all of us in study groups separately to his home and gave us a proposition: that whatever step we were on in our commitment to Judaism—we move up one step. For instance, if we ate *treif* like pork or shellfish, we would stop. If we ate meat out, we would stick to fish or salad and so on. Not everyone wanted to do it, but most said that they would try. At the end of the year we all got together and a few had stayed with it. I thought it was great, but [Rabbi Matt] felt it failed.

He used every opportunity he could to attract people to the "blessed yoke" of Torah and *mitzvot.* He wrote and circulated a series of pamphlets on the "how and why" of many *mitzvot* including: *Shabbat,* prayer, *tefillin, tallit, mezuzah, tzedakah, kashrut,* circumcision, and conducting a *seder.* Other pamphlets covered topics such as: basic *mitzvot,* Torah and business life, how a Jew should spend money, *leshon ha-ra* (on the holiness of speech), *yetzer ha-ra* (the evil inclination), choosing a Jewish name for a newborn, and a Jewish approach to sex. With typical modesty, his name does not appear on these. Here is a short sample, from his pamphlet entitled "What is *tzedakah?*"

> *Tzedakah* does not mean merely "giving charity," in the ordinary sense. It does not mean simply showing how nice one is by handing a few pennies (or a few dollars) to a poor person. For the word *tzedakah* means "righteousness, firmness-in-doing-the-right, steadfast straightness, justice, uprightness." The *mitzvah* of *tzedakah* means that in God's eyes and by His command what I have is not my own but God's and ought to rightfully be shared with God's other children in need, shared lovingly and generously, as with a brother or sister.... To perform the *mitzvah* of *tzedakah* means so freely and lovingly to obey God's command-to-give that one could not imagine doing otherwise.

How much shall I give? The ideal is that "no one has a right to retain for himself more than the necessities of life as long as anyone lacks for these things." If I find this standard to be impossible of fulfillment, then at least I should be guided by my own answers to such questions as these: Which of my luxuries can I eliminate, or at least reduce? Can I give up some of the things that are not necessary for my true welfare, or that are even against my true welfare? Have I yet reached the point in my giving where I am making a painful sacrifice? If it were my own blood brother or sister who were in hunger or pain, what would I find myself able to do?...

In what form shall I give? The ideal would be to give in such a way that the recipient become self-supporting. Since this standard is often impossible, let me give my aid in every form: in money (both loans and gifts), in goods, in work and time and help, by word and smile, by silent companionship and by prayer.

Once, following a *Yom Kippur* service, Rabbi Matt addressed a letter to the entire congregation, inviting them to make a Jewish New Year's resolution and commit themselves to increasing their level of observance in such areas as Torah study, worship, ethics, *kashrut, Shabbat* and festivals. He hoped that the intense experience of *Rosh ha-Shanah* and *Yom Kippur* would carry over to the rest of the calendar year. The letter read in part:

Dear Friend,

If you have to any degree been moved by the services and sermons of the High Holy Days, I hope that you will now give very serious thought to examining the extent and depth of your Jewish living.... I urge you to ... take the combined pledge-and-request form, consider it carefully, see what on it is possible for you to try, fill out one copy and return it to me.... Begin now. It it too late to delay, but it is not too late to begin, or to return to, the holiness and joy of living the Jewish life of Torah and *mitzvot*. In hope and confidence,

Your Rabbi,

Hershel Matt

Another year, he was more specific and more limited in his post-High Holy Day request. He had given a sermon on *Yom Kippur* entitled "How Fasting Can Help Us Eat." Here he had suggested that people "restore into their home life, on a regular basis, the *mitzvah* of uttering a word of thanksgiving before and after our meals." A few days later, the congregants found in their mailboxes two copies of a card containing the *motzi* and the *birkat ha-mazon,* the blessings before and after meals. A letter accompanying the cards included the following thoughts:

> If you have not yet begun, why not begin this day to thank God for the blessing and miracle of our daily bread? Perhaps in this way your table can begin to assume the character of an altar and your home take on a little more of the nature of a sanctuary. What a strange and wonderful paradox: by thanking our Father in Heaven for the bread by which we live, we can learn again that we live not by bread alone.

In Metuchen Rabbi Matt succeeded in initiating about a dozen families into the *mitzvah* of building a *sukkah* on the harvest festival of *Sukkot,* an unusual and delightful *mitzvah.* He took great pleasure in "*sukkah*-hopping" on the holiday, visiting one booth after another, rejoicing with the families, complimenting each one on its fragilely splendid *sukkah.* The days preceding *Sukkot* were wondrous for us, his children. This was the only time all year when our father wore beat-up, old work-clothes; he loomed in front of us like a master carpenter. We worked on the *sukkah* together and then got to sleep out in it a few nights during the holiday. One *Sukkot* there was a thief in the neighborhood, and our house was spared. Perhaps the thief figured we were sleeping out to protect our property.

Shabbat was the highlight of Hershel's week, and of his life. I remember once hearing him speak at Brandeis University on a *Shabbat;* he said that if it weren't for *Shabbat,* he didn't know if he could go on living. The audience was stunned, and silence reigned. I remember thinking, "God, am I lucky to have a father like that!"

Our house was busy, of course, on Friday afternoon. Somehow, we all managed to take a shower or a bath in time for lighting the candles. My father would shine his shoes, cut his fingernails and shave in preparation for greeting the Sabbath Queen. After my mother lit the candles, we would sit down in the living room and chant a chapter from the Song of Songs, the psalms from *Kabbalat Shabbat,* and *Lekhah Dodi,* the mystical poem greeting the royal bride. For the last verse, we walked to the front door and opened it. In wafted the presence of *Shabbat.*

The next twenty-six hours or so were largely devoted to *daven*ing, playing, studying, laughing, walking, talking, relaxing, reading and napping. The *Shabbat* meals were leisurely, sumptuous and spiced with *zemirot,* humor and lively discussion. My father encouraged each of us to question and interpret the weekly Torah portion. It was unusual not to have a guest or a friend with us at the table. On *Shabbat* afternoon, as I mentioned, we kids usually divided our time between playing touch football and studying the Torah portion with my dad. As *Shabbat* drew to a close, family and friends would gather in the living room, singing gentle songs and weaving stories. Hershel used to say that this was a bittersweet time, as when a close friend is about to leave. You don't want her to go, but you are overjoyed that she is still there with you, at least for a little longer. We finally escorted the Queen on her way with *havdalah.*

Rabbi Matt sought to initiate his fellow Jews into the wonder of *Shabbat,* but most of them had other plans for the weekend. The only time they would venture into the synagogue on a Friday night or Saturday morning was if they were invited to a *bar* or *bat mitzvah.* Once he put the following notice in the Temple Bulletin:

> This *Shabbat* is just an "ordinary" *Shabbat*—with no special reason to attend Sabbath services: no *bar mitzvah,* no *bat mitzvah,* no guest preacher, no holiday—not even an *oneg Shabbat* (a reception following the services)! But that's wonderful! Here is a chance for a Jew to come to Sabbath worship *li-shemah,* for its own sake. What greater reward can there be? The reward for a *mitzvah* is in performing the *mitzvah....* This *Shabbat* is an "ordinary" *Shabbat.* But to the faithful Jew, an ordinary *Shabbat* is *Shabbat kodesh,* the Holy Sabbath. Join your fellow Jews in Sabbath worship.

I don't know if there were more people in *shul* that *Shabbat* or not, but over the years Hershel came to realize that it was a hopeless situation. To cite one extreme, poignant case, once a mother approached him with a request that he found impossible to fulfill. Her son attended *Shabbat* services regularly, while the rest of the family came only sporadically. She asked if Rabbi Matt would tell her son not to come to synagogue because Saturday was a time when the family planned to go on outings together. The son's synagogue attendance was damaging family unity! Hershel confided in his cantor, Benjamin Stein, "How could she ask me to do that?!" For Hershel, it was by honoring and celebrating the *Shabbat* together that a Jewish family should draw closer. Usually he declined invitations to *bar* or *bat mitzvah* dinners because they infringed on our own *Shabbat* family meals. Here is a letter he wrote to one couple a few months after arriving in Metuchen:

> Dear Leon and Mildred,
>
> This is a very difficult letter to write, and I know in advance that I will probably not succeed in making myself fully understood.

Gustine and I appreciate very much indeed your invitation to join you for Robert's *bar mitzvah* dinner. To realize that in spite of our short acquaintance you wanted to include us at an affair that is really meant for relatives and friends of long standing has touched us deeply. We really do not deserve to be included and are at a loss to understand your kindness in inviting us.

And yet, in spite of your thoughtfulness and kindness, we are unable to accept your invitation. It is a very deep principle with us never to leave our children at [*Shabbat*] dinner time or in the afternoon. The *mitzvah* of observing *Shabbat* together as a family is so very precious that we would feel we are desecrating the holiness of the day if we were to deprive them (and ourselves) of this sacred aspect of *Shabbat.*

You were generous enough, when I mentioned this, to offer to include the boys in the invitation also. But such an arrangement would not be proper: partly because of the imposition upon you of added trouble, expense and inconvenience; but also because we believe that part of *Shabbat* day should be spent in rest and quiet reading and Torah study and spiritual renewal in an intimate sharing of family life.

Please do not let yourselves feel that we are declining to share in the *bar mitzvah* and its *simhah.* Robert becomes *bar mitzvah* during the service, where we will indeed share the joy and thrill and tears and prayers—of thanksgiving and of hope—for Robert and for you.

We want very much to get to know you better and better, and to come closer and closer to you. We are eager to spend time with you in your home and in ours—so that the relationship between us may, with God's help, grow into an ever deeper and dearer friendship. But this cannot take place at a large dinner where we can hardly even speak to one another or hold any genuine conversation.

Please try to understand and please try not to be offended. We have already begun to admire you and to love you.

Warmly,

Hershel Matt

5

Though he was aware, in part, of his influence on others, Rabbi Matt came to see himself as a failure in the rabbinate. As he confided to Cantor Stein, in words that recall Abraham's arguing with God, "I need to find at least ten in the congregation whose lives I have touched. I haven't. I have failed." Hershel certainly had touched many times ten; a solid core attended services regularly, and there were numerous study groups that met in the synagogue and in people's homes. But this particular rabbi needed a greater number of responsive souls. Solomon Bernards offers these reflections on Hershel's disillusionment:

For those of us who knew him well, and who knew of his magnificent achievements in each of these communities, and who were astonished as to his decisions to leave—it was a deep sense of failure which plagued him all through the years of his congregational rabbinate. Why didn't the congregational leaders take him seriously when he pointed out the need for leaders to be models of piety, of Sabbath observance, of deep commitment to Judaism and Jewish values? He blamed himself for the failures of most of his laity. He must not have been as convincing a model, as persuasive a "Rabbi and Teacher and Preacher," as compelling an advocate [as he could have been]. Therefore he must leave, and try to accomplish his mission elsewhere. But everywhere people were frail morally, and distracted in their convictions and persuasions. Was it an innocence that plagued him and hurt him so deeply? Was it an unalterable demand which he placed upon himself, in the mood of the prophets, single-handedly to build a new universe?

His frustration grew from year to year, but already in his first congregation in Nashua it was strong. In his second year there he gave a sermon entitled "Does Nashua Want a Rabbi?" When he expressed his feelings to his father, Rabbi Matt, Sr. tried to talk him out of searching for greener grass:

> ... About the proposed *shinnui makom* ["change of place"].... You must realize that even the most earnest and consecrated rabbi cannot hope to metamorphose the lives of his people. If they were more responsive during your first and/or second year than in your third year, it is not because you are less effective but because they are probably settling back into their former groove, but it is no reflection on you.... It is like submitting a person to the influence of a stimulant; in time it wears off. Am I ... defeatist? No. It is rather an honest appraisal of the work of the rabbi and of his ministry. There is no doubt that you have done some fine work and you have influenced them, more than you or they realize. [Max] Arzt was here yesterday morning at a Seminary breakfast.... He told me how well thought of you are, and I am sure he didn't hear it from you.

But the compliment did not do the trick. In the first of several letters of resignation to his various congregations, Rabbi Matt outlined the problem:

> Dear Friends,
>
> I am writing to inform you of a decision which I have regretfully come to....: to resign as your rabbi, when my contract is up in August, 1950. You can be sure that I have given this matter much thought and have hesitated a long time before arriving at my decision to leave—for I have been happy in Nashua in many ways. But the situation by now is so

frustrating and depressing that I feel I can no longer be happy or effective in my work.

After two-and-a-half years with you, most of you still do not seem to feel that it is important or worthwhile to learn about the history of our people or its beliefs and practices. Almost no one has come to adult classes, even to give them a try.

What is more important, most of the community do not come to Friday evening services. Though I have tried my best through English prayers, congregational singing, and my sermons to make the services inspiring and effective, these have not succeeded. Most Jews here do not pray or even want to try.

Even in our school, though the children have made some progress, the general spirit has reflected the parents' indifference. "I'm not coming to services; my parents don't go and don't care" is a typical comment. Children are quick to see that what is unimportant for their parents can't really be important for them.

In any case, a rabbi is more than a teacher of children—he is a rabbi for every age. He cannot remain where Judaism is for children only....

Some of the blame is mine, I am sure. I have not done enough; and what I have done I've not done well enough. Perhaps some of the blame is yours, too. In any case, it does not seem likely that there will be a basic, deep-seated change in this community with me as your rabbi. So with deep regret I must resign.

I hope that your next rabbi may succeed, where I have failed, in strengthening in you a desire to worship God, to study His word, and to give Him a central place in your daily life. May God bless you.

Very sincerely,

Hershel Matt

Hershel left Nashua and moved to Troy, New York, where he served for nine years (1950-59). Eventually, the same frustrations drove him to start all over again in Metuchen, New Jersey. Here he stayed longer than anywhere else, from 1959 to 1970. One might conclude that things were different in this pleasant suburb, but actually he threatened to leave already in 1962. He began to conduct what he referred to as the "*Mitzvah* Campaign," asking his congregants to commit themselves to increased religious observance. He felt that without such a commitment he could not serve effectively or honestly as a rabbi. We can follow the progress of this campaign in a remarkable series of letters written by Rabbi Matt to the congregation. Here are some excerpts:

January 23, 1962
Third Day of Torah Portion *Yitro*

Dear Friend,

The problem I presented [at last night's Congregational meeting] is this: What does it mean to be a Jew? to be a member of the Jewish community? to be a member of a synagogue? to have a rabbi? (Also, from the other side, what does it mean to be a rabbi?)

Through the ages it was recognized that to be a Jew means to be a member of that people—Israel—which is under a holy covenant with God, subject to, and guided by, Torah and *mitzvot,* called to live a separate life of holiness, bound by a certain holy discipline, judged by a certain holy standard, loved with a holy love, blessed with a holy joy.... In the pursuit of Torah and *mitzvot* the Jew would find the whole meaning of his life....

What makes our situation dangerous ..., desperately perilous, in fact, is that today even synagogue Jews accept no standard, no obligation, no commitment to the tradition.... If you hear about a Jew that he has joined a congregation, or is even active in one, is on the Board of the Congregation or even an officer—that tells you nothing, absolutely nothing about whether he knows about, cares about, or does anything about such crucial Jewish pursuits as worship of God, study of Torah, observance of the Sabbath, practice of *kashrut.* The fact of his synagogue affiliation tells you nothing, absolutely nothing about the level of his business ethics, the quality of his family life, the measure of his giving *tzedakah....* To be a member of a congregation in the modern world, in the United States, in Metuchen, New Jersey means nothing Jewish in particular—which is to say that it means: nothing!

And so, to be the rabbi of a congregation, in a certain sense, means the same thing: nothing!

"Rabbi" is one of those words in the language that imply their opposite number. Just as the word "husband" implies "wife" (and vice versa),... so too "rabbi" implies "disciple."

The members of our congregation do many wonderful things; they have many wonderful qualities; and they have treated their rabbi in many wonderful ways. But they have not, for the most part, given any indication that they need or want a rabbi; that they have any use for a rabbi; or that they even know what a rabbi is for.

A rabbi's main function and purpose in the world (and in Metuchen) is to learn and teach Torah: that is, his principal task is to lead his people in the pursuit of learning and doing that which the Torah tradition tells us is God's will for the people Israel. If the rabbi does not strive to perform that task, he is no rabbi. If the rabbi is not given the opportunity to perform that task, he is denied the opportunity to be a rabbi. And if the congregation does not provide at least a core group of men and women who acknowledge the supreme importance of this task by offering themselves as the rabbi's disciples and partners in seeking to study the holy tradition and to fulfill the commandments, then there is neither congregation nor rabbi....

As the rabbi, therefore, I am asking you whether *you* are willing to clarify for yourself and to indicate to me where you stand.

Inquire in your heart whether you are willing to accept the double task and the double privilege of being a Jew: the task and privilege of *increasing your knowledge* through the study of Torah and the task and privilege of *increasing your practice* through the fulfillment of *mitzvot....*

Approach the rabbi to discuss your readiness; to seek his help, support, guidance and resources; and possibly to learn of other Jews who are in a similar situation, with whom, if you wish, you can share the search.

Remind yourself that while on the one hand.... you are called to accept the commitment to a life of Torah and *mitzvot* (an "impossible" maximum standard), on the other hand you may begin with a minimum standard: to climb one rung higher than you are at present on the ladder of Jewish holiness.

Are you as a Jew ready to commit yourself to make a genuine effort?...

I write you as the one who officially and nominally is already your rabbi, but who prays that you (and God) will allow me to be your rabbi in a deeper and truer sense.

May I hear from you?

Your Rabbi,

Hershel Matt

About a month later, Rabbi Matt penned a letter to the teenagers in the congregation, encouraging them to become involved in the "great project," with their parents or on their own. Here he was treading on thin ice and did not want to ruin *shelom bayit,* the peacefulness of the household. Still, he made it clear that teenagers had certain rights and responsibilities of their own.

> It's not up to you to make any decisions for the whole family, but I'm sure your parents and you agree with the Jewish tradition that a boy or girl who has reached *bar* or *bat mitzvah* age is old enough to make some decisions about the *mitzvot* for himself.

A few weeks later, in March 1962, Rabbi Matt wrote to the congregation again, noting that "a significant number have responded in significant ways.... Some have begun actually to add to their pattern of Jewish living, and to increase their study and practice of one or more of the *mitzvot....* Some are on the verge; some are taking the plunge." He announced a series of meetings to discuss the commitment to Torah and *mitzvot.* Soon, though, he realized that he had not been specific enough in his campaign for greater observance. In May, he wrote another letter, which read in part:

> A congregation in which membership involves nothing in particular is hardly a congregation at all. When it pretends to be, it commits *hillul ha-shem,* a profanation of God's name.
>
> Something must be done to make membership in our Congregation again mean something—something clear, specific, and worthy.... I am therefore asking our present members to indicate whether they can say the following:
>
> a) We recognize that the primary purposes of a congregation are: worship, Torah study, and fellowship for holy life.
>
> b) We accept the importance of the *mitzvah* of public worship sufficiently to commit ourselves to begin some *regular* pattern of attendance at Sabbath and daily services, as our circumstances permit.
>
> c) We accept the importance of the *mitzvah* of Torah study sufficiently to commit ourselves to begin some *regular* pattern of study, either in a class or privately.
>
> d) We accept the importance of the holy discipline of *mitzvot* sufficiently to begin increasing the scope and depth of our practice of Jewish living....
>
> Your Rabbi,
>
> Hershel Matt

There was enough response to keep Hershel in Metuchen temporarily, but five years later, in 1967, he threatened to resign unless he received pledges of commitment from a significant number of members. Enough people responded to keep him in Metuchen for a few more years, but the underlying problem was apparently unresolvable. Finally, in 1970, he left Temple Neve Shalom and moved on to his last full-time pulpit at The Jewish Center in Princeton. Here he remained for five years. His letter of resignation from Princeton included a p.s. that left a loophole.

> *Erev Shabbat Kodesh Va-Yikra*
> March 14, 1975
>
> Dear [President] Roz,
>
> This coming summer will mark the completion of my twenty-eighth year in the rabbinate. Throughout these many years I have had (thank God) ... numerous moments of deep satisfaction: the satisfaction that comes from trying to guide people in finding in Judaism the resources for living their lives as human beings created-in-the-image and as members of the covenant people of Israel.

I have increasingly found, however, that the structure of the American Jewish congregation is so filled with ambiguities and contradictions that I no longer find it viable as a synagogue or "holy congregation." To continue trying to function as rabbi within the congregation as presently structured is no longer possible for me....

I have therefore decided—after careful thought and with much regret—that I must tender my resignation as Rabbi of the Center, effective August 31, 1975....

Sincerely,

Hershel J. Matt

P.S. If the Center would by chance be interested in considering a radical restructuring—to allow for a) the formation of a *havurah*-type of congregation within the larger Center membership, and b) a changed relationship between the rabbi and each of these two entities—I would be pleased to share my thinking and to explore the possible role for myself in such a restructured Center.

The president and others, not wanting to lose their rabbi, asked Hershel what he had in mind, and he responded immediately with a proposal. He envisioned creating a *havurah* within the larger congregation that would commit itself to a certain standard of Jewish observance and study. The rabbi would divide his energies between the congregation and the *havurah,* devoting approximately 75 percent of his time to the congregation and 25 percent to the *havurah*. Here are some selections from his proposal:

A. Instead of the present single-model membership, there should be a double model: The *Havurah* and the Congregation.

B. The *Havurah* would be conceived as a fellowship of Jews who accept for themselves the basic purposes of the traditional synagogue: the regular study of Torah; the regular worship of God in the Jewish mode, in public and in private; the celebration of prescribed moments in the day, week, month, year, and life cycle; the regular practice of justice and love in their interpersonal relations and in the public arena; and the regular sharing of concern and effort on behalf of the covenant people Israel.

C. Membership in the *Havurah* would involve an acceptance of such purposes and standards, and a commitment to strive to live and help others to live by them.

D. Membership in the Congregation would remain on the present basis.

For a variety of reasons, the proposal did not work out. Some members of the congregation felt that such an arrangement would be too divisive. Two months later, Rabbi Matt submitted his last resignation from full-time congregational work. He circulated a letter offering his reflections.

A RABBI'S REFLECTIONS
ON LEAVING THE CONGREGATIONAL RABBINATE
May, 1975

A number of members, upon hearing of my resignation as Rabbi of the The Jewish Center, have asked about my reasons for resigning; they—and all other members—deserve an answer and an explanation....

I am resigning because I have become increasingly convinced that the congregational rabbinate involves such inherent contradictions that for me it is no longer a viable form of rabbinic service....

A synagogue worthy of the name should consist of members who sense, however vaguely, the transcendent meaning of the Jewish people; who at least dimly know that Israel is a people only for the sake of the Torah and by means of the Torah; who *seek* to live in the holy dimension of Jewish life; who *try* to accept the obligation and find the joy of worshiping God; who *try* to look upon the Torah as somehow containing God's word and the revelation of His will and command and promise; who *try* to find in the study and practice of Judaism their primary source for the strength and joy and meaning, the judgment and the hope, that God provides....

Since the present reality is that affiliation with a congregation, or even election to the Board or to Committees, does not require any such commitment or intention, it is almost inevitable that the vast majority of members will not share the same purposes as the rabbi, and indeed will not even be interested in exposing themselves to the Torah teaching he seeks to bring—which means that he and they will be working at cross-purposes and that he (and perhaps they as well) are likely to find the situation extremely frustrating. After twenty-eight years in the congregational rabbinate, the degree of frustration and the sense of contradiction have for me become unbearable—and the role of congregational rabbi has for me become untenable.

My decision is not at all intended to be an unfavorable reflection on the congregation—its members or its leaders. They are good people.... It is intended only to free myself from continuing to try to function in what I find to be an inherently self-contradictory situation. If it incidentally serves to help some members reexamine the purpose of The Center and the meaning of their affiliation—and if such reexamination leads in turn to a reexamination of what it means to be a Jew—perhaps it will prove to be of slight blessing to them as well.

May God bless each of you and all of you.

Hershel Jonah Matt

In suggesting the idea of a *havurah*, Rabbi Matt had in fact planted seeds in Princeton. Several years after he left, The Jewish Center formed two *havurot,* which are still functioning today.

6

For the remaining years of Hershel's life, from 1975 until 1987, he and Gustine lived in Highland Park, New Jersey. He taught, lectured and wrote. He was enthusiastic about his teaching at two rabbinical seminaries, the Reconstructionist Rabbinical College and the Academy for Jewish Religion. Here he had a powerful and lasting impact; both students and faculty appreciated his wisdom and his presence. Often he engaged in unasked-for research in order to answer the question of a student or a faculty colleague. In class he would invite students to take turns beginning each session with an original prayer. He fully believed what he once wrote: "To study Torah is to worship God."[16] After tending to whatever administrative details demanded his attention, Rabbi Matt frequently announced that it was time to "treat ourselves to some Torah study."

Fellow rabbis and teachers too continued to feel the effects of Hershel's love of Torah. Rabbi Julius Funk, a friend who lived near by, remembers that

> Hershel had the habit of popping by to inquire after my health and peruse my library of Judaica. On one of his quick drop-ins, he left me a sheet of white paper on which he had written on both sides, in tiny script, a schedule of biblical readings for every day of the week—starting with Joshua and ending with the Book of Chronicles. This was a meticulous, painstaking job, and I was momentarily too stunned to ask him—Why? When I returned to normalcy, I knew why. Hershel wanted to help me fulfill the commandment: *ve-hagita bo yomam va-lailah* ("Meditate on it day and night"). He felt that a chart with daily reminders would stimulate me to join the widening circle of Torah devotees.

John Merkle, a Christian scholar who has written widely on Abraham Heschel and who met with Rabbi Matt whenever he could, recalls their last encounter:

> About a half-hour before leaving our home, Hershel asked me if I would like to study a text of Torah with him. This was vintage Hershel! He always called my wandering mind back to God. Of course I wanted to study Torah with Hershel. To do so was to be spiritually renewed. But

16. "The Goals of Teaching Jewish Prayer."

just by being with Hershel I felt spiritually uplifted. Not only was he a
masterful teacher of Torah; his life was a sublime *midrash* on the Torah.
More than anyone I have ever met, Hershel Matt embodied and made real
the heart and core of the Torah.... I am grateful that in our last moments
together, after we had studied a text of Torah, I told Hershel that my ideal
sabbatical would be to study Torah with him daily. After all (this I did not
tell him), he was my *rebbe*. Naturally I longed to study with him as often
as I could; naturally I wanted to imbibe the way of Torah he so beautifully
embodied.

In the 1980s Hershel also devoted himself to chaplaincy in hospitals
and nursing homes. His reflections on this work developed into one of his
last and most moving essays, reprinted below: "Fading Image of God?
Theological Reflections of a Nursing-Home Chaplain." During these years
he *daven*ed regularly at the Highland Park Conservative Temple and
taught numerous classes there. He sometimes missed being a congregational rabbi, and for several years (1976-80) he served as weekend rabbi for
Har Zion Synagogue in Mt. Holly, New Jersey. When he left Har Zion, he
wrote up a fifty-page procedural manual for the incoming rabbi, a step-by-
step guide on how to run a small congregation.

But Hershel, of course, never stopped being a rabbi. When he no longer
served a congregation, he served his fellow Jews and fellow human beings.
Wherever he was, he transmitted Torah, by the way he spoke and listened
and responded, by the gentle yet impassioned way he lived each moment.
His entire life was one uninterrupted teaching. Hank, the superintendent
in his apartment building, used to seek out Rabbi Matt for advice and
counsel. On the morning of Hershel's funeral, Hank told me, "Your father
always had time to answer my questions, my questions about religion.
Now, my teacher is gone." But, as with all great souls, Hershel's death has
not ended his influence. His lifelong friend, Max Ticktin, puts it this way:
"Every recalling of Hershel is a personal *heshbon ha-nefesh* [a moral self-
examination] on who I am, have been, and might be."

Hershel achieved a certain closure toward the end of his life. In his final
few years he offered seminars at the Highland Park Conservative Temple
on his mentors, Abraham Joshua Heschel and Will Herberg. In preparation, he reread much of Herberg and Heschel's entire corpus. One of the
last courses he taught was also at this synagogue, where he focused on
about fifty key Hebrew words in the *siddur*. This brought him great joy
because he felt that he was helping people understand the core of the
*daven*ing.

1987, the year Rabbi Hershel Matt died, was the one-hundredth anniversary of the birth of his father, Rabbi C. David Matt, and Hershel arranged a memorial tribute and lecture in May of that year in Philadelphia. He asked me to give the lecture, and I spoke on the theme of humility. There Hershel reconnected with dozens of friends and relatives.

Hershel's last lecture trip was to his birthplace, Minneapolis, in the fall of 1987, sixty years after his family had moved from there. He visited his cousins and his father's synagogue, Adath Jeshurun. That week, the Minnesota Twins were playing against the St. Louis Cardinals in the World Series. The series went to seven games, and the last game was played in Minneapolis. Even if he had had the opportunity, Hershel would probably not have gone to the game or even watched much of it on TV, but he was not even tempted because he was scheduled to lecture that same evening. His topic was: "Messiah and Life after Death." After the talk, attended by about thirty-five people, Hershel heard the last inning of the game. I imagine he was happy that his home team won, and that he commiserated with the Cardinals.

Hershel Matt passed away a few days after Hanukkah, on the sixth of *Tevet* 5748; December 26, 1987. He died of a heart attack that he suffered on the way home from *Shabbat davening*. His soul departed with the Sabbath Queen, at the beginning of the week of Torah portion *Va-Yehi*, "And he lived." That same afternoon, a few hours before I heard the sad news, I was teaching the *Zohar* on *Va-Yehi*, a passage about good deeds, life and death. The *Zohar* relates that a garment is woven for each person out of the good deeds he has performed or out of the days he has lived in holiness. Robed in this garment of splendor, one passes on from worldly existence to another dimension. At my father's funeral, I related how he used to tell us that our family name is an abbreviation for *ma'asim tovim,* "good deeds." Then I read from the *Zohar:*[17]

> When a human being is created,
> on the day he comes into the world,
> simultaneously, all the days of his life are arranged above.
> One by one, they come flying down into the world
> to alert that human being, day by day....

---

17. *Zohar* 1:224a-b, translated in Daniel C. Matt, *Zohar: The Book of Enlightenment* (Mahwah, New Jersey: Paulist Press, 1983), pp. 91-94.

Come and see:
When those days draw near to the Holy King,
if the person leaving the world is pure
he ascends and enters into those days
and they become a radiant garment for his soul!...

Happy are the righteous!
Their days are all stored up with the Holy King,
woven into radiant garments to be worn in the world that is coming....

Come and see:
Abraham, who was pure, what is written of him?
"He came into days" (Genesis 24:1).
When he left this world
he entered into his very own days and put them on to wear.
Nothing was missing from that radiant garment:
"He came into days"....

Happy are the righteous
for their days are pure and extend to the world that is coming.
When they leave this world, all their days are sewn together,
made into radiant garments for them to wear.
Arrayed in that garment,
they are admitted to the world that is coming
to enjoy its pleasures.
Clothed in that garment,
they are destined to come back to life.

We all sat silently for a few minutes and imagined the garment Hershel's soul is wearing.

The funeral service was packed with people who felt the loss. One person who hadn't attended was curious about the big crowd. He asked the officiating rabbi, Yakov Hilsenrath, "What congregation did Rabbi Matt serve?" Rabbi Hilsenrath responded, *"Kelal Yisra'el,"* the community of Israel. Yes, Hershel served the entire Jewish world, and beyond.

THEOLOGICAL ESSAYS

INTRODUCTION

We have seen how Hershel Matt lived his life and what kind of rabbi he was. His theological writings, most of which originally appeared in various religious journals, can best be appreciated against that background. Rabbi Matt's life and his theology were harmonious and in fact inseparable. That is how it should be. As he wrote, "What one really believes is indicated by the way one lives; the way one lives ... *constitutes* one's belief."[18]

Rabbi Matt's life is a model of how to translate faith into *avodah*: service, work and worship. His theological writing developed out of reflection on his faith, his religious experience, and the problems and possibilities he discovered. He was intensely committed to the Jewish tradition but equally devoted to rendering its insights into a contemporary idiom. He loved to quote the saying: "One who says that the words of the Torah are one thing and the matters of the world another is as if he denies God."[19] By insisting on making the tradition relevant, he helped transform it.

1

Basic to Hershel Matt's life and thought was the concept that human beings have been created in the image of God. In his life, day by day, he cultivated and conveyed his divine image. He once suggested that "creation-in-the-image could form the basis for an entire theology of Judaism."[20] His essays and articles represent the components of such a theology. Since each human being is modeled on divine being, human creation is a "universal, general revelation."[21] We have it in our power to

18. "Dogmas in Judaism."
19. *Midrash Pinhas* (Warsaw, 1876) 4:34, p. 32. See "A Jewish Approach to Sex Education," "Sin, Crime, Sickness, or Alternative Life Style?: A Jewish Approach to Homosexuality."
20. "Not Every Mysticism Is a Jewish Mysticism."
21. "Human Choice and God's Design."

enhance the divine image through acts of love and righteousness; if we sin, then we deface the image.[22]

It is not merely our intellect, as Maimonides taught, or our soul that participates in the divine reality. Our entire being, body and soul, is fashioned in the image of God. The holiness of the body is evident in several areas of Rabbi Matt's thought, including his teaching on life after death. He believed in the truth of bodily resurrection, though he pointed out that he was "speaking not in terms of literal truth but 'mythical' or poetic truth."[23] Especially revealing is his opposition to the notion of the immortality of the soul.

> However widespread this view and however attractive this doctrine, "immortality of the soul" is inadequate and potentially misleading.... If it implies that the soul alone is *worthy* of survival, it thereby disparages the body, which, no less than the "breath of life," went into the formation of Adam, pinnacle of God's good creation and paradigm for all of Adam's descendants.... In any case, the very dichotomy between body and soul impugns the integrity of the whole person, which ... is crucial to the Torah's primary affirmation of creation-in-the-image.[24]

Immortality of the soul "implies that my body is less ... precious, less important,... less 'clean' and pure than the soul." The theory of bodily resurrection offers a more holistic approach. It "affirms that just as in this life and world, so in the life-and-world-to-come, the body no less than the soul is God's creation—and as such is both necessary and good."[25]

The uniqueness and integrity of each individual is also vital to Matt's thought. The theory of the immortality of the soul fails on this count as well, since it may imply "that the soul, upon leaving the body, merges with, and is absorbed by, the divine All-Soul." If so, "the identity and unique personality of this particular person who has died are ... compromised, diminished and even dissolved."[26] For the same reason, Matt was opposed to certain trends within the mystical tradition, despite his own profound spirituality.

> Where mysticism speaks of human beings as *merged* with God, the universe or fellow human beings, it becomes Jewishly inauthentic—since

22. "How Shall a Believing Jew View Christianity?"
23. "An Outline of Jewish Eschatology."
24. "Fading Image of God?"
25. "An Outline of Jewish Eschatology."
26. "Fading Image of God?"

54

the essential biblical teaching, although affirming an ideal unity and harmony among these three, insists upon the uniqueness and integrity of each.[27]

Since the body is a positive religious phenomenon, so is sexuality. "One sees the mysterious power and attraction of human sexuality—and is moved to awe." Ideally, sexuality serves as an opportunity for the deepest, most genuine relationship. "When man and woman unite sexually, their sexual union ... is a distinctively human relationship—an I-Thou relationship."

> Human sexuality, like every human capacity, comes from God and is therefore holy and good—provided that it is exercised in faithful acceptance of God's purpose and in reverent awareness of His presence. The proper sexual relation is that which serves both to express and to further the mutually responsive and responsible love of a man and woman who recognize that each has been created in God's image.[28]

2

But who is this God, in whose image we have been created?

> God is not a person just like us, but He is surely not less of a person than each of us; rather He is more than a person.... He meets us in countless ways, but in all the ways He meets us, He meets us personally—calling us to be, enabling us to be our most human ... loving, sensitive, personal selves.[29]

It is not easy for modern people to talk about God. Sex and death are spoken of openly, even with one's children, but "one subject remains taboo: God." Matt encouraged others to violate that taboo, to engage in speculation or in informal God talk, to listen to the naive questions of their children and to search for answers along with them. Children, after all, "may be open to dimensions of truth and worlds of meaning that are ... closed to us."[30]

For many, the difficulty with talking about God is simply doubt that there is a God. In responding to this pervasive problem, Matt drew on a formulation of his teacher Will Herberg, who, as we have seen, insisted that all people rely on some ultimate. "The question to be asked ... is not,

27. "Not Every Mysticism Is a Jewish Mysticism."
28. "A Jewish Approach to Sex Education."
29. "The Goals of Teaching Jewish Prayer."
30. "Talking with Our Children about God."

'Do you have a god?' but rather, 'Which god is yours?'"[31] But Matt also indicated that doubt can have a positive religious function. "Doubt itself has a fruitful role to play in the life of faith.... Our doubt can help keep us from being glib, insensitive, and self-righteous in professing our faith."[32] Furthermore, doubt can impel us to confront the traditional set of beliefs and dogmas, and to transform them.

> Each generation of Jews that is plagued with doubt, or even given to reflection, must be bold enough to challenge all previous formulation of the dogmas. Each generation must be vigorous enough to formulate into dogmas its own revised understanding of the Torah-teaching. Each generation must then be humble enough to question its own dogmatic formulations, allowing them to remain but tentative formulations.[33]

Matt's thinking on the problem of miracles offers an example of his approach to traditional belief. On the one hand, he expands the category of miracle. For the faithful Jew,

> there is ... no real difference ... between the exceptional event and the regular, ordinary event.... Miracles are happening all the time. A child is born; the sun sets; our body functions; the mind thinks; the rain falls. True, some miracles are more dramatic or come at what seem to be more crucial moments in the life of the individual person or in the life of the whole people and therefore appear to be more decisive. The splitting of the Sea of Reeds is often spoken of in the tradition as the miracle *par excellence,* the greatest ever. True. And yet that very same tradition declares that the provision of our daily food and sustenance is no less miraculous.

He proposes the following definition: "A miracle is any event in which one sees the power and love of God." Matt does not ignore or deny the explanatory power of science, but he refuses to allow a reductionistic approach that blinds us to the wonder of life. He identifies an element within the tradition that keeps us sensitized to the miraculous aspect of the ordinary.

> So often our eyes remain closed to the miracles that God seeks to disclose. We pass through a world of miracles, but allow the miracles to pass us by. When we come upon miracles we reduce them to laws and explain them— and explain them away! Any miracle can be explained *after* it has happened, when it is past. But any miracle can also be relived, making it

---

31. "What Does It Mean to Believe in God?" Cf. above, "The Life of Rabbi."
32. "Talking with Our Children about God."
33. "Dogmas in Judaism."

present again. All we need is: a *berakhah*.

The purpose of a *berakhah* is to help us recapture the miracle, to open our inner eye, to show us the way across the threshold of the world of miracles. It reminds us that we have been there all the time ... without our even knowing it! With the aid of a *berakhah*, uttered with true *kavvanah*,... the ordinary can become holy.... The facts of life and the laws of nature, without being denied, can be seen as "the work of God's creation." They can suddenly become transparent, and the loving power of God shines through.[34]

3

The presence and the power of God are thus available to those who nurture their spiritual awareness. How, though, does God communicate His will? How does humanity discern the divine will? Here too Matt was both traditional and bold, building on the insights of Herberg and Heschel, Rosenzweig and Buber. "Our Torah,... though containing the word of God, cannot be assumed entirely to be the word of God." It is our task, a "continuing and never-ending task,... to identify (with God's help) which among the Torah's words are God's own words and therefore absolutely binding."

Matt identifies the two primary commands of the Torah: "Love *YHVH* your God with all your heart, with all your soul and with all your might" and "Love your neighbor as yourself." As to the remaining commandments, "they are to be considered binding insofar as they are seen, upon humble and careful study, to be alternate formulations or specific instances of the two chief commands." These two central *mitzvot* serve, respectively, as criteria for the two traditional categories of *mitzvot*: interpersonal and ritual.

Whenever any of the other commandments concerning fellow human beings are seen, upon careful study, to constitute an unnecessary denial or restriction of love, they are no longer to be considered as God's command, absolutely binding.... I ought ... to give much attention and weight to the wisdom, experience, and piety of the talmudic and posttalmudic sages (including those of the present age as well), but since I am the "you" who is being commanded, mine is the ultimate human responsibility to decide what it is that I am being commanded.

Similarly, the ritual commands are meant to be instances of the command to "love *YHVH* your God"—and are to be considered binding only insofar as they are seen to be reflections of, vehicles for, or aids to the love of God.[35]

34. "Miracle and *Berakhah*."
35. "What I Believe."

Much, then, is left up to the individual. Ultimately, for the *mitzvah* to be binding, it must be "heard." Note the parenthetical jolt in this formulation: "I have the duty to perform whatever He commands (whatever, that is, I hear Him to be commanding)."[36] Matt is aware of the dangers of such an individualistic approach and of the value of tradition in and of itself, but the personal, existential moment is decisive.

> To increase or to reduce excessively the Torah-ordained pattern of Jewish practice, as understood by the sages of Israel and accepted by the people Israel, is to endanger the solidarity, identity, and survival of His holy people, to dilute my own participation in its holy function, and to constrict the dimensions of my very own being. But ... this ... cannot be the ultimate consideration.... It is I who must acknowledge the command.[37]

Matt recognizes two alternative approaches to the *halakhah,* the daily discipline of holy living. The conservative approach would be to follow *the halakhah,* with all its traditional formulations. The liberal approach would be to follow *a halakhah.* How would the two approaches differ in regard to the dietary laws, for example? The conservative approach would entail a strict adherence to the entire halakhic system of *kashrut.* However, Matt identifies three essential components of *kashrut*: that some creatures are forbidden to be eaten, that permitted animals must be properly slaughtered, and that meat must be kept separate from milk. Those adopting the liberal approach would fill in this outline in various ways.

> They feel sure that God has commanded Israel to hallow its food life as part of Israel's holy way, and yet they feel sure as well that within the main lines set down there is more than one path along that holy way. They seek to walk with *kavvanah,* knowing that within the prescribed limits each person must follow his own heart's direction as he walks.[38]

If the individual exercises religious self-determination, there is a danger that he or she will reject traditional observance simply out of laziness or rationalization. As we have seen, Matt constantly urged his congregants and his fellow Jews to take the *mitzvot* seriously and to cultivate an observant lifestyle, even though he did not insist on one absolute standard. In an article about *kashrut* addressed to teenagers,

36. "What Does It Mean to Believe in God?"
37. "What I Believe."
38. "*Kashrut* and Conservative Judaism."

entitled "What Will You Have?" he encourages them to make a start: "Perhaps you cannot undo your whole background, relive your whole life, remake your whole Jewish self. But with God's help you can summon up enough strength and willpower to make a beginning, to take at least a first little step."[39]

Observance of the *mitzvot,* however, provides no guarantee of sincerity, of *kavvanah.* Matt identifies two pitfalls awaiting the unwary observant Jew: routinization and self-righteousness.

> Ritual acts and gestures, participation in public worship, use of sacred objects and the accoutrements of worship ... can at times be so routinized and externalized that they become not aids but obstacles to true acknowledgment of [God],... not means but substitutes for serving Him.
> In addition to the peril of routine, there is the peril of self-righteous display: of always appearing to say, "Look at me: how pious I am!".... The effort to cultivate consciousness of God's presence ... is no guarantee against *self-consciousness*, and self-consciousness runs the risk of becoming self-righteousness and self-display.[40]

4

A Jew lives out her religion in many contexts: privately, with family and friends, in the Jewish community and in society at large. The synagogue, of course, is the primary institutional center of Jewish spiritual life. As we have seen, Rabbi Matt made bold spiritual demands on his congregants, who, on the whole, were unwilling to commit themselves to a discipline of holiness. In writing about the synagogue, he describes the problem in language that echoes his congregational correspondence:

> To become a synagogue member today ... one need merely be Jewish by the accident of birth (more rarely by conversion)—and pay dues! To learn that a particular Jew is a synagogue member, even an active member ... tells us nothing, absolutely nothing about whether he knows or cares about such crucial *mitzvot* as worship of God, study of Torah, observance of *Shabbat* or practice of *kashrut.* His synagogue affiliation tells us nothing, absolutely nothing, about the level of his business ethics, the quality of his family life or the measure of his charitableness.

Matt proposed that the synagogue require its members to commit themselves to Torah, Israel, humanity, love, justice, social action and

39. "What Will You Have?" (see Bibliography).
40. "Acknowledging the King," "Covering My Jewish Head."

religious observance. All Jews would be welcome, but membership implied a willingness to serve God and neighbor.

> The synagogue must have the courage to require of its members, as a condition of membership, an acceptance of ... a task-and-purpose and a commitment to strive conscientiously to live by it. All other Jews should be invited to attend the synagogue, join in its worship, utilize its facilities, participate in its program.... Official membership ..., however—involving the right to vote and the privilege of setting synagogue program and policy—should be open only to Jews who find themselves able to make the personal covenant-commitment and to accept the personal covenant-obligation.[41]

After leaving the congregational rabbinate, Matt wrote a set of "Guiding Principles and Basic Policies for the Ideal Congregation." Here he listed certain requirements for membership, and also proposed that members engage in periodic self-review and that leaders of the congregation accept a higher standard of commitment. He even maintained that there should be no required dues and no fund raising. "A synagogue ... should depend exclusively upon voluntary support."[42] Needless to say, he did not expect such a congregation to emerge any time soon on the American scene.

As an American rabbi, Matt often confronted the question of the chosenness of Israel and her relation to other faiths. He described the covenant between God and Israel as a privilege, but a privilege that most Jews relate to only in a Kafkaesque manner.

> How great a privilege to belong to the covenant people Israel, the channel through which the message of *YHVH* is carried, to be God's witness and agent in the world, to be "God's stake in history"! But how sad it is to be an agent almost unconsciously; to be a witness almost unawares; to be a messenger who has all but forgotten the name of the One who sends him.[43]

Drawing and expanding on Herberg, he described the dialectical nature of Israel's chosenness.

> The goal of God's choosing Israel was the eventual disappearance of that

41. "Synagogue and Covenant People." Cf. above, "The Life of a Rabbi."
42. "Principles and Policies for the Ideal Congregation."
43. "Acknowledging the King."

Israel—in the messianic day, when "the earth would be filled with the knowledge of God".... Israel's mission having been accomplished—the mission to serve as a light unto the nations and as God's witnesses among humanity—the differences between the people of Israel and the peoples of the world ... will disappear,... the one true religion having by then been accepted by all.[44]

In contrast to Christianity, however, Judaism insists that the Messiah has not yet arrived. Until then, "Israel's own role remains indispensable—to remain apart in holy separation, serving as God's witnesses and resisting the forms of paganism to which Christianity is prey."[45] Still, as Maimonides and others have insisted, neither Christianity nor Islam is a pagan religion. Building on the insight of Franz Rosenzweig, Matt insists that they share in God's covenant with Israel.

Since it is through their religion—and not in spite of it—that they are provided with the knowledge of the true God and His standards for humanity, all Christians and Moslems are to be included in the broad sense of the term "Israel".... In a genuine sense [they] share in God's covenant with Israel.[46]

Through Christianity, "God's covenant with Israel was opened up and made available as the new (form of the) covenant for the non-Jews of the world." Christianity thus represents "a denationalized, de-ethnicized, de-particularized form of Israel.... Judaism for the nations of the world."[47]

But must not a Jew reject the central and distinctive Christian beliefs: Virgin Birth, Incarnation, Resurrection?

A believing Jew need not necessarily deny ... these miracles alleged to have been performed in Christ—at least in their visible, outer form. Surely the theoretical possibility that God could (if He so willed) cause conception to occur without the agency of a human male, or the dead to live again, is not a contradiction but an affirmation of Jewish faith. (Indeed, that God will, in the future, raise the dead to life is ... affirmed to be an essential "article of faith"....) But even the historicity of such wonders need not necessarily be denied by a believing Jew.

44. "What I Believe," "An Outline of Jewish Eschatology."
45. "What I Believe."
46. "An Outline of Jewish Eschatology," "Talking with Our Children about God." Cf. "Acknowledging the King" and "The People Israel and the Peoples of the World as Reflected in the Jewish Prayer Book" (see Bibliography).
47. "Should Christmas Mean Anything to Jews?," "How Shall a Believing Jew View Christianity?"

Whether God was in Christ, whether God has through Christ provided salvation—these are questions not merely of occurrence but of inner meaning and religious authenticity. Here "we are in the realm of personal, existential appropriation; 'the knowing in faith.' And in this realm the whole notion of affirmation *or* denial by one person of the faith-knowledge of another is inappropriate, pointless, and even ridiculous." Such questions are not meaningful questions for a Jew. "The most a Jew can do ... is to acknowledge that in the lives of countless men and women who profess Christ the power and presence of God appear to be evident."

Each of the two faiths has its role to play in the cosmic drama. Until the Messiah comes (or, from the Christian point of view, returns), the two must remain separate and distinct. But for now, the parallels between Judaism and Christianity can "remind the Christian that God's covenant with His people Israel abides unbroken, and remind the Jew that God's covenant promise and providence have been opened up to extend beyond the people Israel."[48]

5

Matt's openness to new ways of thinking and his sense of compassion and justice are exemplified by the stand he took on homosexuality. He acknowledged that the Bible and the tradition clearly oppose homosexuality, but he inquired into the rationale and "whether there are now any changed circumstances or new data in the light of which the Torah's stand today ... might possibly involve changed formulations." Drawing on the scientific literature, Matt wrote:

> It is only in our own generation that homosexual behavior has been found to involve not merely a single, overt act, or a series of such acts, but often to reflect a profound inner condition and basic psychic orientation, involving the deepest levels of personality.... However deep and numerous are the differences among contemporary experts on homosexuality, on one aspect there seems to be near-unanimity: that *for many homosexuals the prospects of change to heterosexuality are almost nil*.... Their homosexuality is established early in life and is for the most part unalterable.

He correlated this finding with the halakhic principle that "when forbidden acts are performed in the absence of voluntary choice and free

---

48. "How Shall a Believing Jew View Christianity?"

decision, or in the absence of other options, the offenders are judged more leniently."[49]

The question, then, is: "Are homosexuals able to choose and to change?" Those who could live a heterosexual life and choose not to, deliberately opting for a homosexual lifestyle, are to be considered in violation of the Torah's prohibition. Similarly, for those homosexuals "who, with professional help or with strenuous effort, could manage to change—the Torah's standard also remains in effect." But probably the majority "are under the constraint of remaining homosexual indefinitely, presumably for life," and for them, a different view is appropriate. If, except for the sexual identity of their mate, they live faithfully by traditional Jewish standards, they should be fully accepted and respected."[50]

Matt insisted that the Jewish community should reach out toward gays and lesbians and vigorously oppose any discrimination or legal penalties. A gay synagogue is legitimate and should be eligible for affiliation with a national union of congregations unless it restricts its membership to gays. A gay person should be allowed to serve as a rabbi in any synagogue, as long as he or she believes, and seeks to convey to others, that "in spite of his or her homosexuality, the Jewish ideal for man and woman is heterosexuality."[51]

The theoretical ideal of the divine order of creation may be heterosexual, but gays and lesbians "are evidently God's exceptions.... With regard to such exceptions, we must strive to echo and to mediate God's full acceptance and approval."[52]

Matt's conclusions were not as radical as the gay community might have wanted, but they were deeply appreciated by most gays and quite controversial in the straight Jewish community. He spoke widely on this topic and was challenged as to how he could so openly contradict the Torah's explicit condemnation of homosexuality. He responded by explicating his view of the nature of Torah, which we have already encountered:

> As for the Torah's condemnation of homosexuality, we follow those teachers who have taught us that though the Torah *contains* God's word,

49. "Sin, Crime, Sickness, or Alternative Life Style?: A Jewish Approach to Homosexuality."
50. Ibid., "A Call for Compassion."
51. "Sin, Crime, Sickness, or Alternative Life Style?: A Jewish Approach to Homosexuality."
52. "Homosexual Rabbis?," "A Call for Compassion."

it is not *identical* with God's word; it is both divine and human. Insofar as the Torah reflects the divine intent, its prohibition of homosexuality could not have had in mind the kind of homosexuality we have been speaking of. Insofar as it reflects mere human attempts to grasp the divine intent, it reflects also a human misunderstanding of the kind of homosexuality that is forbidden.[53]

Hershel Matt was both traditional and radical, humbly devoted yet boldly innovative. In the way he lived and the way he taught, he demonstrated that to be a Jew is to make the tradition one's own, to engage Torah day by day.

53. "Homosexual Rabbis?"

WHAT I BELIEVE[54]

1. In what sense do you believe the Torah to be divine revelation? Are all 613 commandments equally binding on the believing Jew? If not, how is he to decide which to observe? What status would you accord to ritual commandments lacking in ethical or doctrinal content (e.g., the prohibition against clothing made of linen and wool)?

At the center of my religious affirmation is "Torah from Sinai," the conviction that the Torah contains the word of God revealed to Israel in the wilderness. This word, however, though issuing from God, was addressed to human beings, received by humans, transmitted by humans, recorded by humans, copied and recopied by humans—and thus to some degree was subject to human limitations: their inadequacies, inaccuracies, misunderstandings. Our Torah-text, therefore, though containing the word of God, cannot be assumed entirely to be the word of God. Our continuing and never-ending task is to identify (with God's help) which among the Torah's words are God's own words and therefore absolutely binding.

The absolutely minimal statement of God's word in the Torah is "I, YHVH, am your God, who brought you forth from the land of Egypt, from the house of bondage"—and theoretically this would be a sufficient statement: it identifies the God; it affirms the I-Thou relationship between God and us; it implies both God's love and power to redeem and to command, and our privilege and obligation to obey and to respond. Since this minimal statement, however, may be too meager, the basic and all-inclusive affirmation-and-command of the *Shema* should be added: "Hear, Israel, YHVH is our God, YHVH alone. And you shall love YHVH your God with all your heart, with all your soul, and with all your might." (Alternative formulations, of course, could be cited from the Torah, but the *Shema* is most familiar and, because of its absolute "with all," perhaps the most adequate as well.)

The command to "love your neighbor as yourself" is, like all the commandments, included in the command to love God, and theoretically

---

54. In August 1966 *Commentary* magazine published a symposium entitled *The State of Jewish Belief*, in which thirty-eight prominent rabbis were asked to respond to a series of questions. The symposium was republished by Macmillan under the title *The Condition of Jewish Belief*.

need not explicitly be stated in the minimal formulation of God's command. Lest the cynical nonbeliever or the self-righteous believer fail to see the obvious implication, however, it is advisable to make explicit statement of this second great command.

Concerning all the remaining commands of the 613, they are to be considered binding insofar as they are seen, upon humble and careful study, to be alternate formulations or specific instances of the two chief commands. (For this reason it would be proper to say that there is one additional basic command: "Go and study.")

The commandments involving my relations to my fellow human beings are all to be tested against the inclusive "Love your neighbor as yourself"—remembering, of course, that "love" refers here not to romantic feeling, but to the practice of justice in the highest degree; the manifestation of care and concern in the highest measure; full regard for the true welfare of my fellow human as one who is infinitely precious—having, no less than I, been created in the image of God. Whenever any of the other commandments concerning fellow humans are seen, upon careful study, to constitute an unnecessary denial or restriction of love, they are no longer to be considered as God's command, absolutely binding. In boldly asserting the right of such private judgment, I ought, of course, to give much attention and weight to the wisdom, experience, and piety of the talmudic and posttalmudic sages (including those of the present age as well), but since I am the "you" who is being commanded, mine is the ultimate human responsibility to decide what it is that I am being commanded.

Similarly, the "ritual commands" are meant to be instances of the command to "love *YHVH* your God"—and are to be considered binding only insofar as they are seen to be reflections of, vehicles for, or aids to the love of God. Again, much weight should be given to traditional explication and interpretation, but the privilege and obligation to examine and decide are a personal privilege and obligation. Despite the risks of subjectivity, there is no acceptable alternative; indeed, there is ultimately no alternative at all.

And yet, a crucial additional consideration is involved. To some extent, even the "ethical" commands, and to a vast extent the "ritual" commands, are addressed to me by virtue of my membership in the covenant people, Israel. I was commanded, but I was commanded as one of the children of Israel, along with all other children of Israel; we were commanded together, collectively and not only individually; my hearing and responding to God's commands involves and implicates all Israel as well. A crucial dimension of my life—indeed, the whole normal context of my "ritual" life (including Sabbath, holy days, many aspects of sex and diet and clothing, etc.)—is thus the shared way of the people Israel, summoned at Sinai to be a unique and separate "kingdom of priests and holy nation." Whether the particular ritual acts, objects, and occasions were God-originated or God-designated or God-approved, they came to be accepted as God's prescribed way for Israel to respond to Him. To increase or to reduce excessively the Torah-ordained pattern of Jewish practice, as understood by the sages of Israel and accepted by the people Israel, is to endanger the solidarity, identity, and survival of His Holy people, to dilute my own participation in its holy function, and to constrict the dimensions of my very own being. But once again, this collective acceptance of the Torah's commands as God's commands, crucial as it is, cannot be the ultimate consideration. It is as one of Israel, to be sure, that I am commanded, but it is I who must acknowledge the command.

When I fail to see myself commanded to observe such-and-such of the 613 commandments, there are several options available: I can observe the commandment nevertheless, choosing to accept the discipline of Israel's traditional way, even though lacking the conviction that it is God's command (as long, that is, as I do not consider it a violation of God's command!); or I can cease from observing it ("no longer"); or I can hold back from observing it ("not yet"). All three of these options I find myself taking at various times; no one of them is improper—as long as I take it in reverence rather than from indifference, in humility rather than in self-righteousness.

Note, however, that I do not, need not, and dare not say that I will accept only those commandments whose observance I find pleasant or convenient; or whose origins I find identifiable or acceptable; or even whose specific purpose I find understandable. For the very notion of being commanded by God involves the acknowledgment, at least in principle, that God can command that which is contrary to my preference, for reasons that are beyond my understanding. Indeed, I must even grant that since His thoughts are not my thoughts, it is likely that with regard to at least some of His commandments, such will be the case. I am grateful that God, having created me in His image, has enabled me to understand some of His purpose; having given me the Torah, He has enabled me to understand considerably more; having promised to send the Messiah, He has assured me that someday I will understand far more. Often I crave to understand that "far more" here and now; in moments of deepest faith, however, I am able to cease insisting that I understand exactly *why* I am commanded; it is enough for me to know *that* I am commanded and *what* I am commanded. The only "why" I must know now is that whatever I am commanded is for the true welfare of all humans (including me), for the glory of Israel, and for the sake of God's Holy Name.

2. In what sense do you believe that the Jews are the chosen people of God? How do you answer the charge that this doctrine is the model from which various theories of national and racial superiority have been derived?

I believe that *YHVH,* Lord of the universe, has singled out Israel from the nations of the world, establishing a covenant with Israel by which it has been summoned to be "a kingdom of priests, a holy nation.... My firstborn son.... first fruits of His produce.... My servants.... My witnesses.... a light unto the nations."

Is any superiority involved in this singling-out?

In attempting to answer, one must beware of two perils: the peril of chauvinistic self-righteousness and the peril of apologetic equalitarianism.

On the one hand, if any superiority is involved, it does not lie in Israel's greater original merit as grounds for the choosing ("not because of your righteousness"); nor in Israel's lesser obligation as a consequence of the choosing *("therefore* I will visit upon you all your iniquities"); nor in Israel's consistent faithfulness in response to the choosing ("You have been rebellious against the Lord from the day I knew you"); nor in Israel's greater ease and comfort—at least in this world-and-age—as a result of the choosing ("for Thy sake are we slain all day long").

On the other hand, it would be foolhardy and unworthy to deny that Israel's chosenness is meant to constitute supreme honor and blessing—certainly a superiority of sorts. But the choosing was of God's doing: at His initiative, by His will, through His love, in His time and way, for His purposes and only partially open to our understanding.

At least these aspects of the choosing we have been given to understand: The *reason* for God's choosing "an Israel" was that human beings, though created in God's image and thus able to know His will and free to do it, had shown themselves far too disobedient and unfaithful; what was now required was a greater measure and more intimate degree of God's guidance, instruction, discipline—involving more concentrated attention, as it were, upon a smaller segment of humankind. The *purpose* of God's choosing Israel was the enrichment and blessing of all nations. The *goal* of God's choosing Israel was the eventual disappearance of that Israel—in the messianic day, when "the earth will be filled with the knowledge of the Lord."

3. Is Judaism the one true religion, or is it one of several true religions? Does Judaism still have something distinctive—as it once had monotheism—to contribute to the world? In the ethical sphere, the sphere of bein adam la-havero, what distinguishes the believing Jew from the believing Christian, Moslem, or Buddhist—or for that matter, from the unbelieving Jew and the secular humanist?

Since the God who redeemed Israel from Egypt and established the covenant with Israel at Sinai is affirmed to be the only true God, He is thus the God of all human beings, and His word in the Torah is addressed to all of humanity (except for those "ritual" commands that are addressed to Israel in its separation). In one sense, therefore, Judaism—insofar as it faithfully preserves and conveys this word of the one true God—can properly be termed the one true religion, and its ethic, grounded as it is in the word of the one true God, can properly be termed the one true ethic.

But in another sense Judaism should be termed not the one true religion and ethic but the one criterion of true religion and ethics. If non-Jews—in concert with or in contrast to their particular society; in any place or at any time; prior to the Torah, or subsequent to but uninfluenced by the Torah—are found in fact to have enunciated the same truth concerning God and the human being as that contained in the Torah (or some part or measure of that same truth), then their religion and ethics are to that extent also true. (That others should be found to have arrived at this same truth, at least to some degree, should of course not surprise or disturb us; the Torah itself, after all, teaches that *adam,* the-human-being-as-such, every human, is created in God's image, and is thereby endowed with the capacity to hear and respond to God's word concerning how to relate to Him and to other human beings.)

Christianity, however, stemming as it does from Judaism, occupies a very special place among the other religions (Islam too, to some extent). The central "vehicles of revelation" of Judaism and Christianity—the people-Israel-as-bearers-of-the-Torah in the one case, and Christ in the other—are radically different; the two communities are different; their roles are different. But the content of the two faiths, as regards the proper way to relate to God and to other people, is—despite differences in emphasis, tone, and mood—basically the same. Christianity can properly be viewed as a second and equally valid form of God's covenant with Israel—the missionary arm of Israel, serving to bring under the covenant those who, unlike the Jewish people, are not yet under it.

Every believing Jew takes for granted, of course, what few believing Christians can fully grasp: that the people, Israel, is in no sense supplanted by the Church, and that Israel's own role remains indispensable—to remain apart in holy separation, serving as God's witnesses and resisting the forms of paganism to which Christianity is prey; insisting upon the need for justice as the ground of love; constantly exposing the unredeemed character of the present world-and-age; holding up the vision of a truly redeemed world-and-age; and stressing both the human task and the divine role in hastening the establishment of God's Kingdom upon earth.

In that "final day," when God's purpose for humankind will have been fulfilled, the differences between Judaism and Christianity will no longer be necessary, and will therefore disappear—the one true religion having by then been accepted by all.

4. Does Judaism as a religion entail any particular political viewpoint? Can a person be a good Jew and yet, say, support racial segregation? Can one be a good Jew and be a Communist? A Fascist?

As regards the compatibility of Judaism with any particular political, economic, or social system—and advocacy or support thereof—one absolute and several relatives are involved.

The absolute is the Torah's standard of perfect justice, which is love. Every political system, economic arrangement, and social pattern is to be measured against that standard and judged in terms of that ideal. We can thus expect—pending the coming of the Messiah—that every system will be found to be only relatively good, and thus also relatively evil.

But a second relative factor must at once be introduced. Though all systems known to us are relatively evil, they are not equally evil: some involve a greater degree of injustice, or cruelty, or dehumanization, or enslavement than do others. A "good Jew," therefore, must at every moment discriminate among the available alternatives, supporting the least evil of them and working to reduce the degree of evil involved (in addition, of course, to praying for forgiveness for his own complicity even in the unavoidable evil).

It is thus easy to answer whether a "good Jew" can be a segregationist, or a Communist, or a Fascist. Of course he cannot—since to be any of these involves a denial in principle, and a repression in practice, of the basic equality and fundamental rights that belong to all people as created in God's image.

But though it is easy to say who is not a good Jew, it is indeed impossible to say who is. For since almost all available alternatives at a given moment involve at least some degree of evil, there is no complete escape from some taint of evil—and complete noninvolvement is not an available option.

The term "good Jew" should therefore be dropped from our vocabulary; or, rather, it should be held aloft to describe the ideal Jews, but never should it be applied by us to an actual Jew. God alone can and will decide.

5. Does the so-called "God is dead" question have any relevance to Judaism? What aspects of modern thought do you think pose the most serious challenge to Jewish belief?

From the point of view of Judaism, the "God is dead" argument is either relatively meaningless or deeply troublesome or absolutely crucial—depending upon the terms of the argument.

If the statement that "God is dead" is meant to convey the notion that "once God lived, but then He died," it is for Judaism a self-contradiction and thus meaningless. The Living God *YHVH* is eternally living; if He no longer lives, He never lived; if He is not God now, He never was.

If the statement means, however, that God is deathly still and silent, that He does not appear any longer to act in history, that He does not intervene when people defy His will and torture His children—then the challenge is real and profound, and ancient as well. All that the believing Jew can do is to offer an answer to the proximate "why" by pointing to the awesome reality of human freedom to do evil; and to the ultimate "why" by reaffirming one's faith in God's original good purpose in creating the human being; one's trust in the eventual fulfillment of that purpose on "the final day"; and one's "acceptance" of God's "right," in the interim, to hide His face in anger or in anguish, with thoughts that are not ours.

But perhaps "God is dead" means that God is not—and never was— a living being but a force or energy, a system or process, a near-perfect mechanism; that He is not a "he" at all; that all the attributes of a living God were erroneously attributed, were but illusions. To which the believing Jew can of course offer neither rational nor experimental refutation, but only the humble yet confident testimony of his own personal encounter with the living God, of his own reenactment of Israel's encounter at Sinai. And if the believer hesitates to quote to the nonbeliever that "the Lord is near to all who call upon Him in truth"—lest he appear overly self-righteous—he has but to couple his quotation with a twofold confession: first, that often the religious establishment itself has been responsible for exiling God from His house, muffling and stifling His voice; and second, that all too frequently, in the attempted encounter of prayer, the believer herself meets only with dead silence.

Have we now perhaps reached the crux of the whole argument? God's silence may be due not to any defect in His voice but to a defect in our ear! In that case, the very first challenge—that God once lived but now is dead—which I dismissed earlier as meaningless, may be the most meaningful of all. We used to hear the voice of God—in pleading and command, in judgment and forgiveness—but now, because we have for too long turned away and shut our ear, that voice has become almost totally inaudible. How hopeless! But if we once were among those, or even once knew those, who heard the living God and spoke to Him, perhaps there is yet a thread of hope: perhaps—for God is merciful—we, for whom He has become dead because we have become dead to Him, may yet be revived sufficiently to find His living presence once again.

I do not believe that any aspects of modern thought pose an ultimate challenge to Jewish belief, except perhaps to a fundamentalist version of Jewish belief.

Two tendencies of modern *thinkers,* however, pose a challenge by preventing a confrontation. One is the strange tendency of many profound minds and sensitive spirits, who in all other fields approach their subject with creative openness to the multiple dimensions and levels of truth, beauty and meaning, to approach Judaism rigidly, narrowly, literalistically, dogmatically, and one-dimensionally. The other tendency is to overlook existentially what they know intellectually: that the secularist position, no less than the religious, operates with certain assumptions of faith—so that not whether to believe, but what to believe, is the only option open to us.

HUMAN CHOICE AND GOD'S DESIGN: REFLECTIONS ON FREEDOM, JUDGMENT AND PROVIDENCE

For Will Herberg

1

If to be truly human is to be concerned with issues of right and wrong, to be truly Jewish is to be preoccupied with them. For in our traditional Jewish outlook standards of right and wrong constantly enter—and at times tend to dominate—our learning and teaching, our public and personal conduct, our casual conversation, and even our private thoughts.

But to be Jewish in modern times is often to find oneself beset by a host of questions and doubts concerning these traditional standards: Are right and wrong absolute—or are they relative to shifting circumstances and varying situations? Are we truly able to distinguish between right and wrong, to choose between them, and to act on the basis of our choice— or is our behavior, rather, the predetermined product of our heredity and environment, in which case we ought neither to be held responsible nor to be judged? And, what—if anything—does God have to do with any of these: with right and wrong, with human freedom and responsibility, and with judgment?

These are indeed basic questions: troubling, far-reaching, and crucially important. They are also questions to which Judaism claims to provide an answer—or at least the essential keys to an answer.

2

Judaism affirms, first of all, that right and wrong are not relative but absolute—having their source in, and deriving their authority from, God Himself, who is above all the relativities of individual human beings and whole societies.

Judaism also affirms that God, in His love, miraculously creates the human being in His own image, and that by virtue of this creation-in-the-image (a sort of universal, general revelation) all normal humans are endowed with the capacity to know God's absolute standards of right and wrong. This innate capacity involves a double knowing: knowing that because God exists, absolute right and wrong exist; and knowing, at least in broad general terms, whereof the right and wrong consist. "Beloved is the human being in that he is created in the image; even greater love it is that the human being is so informed." The oft-cited "seven command-ments of Noah (or Adam)" are a rabbinic attempt to formulate this universal morality, which is assumed to be known to, hence binding upon, all people in all societies.[55]

Furthermore, Judaism affirms that through the Torah, the people Israel (and through Israel, some would say, Christianity and Islam also) has miraculously been shown a further measure of God's love (a special revelation), whereby it receives both more intensive instruction in the specifics of God's standards of right and wrong and more intense aware-ness of their divine origin. "Beloved are Israel, in that they are called God's children.... and are given the precious instrument of the Torah; even greater love it is that they are so informed." The best-known summary of the Torah's teaching concerning humanity's moral obligation is, of course, the great passage in Leviticus: "Love your neighbor as yourself; I am the Lord." All rules involving relations with others are to be tested against this root principle.

In addition, Judaism affirms that these affirmations are *faith* affirmations: though understandable to human reason, they are not rationally demonstrable; though attested by human experience, they are not empirically verifiable. They involve certainty—not merely feeling, impression, and opinion; but this certainty—that right and wrong are absolute, originating with God and made known to us—is the certainty of faith.

3

This affirmation that one can know God's standards of right and wrong is basic to the whole notion of morality. No less basic is a further affirmation: that not only can one know right from wrong but one can choose between them; to be created in the image is to be able to exercise moral choice. "I have set before you life and death, blessing and curse; choose life." This ability, this freedom, is humanity's unique privilege and glory; it is one of the crucially distinctive marks of our humanness. Every society known to us has some moral code (in part reflected in, and always presupposed by, its legal code), which all of its normal adult members are expected to obey because they are assumed to be able to obey. And with

55. Sociologists and anthropologists attempt in their way to identify a universal morality, pointing, for example, to a "natural solidarity," common to every known society, which involves a significant measure of "mutual forbearance, helpfulness, and trust" and is accepted as binding upon all members of at least that particular society.

regard to choosing between right and wrong, Judaism affirms what all societies and indeed almost all individuals assume: that human beings, unlike all other creatures, are free.

4

But we are not completely free; like all other creatures, we are rooted in nature, restricted by its laws, and subject to its limitations. Our physical endowments and our mental capacity depend, in the first instance, upon our heredity; our survival and growth depend upon a continuing and adequate measure of water, food, sleep, and shelter; our ability to function depends upon the avoidance of, or recovery from, serious injury and illness of body and mind. Thus, to the extent that our ability to make decisions depends upon the ability to function physically and mentally, our moral freedom is obviously limited by natural conditions.

It is also limited by social conditioning. Our parental upbringing, our childhood experiences, our academic training, our relations with neighbors—indeed, all aspects of our social environment—have helped to shape our personality and pattern of behavior. Even in our adult years the impact of our social milieu continues to be great. Although in some measure we are creators of society, responsible for the conditions of society—and are thus free—we are also, in significant measure, creatures of society, conditioned by society—and thus unfree.

Two additional factors, involving both individuals and whole societies, affect our moral freedom: a) our limited knowledge of the factual consequences of the various options available to us at any given point; and b) the combination of beneficial and harmful results of almost every one of these options. How can we be said to be fully free to decide between good and evil, if we are not able to be fully aware of whether, or to what extent, such decisions will, in fact, benefit or harm another—and if what appears, at first, to be a choice between simple good and evil turns out to be, in fact, a choice between two evils?

Our freedom is reduced in still another way: our capacity to make moral decisions in the present is limited by our own decisions, actions, and reactions in the past. "The performance of a commandment draws another in its train; the performance of a transgression—likewise." "At first, sin is an indifferent stranger; later, a welcome guest; finally, the master." "At first it is like a spider's web; in the end it is like a wagon rope." Yes, our freedom to choose between right and wrong, to decide, to act— is indeed limited.

5

And yet, however real the limitations upon our moral freedom, not all of them are necessarily permanent. Even concerning the limitations of our physical nature, science in its various branches enables us to vastly increase the ability to maintain or restore our health, avoid or survive serious accident and injury, prolong our life, correct or replace or compensate for physical or mental defect, and extend our powers of body and mind. And as for the limitations imposed by our ignorance of consequences and by the mixture of beneficial and harmful results, the growth of civilization has expanded, to some extent, both the ability to foresee the consequences of our behavior and the power to reap the benefits of our decisions while mitigating their harmfulness.

Similarly, the limitations imposed upon us by earliest upbringing or subsequent environment can often be reduced. At times, a mere change in environment can relieve the intolerably constricting pressures upon us. At times, counseling and various forms of psychotherapy are able to release us, at least in part, from the chains forged by years of hostile treatment on the part of others or by our own long-established patterns of neurotic behavior. However unfree we are—however "tied up in knots"; depressed or dependent; desperate to escape through fantasy, alcohol, or drugs; compulsively driven or incapacitated by inordinate fear, guilt, hatred, anger, or anxiety—we remain "essentially" and potentially free, possessed as we are of a *margin of freedom.* Using this residual freedom, aided by other human beings who are trained and gifted, we can often manage to transcend, at least to some degree, our previous limitations, and thus enlarge the area of our moral freedom—including the freedom to sin and to be virtuous, the freedom to feel guilty and to repent.

6

Commensurate with our moral freedom is our moral responsibility. Whatever the extent of our freedom—whether we are ninety percent free and ten percent unfree, or vice versa—the freedom is genuine[56] and the

56. The Maimonidean formulation at first sounds extreme: "Every human being may become righteous like Moses, our teacher, or wicked like Jeroboam; wise or foolish, merciful or cruel, niggardly or generous; and so with all other qualities. There is no one that coerces him or decrees what he is to do, or draws him to either of the two ways; but every person turns to the way which he desires, spontaneously and of his own volition." But it is extreme only if taken quantitatively ("free in all regards," "free in all degrees"); if taken qualitatively ("in all seriousness"), the freedom is indeed utter freedom.

responsibility real; what we do with this freedom is what we are responsible for.[57] ("The angel appointed over conception takes the seminal drop,
sets it before the Holy One, blessed be He, and asks: 'Sovereign of the
Universe, what is to become of this drop? Is it to develop into a person
strong or weak, wise or foolish, rich or poor?' But no mention is made of
his becoming wicked or righteous.") Our task-and-obligation as well as our
unique privilege lies in our power to be virtuous by choosing the good or
to be sinful by choosing evil. Our greatest glory lies in being able to sin but
choosing not to.

Again and again, it seems, we tend to avoid the task and evade the
obligation, to abuse the privilege and becloud the glory—for again and
again we succumb to the temptation-to-evil that daily assails us. Indeed,
"the inclination of the human heart from one's very youth is toward evil,
only evil all day long." Yet sin is not inevitable, since (with God's help) we
are able to resist and overcome the temptation to evil. "Though sin
couches at the door and its desire is upon you, you can overcome it." And
even when we have yielded to the temptation to evil and have sinfully
turned away from God's righteous path, we are able (again, with God's
help) to turn back in the turning of repentance *(teshuvah)*. The original
freedom and responsibility to choose between good and evil, though to a
degree limited by the pull of habituation to evil, nevertheless remains.
Indeed, the very fact of temptation and struggle is itself a reflection of our
continuing freedom. And since freedom and responsibility abide, so does
accountability: we are to be judged.

7

By whom are we judged?

By God, of course—for Judaism affirms that God is the God of just
judgment. God judges us here and now, on the basis of our conduct of each
moment; and He judges us hereafter, on the basis of our conduct of a
lifetime. His judgment in this world-and-age is disclosed only in part:
traces of the judgment are evident in what befalls us physically, in

57. The tradition speaks not only of sins committed deliberately and intentionally,
but also of sins committed unintentionally, accidentally, under duress, and from
ignorance. The sin in such sins lies perhaps in the degree of inexcusable ignorance, of
insufficient caution and concern, or of guilt for unintended acts in the present which are
the consequence of deliberate acts in the past.

accordance with "natural law"; in how we are treated socially, in accordance with the "laws" of group behavior; in how we ourselves react, in accordance with the "laws" of individual psychology; and through our own conscience.[58] For the most part, however, concerning the here-and-now we must acknowledge that what God's judgment is—and that it *is* God's judgment—remains concealed. As regards the judgment in the age-and-world-to-come, all that is at present revealed for sure is that it is sure to come and that the judge is surely God.

So, whether here or hereafter, we are judged by God, who is the only true and truly adequate Judge. He alone knows all that must be taken into account: the complete facts of our behavior; the true motives of our behavior; the full consequences of our behavior; and the exact degree of freedom of our behavior. "He is the Discerner, the Judge, the Witness.... in whose presence there is neither crookedness nor forgetfulness nor partiality nor taking of bribes—but all is according to the reckoning."

8

But even though ultimate judgment belongs to God, may proximate judgment properly be made by human beings? We are here faced with a basic dilemma. How can we judge when the requisite knowledge, impartiality, and authority are lacking to us? Yet how dare we not judge when personal life requires moral judgment, when social life requires judicial judgment, and when the Torah itself commands us to exercise both kinds of judgment?

Perhaps the dilemma can be resolved if we distinguish among several senses of the word "judgment."

As regards personally judging our neighbor's behavior, it is clear that we can and we ought to: both in the sense of noting, as accurately as possible, the facts of his behavior and in the sense of evaluating that

---

58. Our conscience, though provided by God and serving as channel for the voice of God, cannot simply be identified with the voice of God. To the extent that our conscience has been shaped by society, by our parents and other authority figures, and by our own selves, it is human and therefore potentially defective and partially corruptible. It can muffle or distort the voice of God and can even serve as a channel for the voice of Satan. (After all, the number of heinous deeds committed with "a perfectly clear conscience" is legion.) Though we are, in the last analysis, always obligated to obey our conscience, we are first obligated scrupulously and continually to examine our conscience for possible defect and corruption.

behavior in terms of Judaism's standards of right and wrong.[59] We can judge at least his overt behavior; we ought to, since we have the moral obligation to decide whether, and in what degree, to emulate him, associate with or avoid him, assist or oppose him, and guide and train our children to do likewise.[60]

As regards judging our neighbor's moral guilt or innocence, it is clear—if not immediately, then upon reflection—that we cannot and ought not to try: we do not know the true motives of his actions; we do not know the full consequences of his actions; we do not know the true degree of his freedom of action and therefore of his responsibility. Our tendency, of course, is to assume that our neighbor is in full control of his actions and is therefore fully responsible for his offensive behavior, but we are really not able to verify that assumption, and cannot, therefore, properly judge his moral guilt or innocence nor thus judge *him*. "Do not judge your fellow till you stand in his place"—which we never fully can.[61]

But what of judicial judgment—judging, through duly authorized courts of justice, the neighbor who is accused of a crime against society? Every society asserts the right and duty so to judge and assumes the prerogative so to judge. On what grounds may society so judge? We do so, in accordance with the Torah's authorization and command, on the sole grounds of society's collective right and duty to protect its members from avoidable harm. ("Pray"—and act—"for the well-being of the government, for were it not for the well-being of the government, people would swallow up one another alive.")

59. This circumlocution, avoiding the use of such a phrase as "evaluating the morality of his behavior," is employed in the interests of precision, since to speak of moral (and immoral) behavior, conduct, action, or deed, is to be less than precise. Morality properly pertains to decision—which, by definition, involves the use of freedom, and not to overt action—which, at least in some measure, may reflect conditioning factors and thus a reduced degree of freedom. The slaying of an infant, for example, when done by an insane person, however horrible and ghastly it is, is *not* immoral; the deliberate humiliation of one person by another *is* immoral.

60. Not, however, to the extent of "smothering" and brainwashing our children. Even assuming that methods of child-rearing could be discovered and applied that would insure a lifetime of correct behavior by our children and guarantee against all deviation, would not such utter success constitute utter failure? If a person could be so successfully trained, "boxed in," "programmed," and automated that he literally could never choose to do evil, would he not be equally unable to *choose* to do *good*, and would not such a human being have thus been deprived of being truly human?

61. On rare occasions, the tradition tends toward the extreme assumption that even the most desperate act (e.g., suicide) must have been done deliberately and should

We initiate the process of judgment by ascertaining, as accurately as possible, the facts of the case: whether the neighbor who has been accused of a criminal act has indeed committed that act. If he has, our right-and-duty to judge him requires us to proceed to make, as accurately and objectively as possible, the following four determinations:

> a) In what manner can the harm done by this particular offender to the particular victim (and to any other members of society) best be counteracted (the loss restored, the injury compensated, the damage repaired, the wound healed, the suffering assuaged, the fear of future crimes allayed, the sense of moral outrage and cynicism alleviated)?

> b) What is the likelihood of recidivism—repetition by the offender of this offense against society, or commission by the offender of other offenses against society—if he is now permitted freedom of movement in society?

> c) If such likelihood is considered to be great, what manner of treatment during his incarceration is best calculated to accomplish his rehabilitation most fully and most promptly and to involve the least possible degradation and dehumanization?

> d) What conditions in our society appear to have influenced[62] the

therefore be "punished" (e.g., by less complete and respectful treatment than in the normal case of mourning for the dead). On rare occasions also, the tradition veers to the opposite assumption that sinful action is due entirely to the "spirit of folly that enters and possesses a person" and that no one "in his right mind" ever acts sinfully. Generally, however, the tradition avoids the assumption of either complete responsibility or of complete lack of responsibility.

62. "Influenced," not "caused" or "determined." Almost never can behavior properly be accounted for entirely in terms of cause. Various circumstances—genetic, psychological, physical, social, economic, or political—may well constitute conditioning factors, leading to a predisposition, tendency, proclivity, or likelihood. But, as long as there remains even a margin of freedom, "causation" and "determination" are not appropriate terms to use. (Recent evidence concerning the double-X chromosome factor is a case in point; this factor constitutes "predisposition" but not "cause.") Use of such a term as "influence" has the advantage of acknowledging both the offender's possible paucity, or absence, of freedom ("sickness") and society's obligation to remove the conditions that have encouraged such antisocial behavior, without the disadvantage of declaring the offenders absolved of their true responsibility, which, though unassessable by other people, is known, at least in part, by the offender and in full by God.

offender to offend—and what alterations in these conditions are most likely to prevent similar offenses by others?[63]

Other attempted judgments are morally unjustifiable. Thus, attempts to judge the moral responsibility of the offender, based on an evaluation of his mental capacity and emotional stability;[64] calculation of his "just deserts"; imposition of punishment as "just retribution" or generalized "payment of debt to society"; resort to vengeance, in the sense of needlessly brutal, humiliating, restrictive, or prolonged treatment; and certainly capital punishment—all of these, even though commonly accepted as part of the theory and practice of criminal law—constitute the "crime and punishment" and are morally heinous; all such attempted judgments constitute a usurpation of God's own prerogative. ("Vengeance and retribution are Mine.")[65] Indeed, even the judgments listed above as justified are only relatively justified, since they too pretend to a degree of wisdom and authority not possessed by human beings; their justification lies only in the aforementioned authorization-and-command that society seek to protect its members from the consequences of each

---

63. Strict treatment of offenders is often explicitly claimed, and even more often implicitly assumed, to be effective as a deterrent to others. Evidence—in distinction from mere assertion—for such a claim is often inconclusive, and in the nature of the case is difficult to come by. That the threat of being apprehended and punished is often an effective deterrent to many people, at least with regard to some types of illegal behavior (e.g., driving an automobile at excessive speed) is attested by their own admission. This case for deterrence, however, must be weighed against the evidence that a) the incidence of some types of crime has no correlation to the gravity of the punishment prescribed by law; b) crimes of violence are often committed in moments of passion; and c) at least some people commit crimes from a psychological need and subconscious desire to be punished!

64. Attempts to draw a distinction between the normal criminal (who, being aware of both his deed and its wrongness, is responsible) and the abnormal criminal (who, being unaware of either or both, is not responsible)—however historically significant as landmarks in the humanization of our approach to criminal justice—are no longer necessary (since only the above determinations need to be made) and hence no longer warranted (since they constitute human pretension to divine wisdom).

65. In the Bible, "vengeance" is usually forbidden to human beings because such vengeance involves an uncontrollableness of emotion and a paucity of wisdom that make truly just judgment impossible. For this reason, "vengeance" is permitted, "belongs," to God alone, since He alone is free from these—as from all—deficiencies. God's "vengeance" is merely another term for true justice and true recompense.

other's harmful acts,[66] and thus to preserve each member's own basic freedom—including each one's own basic freedom to sin!

9

But if human freedom—the ability to choose and the power to act—is genuine, how can God's own power and will be operative? And if human freedom is not genuine, how can God's judgment of humans be just?

There have been attempts to resolve these dilemmas by denying that God's foreknowledge of human decisions in any way determines them; such attempts, however, remain unsatisfying, because they introduce a unique and *ad hoc* meaning for either "knowledge," "decision," or "time." There have also been attempts to invoke the authority—and to glorify the paradox—of the rabbinic statement that "all is foreseen yet free will is granted." This statement, however, is such an extreme self-contradiction and is in such sharp contrast with the dominant view that "everything is in the power of Heaven *except* the fear of Heaven," that the former statement must either be interpreted to mean "all is foreseen *except* for free will, which is granted," or else rejected as unrepresentative and erroneous.[67]

The only adequate key to resolving the above-mentioned dilemmas lies in the concept of divine providence *(hashgahah)*. "Providence" affirms that God has a plan and purpose for humanity, for Israel, for the world—but that in forming this plan and carrying out this purpose God has chosen to limit the operation of His own power by granting humans the power to choose, to decide, and to act.

Why God should have done so—creating a creature with the power to rebel against the Creator and thus to delay the fulfillment of the Creator's plan and purpose, is one of the great mysteries. According to the Midrash, the angels questioned the wisdom, and pointed to the danger, of such

66. Whether society is morally permitted, without an individual's consent, to confine him in order to protect him from the consequences of his own behavior or in order to rehabilitate him, is a difficult question. To the extent that his moral capacity is clearly impaired—by virtue of age or physical or mental condition—society probably does have the right to intervene; to the extent that his moral capacity is unimpaired, society does not have the right—except at the point that the harm he inflicts upon himself causes direct and grave harm to others as well. But to make an accurate assessment of moral capacity is, at times, close to impossible.

67. Ephraim Urbach, in *The Sages* (Jerusalem: Magnes Press, 1979, 1:257), argues that *tzafui* does not here mean "foreseen" but rather, "observed."

creation, but their concern was ignored and their advice rejected. And, according to the Talmud, the schools of Hillel and Shammai also debated the wisdom of the creation of the human species; but their verdict—that it would have been better for humans never to have been created—was of little use, being long after the fact! Evidently, God in His divine wisdom, wanted—and wants—to take the risk.

The human power to deny God and to defy His will is not sufficient, however, to prevent the consummation of the divine plan; indeed, the very attempts to deny and to defy will themselves be incorporated into the consummation. For the plan, known to the Creator from the Beginning and fully to be accomplished in the messianic End, takes seriously into account all the multitudinous details of human history in between. This history, consisting of what happens *to* people (through God-ordained "natural law") and what is decided *by* people (through God-given freedom) is the arena on which God's plan is carried forward. Each move made by any human being is met by God's own move and, together with all other human moves, is fitted into the divine scheme—as in a cosmic game of checkers or chess, some one has suggested—God playing simultaneously with each person individually and everyone collectively. God summons us to hear His word, follow His command, and walk in His way; He gives us freedom to do so; He hopes that we will faithfully obey; but whether we obey or disobey, God takes all human decisions and their consequences and incorporates them into the divine economy; using all of our good and evil deeds, He allows the game to proceed.

The Bible is filled with references to God's plan and purpose and with allusions to the human decisions and actions that are woven into God's designs; indeed, the Bible, as a whole, may be said to constitute an account of their interweaving. Joseph, for example, sees (concerning his brothers' conduct) that "you intended it for evil, but God made it count for good.... it was not you but God who sent me here, that life might be preserved." Moses sees how Pharaoh's ever-increasing hardness of heart, brought about by the combined workings of Pharaoh's will and God's will, holds Pharaoh back from the one possibility of his own deliverance and propels him forward to his own doom. Isaiah sees in "Assyria the rod of God's wrath.... sent against an ungodly nation.... though he [Assyria] does not mean it so, nor does his heart intend so; in his heart is merely to destroy.... And he says, 'By the strength of my own hand I have done it and by my wisdom'—but should the axe boast itself over its wielder?" The unknown prophet of the Exile sees in Cyrus the one "whose right hand I [the Lord] have taken hold of, to subdue nations and kings.... I have called you by name though you have not known Me."

Yes, the prophet is enabled to see, and seeks to transmit to the people, a vision of particular aspects of this divine-human drama in its unfolding. The prophet is enabled to hear, and seeks to transmit to the people, a proclamation of what God is doing and what humans have done, or have failed to do but still can do, toward the accomplishment of His purpose. And everyone ever since who reads the Bible with the eyes of faith and hears the Word with the ears of faith, is granted at least a glimpse of the vision and a whisper of the proclamation.

The full measure of revelation, however—involving full judgment and recompense by God and full awareness by human beings—is reserved for the world-and-age-to-come. Only then-and-there will the true measure and true consequences of human freedom in the here-and-now be made known. "In the hereafter, the Holy One, blessed be He, will bring the evil impulse and slay it in the presence of the righteous and the wicked. To the righteous it will appear like a high mountain, to the wicked like a single hair. Both will weep. The righteous will weep and exclaim: 'How were we able to subdue such a lofty mountain?!' The wicked will weep and exclaim: 'How were we unable to subdue a single hair like this?!'" Thereafter, people will always choose the right and never the wrong—the power of the evil inclination having been utterly overcome.[68]

Until the coming of that Final Day, however, we are able to know in faith the only two truths we need to know: that our freedom to distinguish and choose between right and wrong, however limited, is genuine; and that every use we make of that freedom is of genuine significance for furthering God's design and affecting our own destiny.

---

68. This messianic conquest of the evil inclination presents a paradox: On the one hand, since human beings will, at last, be perfectly moral, will they not inevitably choose only the good? On the other hand, does not choosing the good, if it is genuine choosing, involve the temptation and the power to choose also the evil? We should therefore say that the human choice of good in the messianic era will be not "inevitable" but "unfailing."

WHAT DOES IT MEAN TO BELIEVE IN GOD?
Dedicated to Abraham Joshua Heschel: teacher, model, friend

To believe means to act out one's affirmations, to testify to one's belief through the way one acts; the test of one's faith is the degree to which it is embodied in the actual life one lives.

In our survey-surfeited age there is hardly an area of life untouched by the public opinion polls. Our voting and housekeeping, our eating and sleeping and traveling, our saving and borrowing and spending, our sexual practices and religious observance—all aspects of our public and private behavior—are endlessly explored. The results of the polls and surveys are at times helpful and useful, at times encouraging and reassuring, at times instructive and enlightening, at times disturbing and frightening, at times confusing—and at times amusing.

"Amusing" is the word to describe not only some of the answers but also some of the questions; and with regard to some of the subjects explored, "amusing"—or even "ludicrous"—is the word to describe the very notion that one can arrive at meaningful findings through a simple poll or questionnaire.

Such is the case with the question asked in many polls: "Do you believe in God?" Both terms, "believe" and "God," are so complex and so profound that a one-word response is neither appropriate nor useful; an on-the-spot yes-or-no answer tells us nothing significant or helpful—since everything depends upon the meaning attached to these key words.

What *do* these words mean? What *does* it mean to believe in God?

1

There are a number of misconceptions about what it means to believe in God that are so widespread and so deep-seated that we might best begin by stating what it does *not* mean.

To believe in God does not mean simply to know and repeat what either my ancestors or my parents believed, what my teachers taught me, or what the tradition says. The question often posed to a religious instructor, "What do we believe about such-and-such?" implies that when the instructor provides the official answer, the inquirer will then know what he, the inquirer, believes. This procedure externalizes belief outrageously.

Similarly, to believe in God does not mean simply to *say* "I believe." (After all, I may simply be mouthing someone else's views, pretending to believe.)

Indeed, to believe in God does not necessarily mean to talk about God at all. Talking about God—theology—does have important roles to play in the life of many believers. It clarifies the content of belief; it facilitates comparison of one's own personal belief with traditional beliefs or the beliefs of one's contemporaries; it aids in revising and refining, explicating and communicating belief, etc. These roles, however, are secondary and dispensable; to believe does not mean to theologize.

Furthermore, the verb "to believe," when used in a religious context, does not mean what it means in most other contexts; "believing *in*" is much different from "believing *that*." "Believing *that*" reflects either tentativeness and uncertainty ("I believe it's so, but I'm not sure") or admittedly subjective opinion ("I believe that such-and-such color or style is more attractive or satisfying, but *she* believes a different one is"). "Believing *in*," by contrast, involves an affirmation of sure conviction and absolute truth.

Despite this certainty, to believe in God does not mean that one claims to be able logically to prove or empirically to demonstrate to others the validity of one's own belief. Indeed, the true believer will readily agree that his beliefs can never be proved; he will even insist that they are in principle and inherently not susceptible of proof—or, of course, of disproof.

To believe in God does not mean even that one claims to have "all the answers" oneself. However much the believer claims to know, he readily admits that his knowledge about God is far exceeded by his ignorance. His faith does not rest upon the few and fragmentary answers known to him but upon the certainty that all answers are known to God.

Finally, to believe in God—contrary to popular impression and commonly attempted practice—does not mean that the believer ever has the power to impose his belief, or the moral or religious right to try. He does not have the power, since belief by its very nature is a matter of free assent and inner decision—and thus cannot be coerced. He does not have the moral right to try, because in the very attempt to coerce he may well cause the "object" of his attempt much needless pain and anguish, and may well mar and scar his personality for life. He does not have even a religious justification, because the one whose "soul" he is trying to "save" may be so alienated by this religious imperialism that he will be discouraged from pursuing his own religious search and making his own religious decision.

2

From these indications of what it does *not* mean to believe in God, what it *does* mean is perhaps apparent. To believe in God means to make, from the depths of one's being, a series of basic affirmations—which are affirmed to be both utterly true and crucially important for one's whole existence.

What are these affirmations that I make when I believe in God?

Since I am a Jew who has been exposed to the Torah tradition and in significant measure shaped by it, when I believe in God I believe as a Jew. I affirm my faith in the One who graciously established His covenant with the people Israel, miraculously redeemed and preserved Israel through the ages, and who, in and through the Torah, has revealed to Israel (including me) His word and will and way for Israel (again, including me) and for all humankind. A non-Jew may of course believe in the same One God. If he is a Christian who has been exposed to and shaped by Christian tradition, he believes in God as revealed through Christ. If he is a non-Christian, he can believe in God by virtue of the image of God in which all human beings are created. If he is a born Jew or baptized Christian who has not been reared in his tradition, he can believe in God by virtue of that same creation-in-the-image.

When I believe in God, I affirm my faith in the One who, through His perfect wisdom and absolute power, is the ultimate Creator of the universe and all that it contains—including me. The ultimacy of the Creation involves both the original miraculous act of calling into existence and the miraculous maintenance in existence—a renewal of creation day by day and moment by moment. The world is here because of God, and I am here because of God. The ultimacy of Creation also involves both the original intention and the final goal; all creatures exist within God's plan and purpose; all—including me—have a role to play.

When I believe in God, I affirm my faith in the One who is my ultimate Lord and Master: the only one whose absolute sovereignty I accept, the only one to whom I owe absolute allegiance and acknowledge absolute obligation. He alone has absolute claim upon me. Of course, there are other authorities in my life—parents, teachers, leaders, officials, governments—to whom I owe obedience and loyalty; but their authority has limits; God's has none. He has the right to command whatever He wills and to address His command to Israel alone or to all humankind; I have the duty to perform whatever He commands (whatever, that is, I hear Him to be commanding). He is the only one for whom I should do anything, sacrifice everything. He is my absolute King—whose absoluteness involves both the all-encompassing extent of His authority (no aspect of life lies outside it) and the supremacy and finality of His authority (all conflicting commands of other authorities are overruled). Whenever any lesser authority tries to usurp His throne and lord it over me, my response should be: "Who do you think you are—God almighty?!" Whenever I myself am tempted to play God, my response should be: "Thy will, O God—not my will—be done."

When I believe in God, I affirm my faith in the One who is the ultimate source, arbiter, and revealer of ultimate ought: of that which is morally right and wrong for all human beings and of that which is ritually prescribed, permitted, and forbidden for the people Israel. He is the one who has established the standards, for His will alone determines them. He is the One against whose standards all other proposed standards are to be tested. He is the One who reveals these standards to human beings—through both the moral capacity which is granted to each of us by creation-in-the image and through the fuller measure of instruction, admonition, and assurance which is granted to the covenant people Israel in the Torah. My conscience, through which that moral capacity functions, is of course fallible and corruptible; my intelligence, through which that Torah is apprehended, is limited and imperfect. Nevertheless, in my dual role of creature-in-the-image and child-of-the-covenant-people, I am to a significant degree able to know the difference, and to a significant degree free to choose, between the right and wrong in any given situation.

Insofar as I am able to know and to choose, I am responsible for the choices I make and the deeds I do—responsible to other human beings but responsible ultimately to God. Human judges may call me to account, but when I believe in God, I affirm my faith in the one judge before whom alone I am ultimately accountable. He is the one judge from whom nothing is concealed, to whom everything is revealed—my deeds and words and thoughts and motives, and thus the measure of my responsibility and culpability. From Him alone is a judgment of true justice possible. He is also the one judge who is absolutely incorruptible; He alone cannot be bought or bribed or bluffed; hence, from Him alone is a judgment of true justice assured.

But judgment involves not only evaluation and verdict; it involves the imposition of consequences as well. So, when I believe in God, I affirm my faith in the One who is the ultimate source and guarantor of consequences, the ultimate dispenser of reward and punishment. This reward-and-punishment takes may forms; it operates on various levels and in various dimensions; it works itself out at many different times and places. Sometimes I think I can discern the outlines, or discern at least some evidence, of God's justice as it works itself out; I then try to formulate a pattern of God's providence and to incorporate the bits of evidence into various types of "laws" that are at work in the world: laws of nature, laws of history, laws of individual behavior, laws of social psychology and social dynamics. In my deepest moments of faith, however, I admit the tentativeness and fragmentariness of all such laws—and acknowledge the presumptuousness and fruitlessness of all attempts to fathom the depths or trace the paths of God's justice. In any event, even at my most daring and discerning moments, I readily confess that more—far more—of the workings of God's reward-and-punishment remain concealed than are revealed. Nevertheless, even when injustice apparently prevails and wickedness triumphs, I stoutly affirm my faith in the righteousness of His judgment and in the certainty of its eventual fulfillment.

3

How awesome this God must appear, this God in whom I believe—Creator, Lord and King, Judge of right and wrong, Dispenser of reward and punishment; indeed, how awesome He is! Often I stand before Him in fear and trembling. And yet, when I believe in God, I know Him to be not only awesome but caring and compassionate as well. Far from being my enemy, He is my truest companion and friend. Since He is always present, I am never alone. He loves me when others—and even I myself—find me unlovable; He accepts me when others—and even I myself—find me unacceptable; He waits for me, even when I have turned my back on Him, disobeyed His commands, and gone astray. He has provided me with a conscience, with the capacity to feel remorse and guilt, with the ability to turn back in repentance so that I may know His forgiveness; all these are tokens of His love. (The commandments themselves are tokens of His love.) Even when He punishes me, it is not out of hate or cruelty but out of the reluctance, pain, and anguish of one who suffers with and for His children (indications of the "divine pathos"); His punishment is corrective, His chastisement is purifying and refining—a blessing in disguise.

Indeed, when I believe in God, I affirm my faith in the One who is the ultimate source of all my blessings—who constantly showers me with benefits and supplies all my needs. At moments of deepest faith I discover miracles all around me and am filled with wonder and amazement at the blessings of both "nature" and "society": of earth and sky, of life and food and health and strength, of shelter and clothing, of family and friends, of deliverance from danger and recovery from illness—all of them beyond my sole power to provide, beyond my desert. These blessings may appear to come—on one level they do come—from a combination of the world about me and the resources within me; ultimately, however, they come from God, who provides whatever I need. If at moments I find myself still lacking something, when I believe in God I know that I have only to turn to Him in prayer—and He is sure to respond. At times He responds by providing what I have asked for; at times, by providing something equally good, or better; at times, by strengthening my will to acquire for myself that which I lack; at times, by increasing my patience to wait; at times, by helping me understand that what I had asked for is unnecessary or harmful, against my true well-being or that of my brothers or sisters. But always, if I turn to Him in truth, He responds; upon Him I can always depend.

Yes, when I believe in God, I affirm my faith in the One upon whom alone I can ultimately depend. There are many powers (including my own) and many persons (including myself) upon whom I depend, to whom I turn, in whom I trust. But any and all of them—including my nearest and dearest, including even myself—may someday fail. Through loss of strength or courage or will or resources or interest; through bankruptcy of one kind or another; through neglect or desertion, rejection or disloyalty; through collapse or disappearance or death—all may prove themselves no longer dependable. In God alone do I dare put my absolute trust, for He alone is absolutely trustworthy. On His ever-present and all-sufficient power and wisdom and justice and love do I rest my hopes.

When I believe in God, I affirm my faith in the One who is the ultimate hope: for me, the people Israel, and all humankind. When all goes wrong, within me and around me; when war and hatred, jealousy and cruelty rage; when hunger and poverty, sickness and suffering abound; when storm and flood and earthquake roar; when failure and defeat and death stare me in the face—God alone is my rock and refuge; He is my redeemer. Even when He hides His face in anger and disappointment, my hope is not crushed and I need not despair. For when I believe in God, I know that however vast and horrible and—as far as I can judge—unmerited are the pain and evil that I and others suffer, these do not vanquish God, or render Him impotent, or utterly frustrate His plan and purpose. Some of the evil I can account for as the result of human sins—my own and others—sins of both omission and commission; some as the result of the solidarity through which the fate of human beings (for good and ill) is linked; some as the necessary means for teaching us and for correcting us in our stubbornness and perversity. But even when the vastness and the horribleness of suffering defy all human attempts at explanation and theodicy, I still do not surrender hope.

I admit I cannot fully understand His ways in the past and present, but for that reason I do not forget His covenant promises for the future. I take those promises seriously. Through His promise that all who put their hope and trust in Him will be delivered; through His promise that the Messiah will come, the world will be perfected, and His kingdom established; through His promise that the nations of the world will one day accept His Torah and live by it; through His promise that the people of Israel will be vindicated and restored to the land of Israel; through His promise that the Holy Temple in Jerusalem will be rebuilt, the dead brought to life for judgment, and death swallowed up forever—through these promises He saves me from despair and redeems my life from meaninglessness. The mystery of the present remains unfathomable, but I am able to affirm that beyond the mystery is meaning.

4

The above will perhaps suffice to explain what it means to believe *in God,* but surely it will not suffice to explain what it means *to believe.* We have said that to believe means to make, from the depths of one's being, a series of basic affirmations. But *how* does one make these affirmations? They must be more than verbal affirmations, more than merely *saying* "I believe." Furthermore, our statement that these affirmations are crucially important ones, made from the depths of one's being, implies that these are not merely intellectual affirmations, for we are more than intellect. Even to add that they are made with deep emotional feeling is not enough—for we are more than feeling and emotion. To believe in God involves much more; it involves inner moral decision and commitment. But even this does not go far enough, for if to believe means to affirm with one's whole being, then it must involve all dimensions of one's being—including the dimension of overt deed and observable behavior (both moral-ethical and ritual). *To believe, then, means to act out one's affirmations, to testify to one's belief through the way one acts;* the test of one's faith is the degree to which it is embodied in the actual life one lives and the deeds one does. In Martin Buber's phrase, based on the Hebrew word *emunah,* "faith is faithfulness." How overpowering it is to realize that one's religious belief, which is of all things the most private, is so publicly discernible!

5

If this is what it means to believe in God, it must be granted by all—even by a believer—that no one is a complete believer, since no human being known to us lives up to his faith commitment at all moments and in all regards with perfect faithfulness. That is why, in the earlier sections, we took care again and again to use the phrase *"when* I believe"—that is to say, "at those moments I believe, for I do not always; to the degree that I believe, for I do not fully." What disturbing and humbling news this should be for all professed believers who are self-righteous in their profession of belief! If their behavior belies their profession of belief, then their vaunted faith is exposed as faithlessness. And what comforting news this should be for all believers who are tempted to despair about the lapses in their own belief! If their unworthy behavior has exposed their unbelief of the moment, then their repentance and return to worthy behavior will mean a renewal of faithfulness. But what sort of news will this be for those who have long considered themselves—whether reluctantly or readily, proudly or despairingly—to be nonbelievers? Is this insistence upon the inherent connection between behavior and belief likely to bring about any change in their nonbelief?

Let us ask the nonbeliever himself.

The nonbeliever says: "Since you yourself, believer, apparently admit that behavior—externally observable behavior—is what is crucial to belief in God, why not restrict your attention and your affirmation to behavior alone? Why insist on bringing in 'God'—a needless addition, a needless label, a needless name?" To which the believer replies: "Behavior is crucial, but it is crucial as the outer expression and test of my inner acceptance of God, my inner commitment to God, who is the invisible and ultimate One; without that inner acceptance and commitment—without that ultimate One—the ground of my behavior becomes shaky and my step is no longer firm; my whole world totters."

But the nonbeliever presses further, for his doubts go deeper. "I acknowledge no ultimate or absolutes. Whatever leads to happiness and self-fulfillment for the individual, whatever promotes the greatest good for the greatest number—these are the only grounds I find for behavior. I see no need for any god, and I believe in none." How does the believer respond to this more basic challenge? By returning the challenge: "Are you so sure that there are no absolutes or ultimates in your life? Your 'whatever leads' and 'whatever promotes' imply both absolute degree and ultimate criteria as the ideal. Besides, look carefully at your own life—both at your innermost convictions and their outer expression; is it not true that you too at least sometimes acknowledge, and almost always presuppose, a host of ultimates: ultimate beginnings, ultimate wisdom and power, ultimate authority, ultimate right and wrong, ultimate judgment and accountability, ultimate consequences, ultimate source of blessing, ultimate support, and ultimate hope? Every human being has his ultimates. They are what give ultimate meaning to his life. Every person has his absolutes. They are the antidotes to absolute desperation. So, everyone has his god. Whatever or whoever actually functions as the object of your absolute loyalty or gratitude or guilt, of your deepest fear or trust or hope; whatever or whomever you'd do anything for, give everything for—that is your god. The question to be asked, therefore, as Will Herberg says, is not, 'Do you have a god?' but rather, 'Which god is yours?'"

The nonbeliever may now perhaps recant; acknowledging that the dimension of the absolute is present in his own life too, he may now acknowledge the absolute God. Or at least he may be on the way; as he finds that various absolutes prove to be false absolutes, he may come at least to acknowledge the truly absolute One.

Or he may pursue the argument still further: "Even if I am able to acknowledge the absolute, ultimate One, you and I, believer, are still worlds apart. For unlike you I cannot speak of 'God.' And it's not just a matter of semantics. I cannot speak *of* God, because I cannot speak *to* God, and He does not speak to me. Nor does He hear. In fact, He is not a 'He' (or a 'She') at all. No ultimate which I can affirm is the personal, living God whom you affirm, whom you address whenever you utter His name." This final challenge is the most difficult one for a believer to meet; unlike the previous two challenges, this one cannot be met by mere clarification or by reference to the ultimates that every person at some point finds himself ready to affirm. This challenge is far more basic, for it concerns the relationship between the I and the eternal Thou, which the believer finds to be at the core of his existence but which the nonbeliever denies as being at the core of his.

How, then, can the believer respond at all?

First, he must readily acknowledge that the living personal God is in crucial ways unlike any living person we know. He is not subject to any of our weaknesses of body or mind, or to any limitations of time or space; He is not subject to any of our vices, pettinesses, or temptations. He created us in His likeness but not like Him. In this sense, and perhaps in others as well, God is not "a person"; yet He is known to us personally. Surely, the believer must insist, God cannot be less personal than all persons created in His image; indeed, He is more personal—more alive, more active, more conscious and aware, more knowing and more caring, more available and accessible, more present—than any of the persons whom we know.

Secondly, the believer must acknowledge that the gap between himself and the nonbeliever is not unbridgeable, since their actual experiences are not incommensurable. After all, the nonbeliever in his own life surely knows, no less than the believer, the reality of I-Thou relationship with fellow human beings. Whenever any two persons meet in true relationship and dialogue, in genuine responsiveness, genuine care and concern, genuine giving-and-receiving, genuine trust and confidence, genuine acceptance and mutual confirming, they meet as I and Thou. Since, as Buber puts it, whenever any two persons meet as I and Thou the eternal Thou is also present, then the avowed nonbeliever, in spite of his avowal, knows the reality—the face, if not the name; the presence, if not the title—of the ever-present, living personal God. The awe-and-gratitude experienced by every pair of human beings when they know true companionship—the love and loyalty and trust of husband-and-wife, of parent-and-child, of brother-and-sister, of friend-and-friend—is both token of, and pathway to, God's presence; for the way to encounter with God, more often than not, leads through the moments of genuine human meeting. Calling upon God by name is far from unimportant, for the act of professing and addressing Him serves in itself to deepen—and, after moments of separation, to rediscover and renew—the divine-human encounter. Nevertheless, the mysteriousness of God's presence is such that it can be known even when it is not articulated.

Lastly, the believer, mindful of how the actual behavior of so many nominal believers (including himself) has often alienated people from God and brought God's name into disrepute, will strive to act in such a way with all the Thous he meets upon life's path that his behavior not only will reflect how a believer loves God, but will serve to make God beloved of self-styled nonbelievers as well.

DOGMAS IN JUDAISM

Are there dogmas in Judaism?

Some may be surprised that the question is even raised. For would it not seem obvious that a religion that is rooted in a Bible that speaks constantly about God would naturally have dogmas about God? And yet, at least in modern times, there has been continuing debate as to whether there are dogmas in Judaism at all.

Those who have argued that Judaism surely does have dogmas have been able readily to list a whole series of religious affirmations that, they assert, are absolutely basic to Judaism: that God created the universe by His will and the human being in His image; that God established a covenant with Abraham, redeemed Israel from Egyptian bondage, and spoke to Israel at Sinai, giving them the Torah; that God hears human prayer and responds, that He rewards and punishes and forgives; that God assures both judgment and redemption in the Final Day. Without these and other basic beliefs, it is argued, Judaism is unrecognizable and indeed inconceivable.

Others, however, have argued that in Judaism such beliefs are not really dogmas. After all, they insist, there are many Jews today, and there have been at least some Jews in the past, who deny one or several or perhaps even all of these basic beliefs—and are nevertheless everywhere recognized as Jews: by non-Jews, by fellow Jews, by themselves, and even by Jewish religious law-and-tradition! How can Judaism be said to have dogmas when those who do not accept these so-called dogmas are yet universally recognized as Jews?

A good case can clearly be made for each of the two sides in this debate, and the discussion is likely to remain at an impasse—unless and until the question "Are there dogmas in Judaism?" has been clarified and a basic distinction has been made. If the question means "Are there any beliefs that every Jew must accept in order to be considered a member of the Jewish people?"—the answer must be "no." For being a Jew does not depend upon an individual's beliefs (except, perhaps, in the case of a Jew who comes to affirm the distinctive beliefs of, say, Christianity), but depends rather upon his birth to a Jewish mother or (if his mother was not Jewish) upon his entrance through conversion into the community of the Jewish people. If the question, however, means "Are there any beliefs that every Jew must accept in order to be considered a faithful, authentic, traditional, Torah-true Jew?"—the answer is "yes." Yes, there are dogmas in Judaism—in the sense of fundamental religious affirmations, basic religious beliefs, which through the ages have been recognized, with an amazing consistency, to be essential to Judaism. All of them are rooted in the written Torah, all of them are elaborated in the Talmud, and all of them have through the centuries, at least until our grandparents' day, been considered to be basic to the Jewish outlook. Surely this should be evidence enough that there are dogmas in Judaism.

And yet, when we seek to list the dogmas, in clear form and exact formulation, we meet with almost insurmountable difficulty. The giants of our faith, in past and present, who have attempted to set down the root principles of faith, have been far from agreement with one another. They have differed on almost every aspect of the subject: the number, order, and arrangement of the dogmas have been argued; their precise wording has been debated; their exact meaning has been questioned; the relative importance of the various dogmas has been disputed; and even the very inclusion or exclusion of the items from the list of dogmas has been challenged. Does not this continuing and thoroughgoing debate give evidence that Judaism really has no dogmas after all? If even the experts and authorities cannot agree on what the dogmas are, must we not conclude that there are none at all?

But then again, perhaps the opposite conclusion is to be drawn: perhaps the very fact that so many authorities have felt called upon to attempt a formulation of the basic beliefs of Judaism indicates, in spite of all dissension, a decisive consensus that such basic beliefs do in fact exist. However great the differences of dogmatic formulation and interpretation among these great religious thinkers, their differences cannot conceal their unanimous agreement that Judaism is unthinkable without at least a core of religious affirmation. To assert that one has produced or can produce a universally acceptable and fully adequate formulation of the basic beliefs is to claim too much, but to deny that such basic beliefs exist is to claim too little. The undeniable variety of opinions as to exactly what the dogmas are and mean may simply indicate that divine truth—in the double sense of truth from God and truth about God—must inevitably resist a truly adequate human formulation.

Indeed, it is no wonder that in Judaism, almost as soon as dogmas are presented, they are immediately challenged; almost as soon as they are formulated, they are revised. But the presentation and the challenge, the formulation and the revision, are both essential. For to deny that there are dogmas in Judaism would be almost to assert that God has not spoken to humanity, not spoken to Israel—or that humanity has not heard, that Israel has not heard, at all. (Are all the words of the Torah simply of human origin?) And to deny that the dogmas of Judaism may and should be challenged would be to assert that humans can hear exactly, that Israel has understood fully, the word and will of God. (Are all the words of the Torah simply and literally from God?) Each generation of Jews that is plagued with doubt, or even given to reflection, must be bold enough to challenge all previous formulation of the dogmas; each generation must be vigorous enough to formulate into dogmas its own revised understanding of the Torah-teaching; each generation must then be humble enough to question its own dogmatic formulations, allowing them to remain but tentative formulations. Thus two perils will be avoided: the peril of a spineless Judaism without principles and the peril of a brazen Judaism without prudence. Both dangers inherent in the problem of dogmas having been forestalled, a valid role for dogma in Judaism has been assured.

But now another danger lurks, most perilous of all. Till now we have spoken about acceptance and rejection of dogmas as if only correct verbal formulation were involved. We have thereby left Judaism open to the devastating charge that it requires of the individual Jew merely to give verbal assent or intellectual acceptance to its dogmas. But is it indeed sufficient for a Jew verbally to affirm the Jewish creed? Is this all that God requires of us? Suppose an individual Jew openly affirms his belief in God as creator of the universe and of human beings, his faith in God as giver of the Torah-and-commandments and then proceeds to live a life of wickedness and viciousness and violence, of meanness and cruelty, of deceit and exploitation. If it is possible to accept the basic dogmas of our religion and yet live such an irreligious life—the whole case for "dogmas in Judaism" has fallen to the ground. And well it might. For does not true Judaism, authentic Judaism, stress not creed but deed, not belief but behavior, not affirmation but action, not catechism but character and conduct? Surely Judaism has always emphasized how we are to live rather than what we are to believe. Its motto may be said to have been not "Believe and be saved" but "Be righteous and be saved." In Judaism, then, belief and faith are not especially important. Dogma has no important role. The issue has now been resolved.

And yet not quite. Granted that our thinking on this theme of dogma has involved an error. But perhaps the error lies not in the assertion that Judaism *has* dogmas, but rather, in misunderstanding what is involved in *accepting* dogmas. Perhaps our failure has been a failure to indicate what is meant by belief and faith and dogma. For surely, to believe means more than merely to say "I believe"; true faith is more than lip service. Indeed, to believe, in the religious sense, means more even than to hold an opinion that something is true or to accept the intellectual validity of a statement. The key to Jewish belief and faith—and then to the whole notion of dogma in Judaism—lies in the Hebrew word for belief and faith: the noun *emunah,* the adjective *ne'eman,* and the verb *ma'amin.* This Hebrew word means "faith" but also "faithfulness"; it means "trust" but also "trustworthiness"; it means "affirmation" but also "holding firmly to the truth." To believe thus means to affirm with one's whole being; to act out one's faith in deed and word and even thought; to speak the truth and live the truth. The test of one's faith is thus the degree of one's faithfulness in embodying the belief one professes in the life that one lives. That shamefully incriminating gap between word and deed, between intent and act, between resolve and execution, is thus closed. What one really believes is indicated by the way one lives; the way one lives reflects one's actual belief, indeed *constitutes* one's belief.

The meaning of belief and faith in Judaism has now been clarified, the importance of its role has been restored. And so the case for "dogma in Judaism" has been won.

But wait: perhaps it has been lost! If inner belief points outward, to be acted out in life; if outer behavior points inward, testifying to one's actual faith—then what need for dogma after all? Dogma and faith are now seen not to be the same thing; we have been guilty of carelessness in using the two terms interchangeably, as synonyms. Dogma, after all, is not faith or belief; dogma is a statement in words of what one believes. And what need now for a statement in words, when (as we have seen) actions speak louder than words. What need for a creed? Let us heed but the deed. "Deed," of course, includes the mood and spirit and intent in which the deed is performed, but dogma seems no longer necessary. Yes, the vindication of belief appears to be the defeat of dogma.

And yet—one last yet—perhaps dogma may still have a role. Granted that belief-acted-out-in-life is the crucial thing in Judaism. And yet the need for dogma as a statement of belief does not for that reason disappear. Dogmas are attempts to state in words the beliefs that the Torah presents for individual Jews to believe. Dogmas are ways of reminding, of referring, of suggesting, of hinting, of alluding—to the truths by which the Torah directs us to live. Dogmas are pointers; dogmas are signs; dogmas are handles and hooks. Dogmas enable us to talk about our beliefs to others and to ourselves, so that we and they may be helped to express and examine, to clarify and correct, to illumine and refine the truths which are to govern our lives. Dogmas give us the opportunity to compare our beliefs with those held by other people and other religions; but dogmas give us an even more precious opportunity: the opportunity to compare our personal formulation of belief with the Torah's formulation, and to compare our personal profession with our personal practice.

In this world and in this life, both belief and dogma have their respective roles to play. In the world-to-come and in the life-to-come, belief will no longer need dogma, for there will be no difference among the beliefs of individuals and nations (all will share the one true, common faith); there will be no gap between belief and practice (all will practice what they preach, the evil inclination having been uprooted from the human heart). Dogma, therefore, will disappear; belief alone will remain. Or should we rather say, the two will have become one.

AN OUTLINE OF JEWISH ESCHATOLOGY

What does Judaism teach about death and death's aftermath? What does Judaism say about immortality, the soul, the final judgment, heaven and hell? What is the Jewish doctrine concerning the coming of the Messiah and the world-to-come? Is Judaism basically a this-worldly or an otherworldly religion?

These questions are frequently posed to rabbis by Jews and non-Jews alike, by children, adults and college students, by those at home in the synagogue as well as those estranged, by the learned and the unlearned. Everyone, it seems, takes for granted that the Jewish tradition has something to say on these subjects; and yet adequate answers are seldom forthcoming.

Why is it that this question, more than almost any other question of Jewish belief, so rarely elicits an unequivocal answer? It is partly because Judaism, with its stress on collective Israel and the covenant promise of Israel's survival as a people, was in early ages relatively silent about the fate of the individual after death. It is partly because classic Jewish sources record such wealth of detail and such variety of expression on almost every aspect of this subject that it appears difficult to formulate an answer that does justice to them all. It is partly because many Jewish writers and teachers, noting sharp differences among modern Jews on this issue of Jewish faith, tend unconsciously to read back this division too simply into the past—overlooking the large degree of consensus which, in spite of the diversity in detail, yet characterizes the classic literature.[69] And it is also—perhaps mainly—because even many who realize that the tradition provides a fairly consistent answer hesitate forthrightly to present that answer out of embarrassment over what they find to be its hopeless naiveté.

69. This is not to assert that the vast corpus of biblical-rabbinic teaching is completely self-consistent and unanimous. Such an assertion would be obviously false. What is being asserted is that a) considering the voluminousness of the literature, the great timespan of its composition, and the multiplicity of its authorship, there is an amazing degree of unanimity in its major affirmations; b) many of the varying views are not mutually exclusive but refer to different aspects of a complex reality—often to be seen in a relationship that is "dialectical" or "organic"; and c) where differences of view cannot be so accommodated, the tradition itself usually indicates—sometimes forthrightly, sometimes subtly—which view is authentic and which is "heretical."

But none of these reasons—and certainly not the fear of naiveté—should prevent us from examining the teaching of the authentic, classic tradition[70] on this (or any other) subject and from confronting it squarely. Indeed, naiveté is often a key to deep faith and profound insight, which can in turn be transposed to a new key.

1

The first thing that Jewish tradition says about death is that it is real: when we die, we are really dead. This first word, however obvious it may appear, needs to be said; it is not mere tautology, for it comes to deny the notion, common among ancients and moderns alike, that when we apparently die we do not really die. ("I can't believe he's really dead; it's all a bad dream. If he did die, it's only his body that died; he is really still living.") Such a notion is declared by Judaism to be wishful thinking and illusion. Instead, Judaism insists on accepting death its all its starkness: when the body dies (as it obviously does) and is buried in the grave to "return to dust," the person has died. Life has ended; death has begun—the state in which the human being has ceased to function, to act or to do, to know or to care, to be aware of anything—even of reward or punishment—or of anyone—even of God. "Dust you are; to dust you shall return" (Genesis 3:19). "When his breath leaves, he returns to the ground. In that very day his designs perish" (Psalms 146:4). "The dead do not praise God, nor any who go down into silence" (Psalms 115:17).

Thus, any doctrine about death, if it is to be considered authentically Jewish, must first of all affirm death's reality.

---

70. By "authentic, classic tradition" we mean the rabbinic (talmudic) body of teaching. Why should the rabbinic version of Judaism be considered the authentic version? This question, often posed also as a challenge, really includes two questions: a) "Why not the biblical version instead?"; and b) "Why not also extra- and postrabbinic versions?" The answer to the first question is in part historical and in part theological: historical, in that the only groups of Jews to have survived and flourished as Jews have been those who accepted as authoritative, at least in its main outlines, the rabbinic understanding of biblical faith and the rabbinic interpretation of biblical law; theological, in that it is rabbinic Judaism that decided what constitutes the Bible—both in the sense of which books were to be considered Holy Scriptures and were therefore to be included in the canon and also in the sense of what the text of these Holy Scriptures means. The answer to the second question is implied, perhaps, in the answer to the first: the validity of any other version of Judaism must be judged in terms of its consistency with rabbinic Judaism.

2

But if Judaism's first word is an affirmation of death's reality, its second word is a denial of death's finality. The drama of my life is ended; I have exited from the stage. But life is a two-act drama: it is only the first act that has ended; the second act is yet to come.

Why must there be a second act? Because our God is the God of the Torah.

To believe in the God who created the world is to believe that God has a purpose, that history has a goal, that life has a meaning, and that the world is good. To believe in the God who created us in His image is to believe that we have a part in that purpose, a share in that goal, an insight into that meaning, and a view of that goodness. To believe in the God who gave the Torah to Israel is to believe that Israel has been given a special role in that purpose and goal and a special perspective into that meaning and goodness. But so very much about this life and this world appears, even for the children of Israel, to be meaningless, purposeless, incomplete, defective, evil. There is some improvement, to be sure; some progress is made in solving problems in various areas and on various levels; and some evils are overcome or at least reduced. But whatever progress occurs cannot conceal—indeed, it often more fully reveals—the larger amount of evil, suffering, injustice and senselessness that remains. And it seems clear that not all of this evil and suffering, injustice, and senselessness will be overcome—within my lifetime, or the lifetime of my children or grand-children, or ever within the course of human history. To believe in the Creator-God of the Torah, therefore, is to trust in a fulfillment of our life that is beyond our life, and a consummation of history that is beyond history—which means to trust in what the tradition calls, variously, the End of Days, the Coming of the Messiah, the Future to Come, or the Life of the World-to-Come.[71] This, it appears, is what is meant by the rabbinic teaching that "from the beginning of the world, King Messiah was born, for he entered the mind of the Creator even before the world was created" (*Pesikta Rabbati* 152b).

---

71. Although attempts have been made to distinguish among these and other terms and to trace the sequential stages which they are said to designate, these attempts are not convincing: the terms are often used inconsistently in the sources and at times inter-changeably. A more fruitful approach is to consider these terms as embodying, at most, different aspects, different "faces"—rather than different stages—of the messianic reality.

3

To affirm such a culmination of history and such a resolution of its problems may not seem at first necessarily to involve the further affirmation that the dead must themselves somehow share in that messianic event. Indeed, sometimes it is claimed that it would be much less selfish not to insist that I must personally witness the promised redemption and personally share in the promised reward. Is it not reward enough that the group will survive and that my descendants in the last generation will participate in the messianic redemption?

Whether it is less or more selfish to forego any aspiration for personal participation is debatable; after all, my protestation that I do not crave any personal messianic reward may be a cover-up for my fear of the messianic punishment! ("Let not your evil inclination allow you the false assurance that the grave will be a refuge for you" [*Avot* 4:22]). But whatever the verdict on the issue of selfishness vs. selflessness, there would seem to be no doubt concerning the issue of selfhood: to be a true self, to be a full person, involves responsibility and accountability—not only knowing in advance the consequences of my behavior, but facing those consequences; not only knowing that I am under judgment, but hearing the pronouncement of the judgment and experiencing the execution of the judgment. Selfhood and personality thus require personal appearance and confrontation. Since such personal appearance for full judgment and such personal experience of full judgment do not occur during life or during death, the judgment must occur in a life after death.

We may therefore say with assurance that just as any authentic version of Judaism must affirm the reality of personal death, so it must affirm the reality of personal life after death.

4

What will be the nature of this life after death?[72]

On the one hand, contrary to popular opinion in medieval and modern times, the main line of rabbinic Judaism does not teach the survival of the individual soul—in the sense of the continued existence of an ethereal

---

72. It is tempting to respond to this question by dismissing it—with the plea of ignorance. And indeed, concerning the details of what is in store for us after death, all humans must confess ignorance; even the rabbinic tradition, for all its wealth and vividness of description, must grant that "no eye has seen...." (*Berakhot* 34b). Humble

entity, devoid of body but continuing to function with awareness and response.[73]

On the other hand, what rabbinic Judaism does affirm is *tehiyat ha-metim,* the revival of the body—a transformed body, perhaps, but a genuine and recognizable body.[74] It not simply affirms; it stresses. In the face of challenges by both those who denied any form of life after death and those who affirmed such life but in the form of a spiritualized continuation of a life of the soul, rabbinic Judaism insisted, as one of its few dogmas, that the dead are to be resurrected, body and soul. (It included in the early morning prayers: "You will in the future take my soul from me and will restore it to me in the life-to-come.... Blessed are You, *YHVH,* who restores souls to dead bodies." It included in the mandatory *Amidah,* recited thrice daily: "You are forever mighty, *YHVH,* bringing alive the dead.... in Your abundant compassion.... You keep faith with those who sleep in the dust.... You are dependable to revive the dead." And it firmly asserted that "one who denies *tehiyat ha-metim* has no share in the world-to-come"!)[75]

confession of ignorance concerning the main issue of life after death, however, is really beside the point; indeed it is a mark not of praiseworthy humility but of lack of trust. For we are dealing here with a religions issue on which the tradition makes a clear and firm affirmation of faith, whose validity—as in all essential faith affirmations, even those concerning the things of this world—is not susceptible of empirical or logical demonstration. The validity of a religious affirmation cannot be proved—nor, let us remember, disproved.

73. The one valid sense in which the dead can be said to live on—in addition, that is, to the figurative sense of living on in the memory of, and influence upon, their survivors—is that they are never lost to God's unfailing memory and continuing concern. As regards consciousness, awareness, and response, however, the essential affirmation of rabbinic Judaism is that those who have died are indeed dead.

74. The frequent assertion that this teaching of rabbinic Judaism has little biblical basis, since biblical references to resurrection of the dead are few, late, and of foreign origin—however correct it may be and however illuminating in terms of cultural history and transmission—is for three reasons theologically almost irrelevant: a) a case can be made that the paucity, lateness, and foreignness explain merely the circumstances under which what was implied from the beginning now became explicit; b) in any case, their very inclusion in the Bible requires that such passages be given no less consideration as possible vehicles of revelation than passages containing other faith affirmations which happen to be more numerous, more ancient, more "native"; c) for any authentic Judaism the Bible must be read, at least on one level, through the eyes of the Rabbis.

75. In current editions this passage from the Mishnah reads: "One who says that *tehiyat ha-metim is not derived from the Torah....*" (M. *Sanhedrin* 10:1), but at least one early

5

Why this stress on bodily resurrection rather than on immortality of the soul?

For one thing, the concept of the soul's immortality tends to deny the reality of death ("death is but an illusion; it's only my body that dies; my soul, the real me, lives on") and thus, in a subtle way, to deny also God's right and God's power to take my life, whereas resurrection affirms the contrary: that my death is real, that God has the authority to take my life, and has the power and love to restore it.[76]

Furthermore, immortality of the soul implies that my body is less worthwhile and precious, less important and necessary, less "clean" and pure, than the soul; whereas resurrection affirms that just as in this life and world, so in the life-and-world-to-come the body no less than the soul is God's creation—and as such is both necessary and good.

Besides, the very notion of a bodiless soul runs counter to my experience of myself and of other persons—who are always unitary, body-soul persons and whose very personality is known to me, and indeed conceivable to me, only in such a psychosomatic combination.

Then too, the notion of a disembodied soul tends toward the notion that this soul will merge with other souls into the divine, ethereal stuff of an All-Soul—thus denying both the irreducible significance of the individual personality and the forever unbridgeable gap between humans and God.

In addition, while affirming the ultimate significance and unitary integrity of the individual person, resurrection likewise affirms the significance of human society: I, who am a person with no dichotomy of body and soul, function as a person, and indeed become a person, only in the society of other body-soul persons—meeting with them, relating to them, but remaining distinct from them.

---

manuscript does not include this limitation, which is therefore evidently a later addition. There are a number of passages, however, which midrashically deduce *tehiyat ha-metim* from the Torah, and a case can be made that *tehiyat ha-metim* is implied in a number of places. Indeed, one midrash claims that "there is not a single chapter of the Torah that does not contain the doctrine of resurrection, but it is we who have not the power to discern the true interpretation" (*Sifre Deuteronomy*, 306).

76. It is this triple affirmation that forms the basis for the authentic Jewish response to death: grief over the reality of a loss and separation that are permanent in this life; loyal acceptance of the decree of the True Judge, who has authority over life and death; and comfort in the divine assurance of resurrection in the world-to-come.

For all these reasons—and perhaps for others as well—bodily resurrection, and not immortality of the soul, is a necessary affirmation of any Judaism that claims to be authentic.[77]

6

When human beings are raised from the dead and restored to bodily life, what is in store for them? What is the essential nature and content of the resurrected life?

Since, as we have seen, the whole point of revival in the world-and-age-to-come is to enable humans to grasp in fuller measure God's original purpose for the world, for humankind, and for Israel, and to enable each person more fully to grasp the meaning of his own life in relation to that purpose, it is to be expected that the content of the resurrected life in the world-and-age-to-come will consist of the full disclosure of God's purpose, a full exposure to God's presence, and the full imposition of God's judgment.[78]

77. The concept of bodily resurrection—as of many other aspects of the messianic fulfillment—immediately elicits from many people the question: "How can this be true?" The question is really ambiguous. If it refers to the *ability of God* to perform the miracle, faith's answer must be: Since God is God He can perform any miracle; He is not bound by the "laws of nature"; as Creator He made them—and can change them or make exceptions. If it refers to the *manner of God's performance* of the miracle, the answer must be: "My thoughts are not your thoughts, nor your ways My ways" (Isa. 55:8). If it refers to the *kind of truth* which is being affirmed, the answer is: We are speaking not in terms of literal truth, but "mythical" or poetic truth. A "mythical" or poetic statement seeks to point to a truth and to affirm a truth which is beyond the power of science to demonstrate, beyond the power of experience fully to confirm, beyond the power of logic to prove, beyond the power of rational discourse to convey. The truth here being affirmed by the concept of *tehiyat ha-metim* includes these affirmations: that God's purpose for us is not ultimately fulfilled in this life; that it is not ultimately defeated, however, by death; that the ultimate fulfillment is beyond death and beyond history; and that this fulfillment involves full awareness by a real person that being in God's presence and under His judgment, he must accept the full responsibility and full consequences for his life. I am aware of no better concept than *tehiyat ha-metim* for conveying these affirmations.

78. There are passages in rabbinic literature that speak of a judgment that is apparently rendered immediately after death and thus before the bodily resurrection. Such passages should be taken as stressing the affirmation that the record of human behavior, upon which the judgment is based, is complete immediately upon death; there being no opportunity for further acts of righteousness or sin or repentance, God's judgment is ready to be pronounced. One's ability to hear the pronouncement and experience the execution of the judgment, however, comes only with the resurrection.

As regards the identity of the judge—it is, of course, to be God Himself, acting either directly or through the Messiah, anointed descendant of David, serving as the truly righteous king, God's trustworthy agent and symbol of Israel's vindication.

As regards the identity of those who are to be raised for judgment— since God has given to Israel "the Torah of truth, thus planting everlasting life in our midst" (second of the two blessings recited over the Torah), "all Israel have a share in the world-to-come" (M. *Sanhedrin* 10:1), plus at least "the righteous ["pious"] from among the nations of the world" (Maimonides, *Hilkhot Teshuvah* 3:5, based presumably on *Tosefta Sanhedrin* 13:2).[79]

As regards the extent of the judgment—it is to include the righting of all wrongs; punishment of all sins of thought and word and deed—sins of commission and omission (including passive complicity in evil); the reward for all good performed; the vindication of all innocent suffering.

As regards the nature of the reward and punishment—numerous, varied, and vivid images are found in the classic sources, but there seem to be two main themes: the reward consists essentially in a life of perfect blessing—plenty, wholeness, love, tranquility—revealing the full measure of God's favor and nearness; the punishment consists essentially in the denial of these—but constitutes also a preparation for the enjoyment of these, through correction, purgation, and refinement. Indeed, the same reality constitutes heavenly reward for the righteous, hellish punishment

79. Since, on the one hand, "all of Israel" are included, the "share of the world-to-come" obviously involves not merely reward for righteousness but also punishment for wickedness, for surely most, if not all, of Israel have in some measure sinned. Since, on the other hand, only "the righteous ["pious"] from among the [pagan] nations" are included, perhaps "righteous" ["pious"] has here a special meaning, referring not to actual moral and religious behavior but to the awareness of being under the judgment and mercy of the one true God. "All Israel," by virtue of the covenant and the Torah, are assumed to have that awareness. Those among the nations who, in spite of their pagan upbringing and surroundings, are able sufficiently to rise above that paganism and to acknowledge the one true God as their Lord and Master—and His standards as their standards—are also eligible. What is referred to in the promised "share" is thus not reward in the usual sense but eligibility for judgment. Standing *for* judgment is what is here promised; one's standing *in* the judgment will depend on the record of life in this world (as well, of course, as upon God's mercy). As for Christians and Moslems, we would say that since it is through their religion—and not in spite of it—that they are provided with the knowledge of the true God and His standards for humanity, all Christians and Moslems are to be included in the broad sense of the term "Israel" and all of them, therefore, have a share in the world-to-come.

for the wicked, and the transformation of at least some of the wicked into righteous.

As regards the nature of humanity thereafter—individuals will be free from sin or fault of any kind, lacking even the temptation to do evil, the *yetzer ha-ra* (inclination to evil) having been completely conquered; while humanity as a whole will constitute the ideal society of perfect justice and harmonious love, a true brotherhood.

As regards the duration of the resurrected life in the redeemed world—it is to last forever.

Galut in every respect and in every dimension—the exile of humanity, of Israel, of the universe, of God's own presence—will be gone forever.

7

Where is this all to take place?

Contrary to popular opinion, it will not be in an ethereal heaven, for the life-to-come, as we have seen, is not a spiritual realm of disembodied souls but a society of resurrected, body-soul persons. It will take place, rather, in this world and upon this earth, which will be, however, a transformed world and earth; the Garden of Eden restored; the world as it was intended from the beginning to be—with all imperfections and defects eliminated, all sicknesses and disabilities cured, all natural catastrophes removed, all lacks supplied, the fruitfulness and productivity of nature marvelously increased.[80]

And where on this earth?

In one sense, the locale of the redemption is to be the land of Israel—with Jerusalem rebuilt, the Temple restored, and the scattered people

---

80. It is sometimes claimed that the biblical and rabbinic picture of messianic abundance and perfection need not necessarily involve any supernatural or even radical change in the order of nature. In addition to discounting many expressions as hyperbole, it is argued that the present state of technological advancement has brought much of what was until now only prophecy into accomplished reality—and has opened up the way for visualizing future achievement, through human means, of what has not yet been accomplished. Even assuming that this verdict is correct, two points should be made: a) the miraculous and the human-natural are by no means mutually exclusive: the latter becomes the former when seen in religious perspective; and b) much more radical, in the messianic picture, than the transformation of physical nature is the transformation of human nature. Human experience to date provides little assurance of any unilinear or unambiguous improvement in basic human character; the fulfillment of the messianic promise in this regard would thus seem to call for no less radical and no less supernatural a transformation than has been heretofore envisaged.

Israel gathered again in the land of their ancestors—for the redemption involves the vindication of Israel as people of the covenant.

In another sense, however, the messianic redemption will not be limited to any one location—for the nations of the world, having been punished for their sins and having turned away from their idolatry and arrogance, will have accepted God as their King and His holy Torah as their law. All humankind having thus formed one band, the whole earth will be one land; the Kingdom of God, established at last upon earth, will extend over all the earth. Indeed, Israel's mission having been accomplished—the mission to serve as a light unto the nations and as God's witnesses among humanity—the differences between the people of Israel and the peoples of the world, and the differences between the land of Israel and the lands of the world, will disappear.

8

And when will this all come about?

How it is calculated from God's own point of view we cannot say; perhaps for Him the question of "when" is not even an appropriate question: though concerned with history and entering history, He inhabits eternity.

From the point of view of those who have died, redemption will come at the very next moment of their awareness—for whatever the length of historical time which has elapsed since their death brought Act One to an end, the sleep of death has consumed the entire intermission; Act Two begins at the very moment of their awakening.

From the point of view of those, however, who are living and not dead, living but not God, how is the question of "when" to be answered?

One could answer, on the basis of many classic sources, that the messianic redemption will come in the distant, even remote, future. But this answer is not fully adequate, for it assumes that the date of the messianic culmination has already been unchangeably determined by God. But perhaps it has not been, for on the basis of other passages in the classic literature we may say that the coming of the Messiah has been allowed by God to depend, at least in some measure, upon humanity. Even though it is not given to us actually to bring the Messiah, it is given to us to hasten or to delay his coming. Human actions in society, the conduct of the Jewish people, the behavior of a single person, can advance or retard the redemption. In principle, therefore, the redemption could occur tomorrow—or even today.

Indeed, in a significant sense it is already occurring—for not only does our this-worldly life affect our life in the world-to-come, but it also offers here and now a sample of that world-to-come. To those who are sufficiently perceptive, concerned and "open," a foretaste of the messianic fare is available at this very moment and in this very place. Whenever we are truly aware that we stand in God's holy presence, we can catch from within time a glimpse of eternity. The reality of hell is known to us in moments of idolatry, arrogance, selfishness, cruelty, war, hatred, and anger—or at least in the moments that immediately follow upon such moments! The reality of heavenly paradise is known in the moment of radical amazement at the grandeur of God's creation; at the moment of true gratitude for undeserved blessing; at the moment of turning to God in true prayer and finding Him; at the moment of genuine love of God and utter obedience to His will; at the moment of perfectly unselfish love for anyone in need or in distress; at the moment of delicious reconciliation with a dear one after deep estrangement; at the moment of genuine repentance for sin and the ensuing assuredness of God's forgiveness; at the moment of true joy in the performance of any *mitzvah*—particularly in the bliss of the Sabbath observed faithfully at week's end, a foretaste of the bliss at time's end, which will be all-Sabbath.

A hint even of the resurrection itself is afforded in this world by the experience of awakening each morning from a sleep during which, in so many regards, we are dead to the world. No wonder the tradition prescribes that upon awakening each day a Jew should at once declare: "I give thanks to You, O living and eternal King, who has restored my soul to me in mercy; great is Your faithfulness."

Truly "a foretaste of all that the Holy One, blessed be He, will bring to pass in the time-to-come He provides in this world in the life of the righteous" (*Va-Yikra Rabbah* 27)—and of the wicked!

9

Is Judaism, then, a this-worldly or an otherworldly religion? Neither the one nor the other, but both. Both worlds are involuntary; both are crucial; both are precious.

Both are involuntary, for "without your consent you are formed; without your consent you are born; without your consent you live; without your consent you die; and without your consent you will in the future render account before the Holy One, blessed be He" (*Avot* 4:22).

Both are crucial: as the time-and-place for preparation, this world-and-age is crucial; as the time-and-place for fulfillment, the world-and-age-to-come is crucial. What we will be likely to find in the age-to-come, what we will be like in the age-to-come, depends largely on what, in this age, we have accustomed ourselves to do and to say, to think and to see, to enjoy and to avoid, to love and to hate, to concern ourselves with and about. "This world is like the vestibule to the world-to-come; prepare yourself in the vestibule so that you may enter the banquet hall" (*Avot* 4:16).

Both are precious: "Better one hour of repentance and good deeds in this world than the whole life of the world-to-come; better one hour of tranquility in the world-to-come than all the life of this world" (*Avot* 4:17).

And, as we have seen, the two worlds are by no means discontinuous: they overlap and interpenetrate. Indeed, the only three factors essential to life are common to both: the world, God's presence, and our awareness. The only crucial difference between this life and the life-to-come is that in this life we, though able to be aware of God's presence, are also able, in some measure and for some moments, to suppress that awareness and be separated from that presence; in the life-to-come there is neither separation nor suppression, only encounter: we and God, eternally face to face.

TALKING WITH OUR CHILDREN ABOUT GOD

Now that many of us have become less uncomfortable in talking with our children about sex and have even brought ourselves to discuss issues surrounding death and dying, one subject remains taboo: God. And there are a host of reasons for our deep and widespread reluctance to broach the subject.

Some of us defend ourselves by saying, "In Judaism, belief in God has not been stressed; behavior is what's important." At the same time, others claim that if we teach our children the beliefs of their own tradition, they'll be confused and troubled by the different, perhaps contradictory beliefs they encounter from children of different religious backgrounds. Still others say that religious concepts are too profound and too abstract for immature minds. Children are not ready for such things; there'll be time enough for that later on; why bother them now? And finally, we sometimes question whether we have a right to indoctrinate our children at all; shouldn't they be allowed to grow up and then arrive at their own religious conclusions, make their own faith decisions—unbiased, unprejudiced, unprogrammed?

The truth is that often we try to avoid engaging in God talk with our children because of our feelings of inadequacy about our own Jewish backgrounds and knowledge. We refrain from bringing up the subject of God and hope our children will too. When they do ask religious questions, we try to change the subject or stall. When they confront us directly and insistently, having become puzzled or troubled or intrigued or excited by some religious issue that has come to their attention, we find ourselves saying, "Let's go down to the library and take out some books on the subject," or "Guess it's time to enroll our children in religious school," or "Let's ask the Rabbi; he (or she) should be able to provide the answer." Now, these are all good things to do, but what a shame to have to depend on others and delegate to them what we could do ourselves. In any case, the influence of our own teaching and example, including that which comes through our neglect and silence, is likely to be at least as significant as the influence of others.

As for the other issues we raise, each deserves serious consideration. Certainly, it is true that mere verbal profession of belief, not accompanied by deeds, is faithlessness; it is also true that a nonbelieving Jew is still a Jew. But sincere faith in God is and always has been of central importance in traditional Judaism; and while religious doctrines are often abstract, they need not necessarily be remote. Children can display a keen interest in religious subjects; they are full of questions about God and prayer and miracles and creation. They often demonstrate, in childish form, a deep awareness of the mysteries of religion and a striking grasp of its profundities. It may be that some concepts cannot be grasped as well at one age as another; experts on children's intellectual and moral development differ on what is appropriate at which stage. But even given the individual difference of all children, what they cannot understand of what they are taught now, they will come to understand later. Almost any religious issue, when formulated in simple terms, can be accessible to most children at some stage of their development. And it is important to make such issues accessible, if only because the children are less likely to be confused if they *do* know what their parents' tradition teaches. To the degree that they can verbalize their family's beliefs, they are helped to know what *they* believe, who they are, and where they stand.

But what about the issue of free choice? Here we come face to face with what is indeed a paradox. Religious faith, by definition, is a matter of free choice and personal decision by a mature person. But faith decisions are often shaped and influenced by the training, environment, and atmosphere in which a person has been reared and by the models to whom she or he has been exposed. Since our children's religious faith will inevitably be influenced by circumstances, relationships, and "significant others" of their childhood years, we parents certainly have the right—even the obligation—to seek consciously to influence our children's faith along the lines of what we ourselves affirm to be true.

Silence on such important issues can only give our children the message we want to avoid. Even when we have our own doubts about God, we have to see that not teaching anything does the children an injustice. Those people who believe children should never be taught anything that they'll later have to unlearn or that they'll discover upon growing up is not true often feel that the disillusionment and resentment children will feel toward both their parents and their religious tradition will be psychologically, morally, and religiously harmful. Granted, we should not teach our children anything—and surely anything about God—that we deem to be false. It is important, however, crucially important, to remind ourselves and help our children understand—to the extent and at the pace they are able to—that there are various dimensions of truth; that language has multiple levels of meaning; that words are multivocal. Even in prose, to some extent, and all the more so in poetry, the expressions we employ are often metaphorical, symbolic, figurative. In religious discourse, this is particularly true. The tradition, for example, sometimes speaks of the Lord, Ancient of Days, sitting upon His heavenly throne, high and exalted, observing all who are on earth beneath, writing in His book the fate of each of us. Yet a Jew who recites these words and affirms them to be true need not be claiming that God has a body and a beard or is a man; or that His throne is of gold or ivory or some other material; or that the book is of a certain size or that its pages are of paper or of parchment; or that He and His throne and His book are a certain number of miles "up there" and could be located, reached, touched, or photographed if we traveled enough light years in the right direction with the right equipment. The validity of one's religious affirmation does not depend on the literal truth of the words in which the affirmation is couched. It may well be that a child, having been taught those graphic and boldly anthropomorphic words, may, as a child, take them literally and, upon maturing, may come to no longer take them literally. She or he need not, however, consider them false and unlearn them. The words can still be accepted as true, but true in a different sense. (Many adults I know have grappled with and worked through their own religious questions by means of a renewed awareness of such nonliteral truth.)

I believe that doubt itself has a fruitful role to play in the life of faith and in our efforts to nurture faith in our children. Our doubt can help keep us from being glib, insensitive, and self-righteous in professing our faith. When openly shared with our children, doubt can help us rear them to be alert to such moral and spiritual perils. (We and they will never boast that "we're religious and 'those people' aren't.") Furthermore, doubt can serve as a humbling reminder that being human, we can never attain a full understanding of God's thoughts and ways. ("*We* don't understand, but then we're not God.") Doubt can thus even deepen our sense of wonder at the mysterious paradox of God's transcendence and presence. ("Yes, darling, it's hard to understand how God can be 'out there' and yet so near to us; I also don't understand exactly what that means.")

Our concern to be honest with ourselves and with our children can, if we summon up the courage and temporarily suspend our own disbelief, be directed into a shared religious search into the various possible meanings of the traditional formulations of Jewish faith. ("Now what might this passage mean? What could that story be trying to tell us? Let's read it over again and think about it some more.") In order to maintain our self-respect, of course, we will want to keep ourselves from being *childish,* but in order to grow in spiritual insight, it may be helpful to be *childlike,* at least for a while. (For those who find themselves unable to make such a distinction and find that trying to be childlike is childish, we offer another possible approach—in the last section of this essay.)

What are some of the ways in which our tradition has been accustomed to speak of God? What are some of the word pictures by which it has sought to portray Him?

Judaism frequently speaks of God as the Creator, who called the universe into being. When our child asks us, in challenge or in wonderment, "But who created God?" or "How old is He?" we can respond, in explanation but also in shared wonderment, "God is the only one who wasn't created, who had no beginning but was always there. There was a time when there was no world or anything, only God." And then we can proceed, on various occasions and in various connections, to spell out on a child's level and in a child's language some of the many implications of creation; that it didn't "just happen," but that God planned the universe and arranged it to function in orderly patterns; that theoretically He could interrupt its workings, since the Creator is not bound by the "laws" of His Creation but that He prefers to maintain its regularities; that not only did He create it in the beginning, He renews each day the work of Creation, in accordance with His plan for the advancement of His purpose; that God's Creation is good; that *Shabbat* is the climax of Creation, constituting the goal and purpose of it all. And if at times our child asks a question about Creation for which we have no answer ("Why did God create earthquakes, floods, and hurricanes?"), we can acknowledge our shared ignorance and then add, "Even if we do not know the answer, God does; and maybe someday we'll know too."

Not only did God create the universe in all its vastness and variety, but He also created human beings, multitudes of us; yet every single one He created in His image, including you and me. How rich is this concept of Creation-in-the-image, richness that can be shared at every stage of our child's growth. We can point to the capacity of every normal human being to think, reason, learn, remember, and imagine; to be aware of self and others; to communicate with others; to know right from wrong and choose between them; to be responsible for choices made; to regret, repent, and change; to be aware of God and pray to Him. There are also many implications of the doctrine of Creation-in-the-image for the worth of every human being. Each human being is unique and infinitely precious, to be loved, to be held in awe as a symbol of God. No one is to be abused, degraded, disdained, treated as a thing, used merely as a means to our own advancement. Once again, our children will raise problems: "image and likeness" may make God too anthropomorphic, even corporeal ("How tall or strong is He? What does He look like?"). Substituting "spirit" may make him too ethereal or too pantheistic ("If He's everywhere, He's in everything, so He can be hit or burned or even flushed down the toilet!"). If all that God created is good, what about the imperfections ("Why are some children born blind or deaf or deformed or mentally retarded or dead; why are some people cruel and evil?"). But, once again, we can be honest enough to share our children's ignorance and bewilderment before Creation's seeming imperfections and try to let them know that our faith can encompass our doubt.

The Torah tradition also speaks of God as Lord and Master, as our King. What are some of the implications of these titles that we might include in our God talk with our children?

If God truly is our Lord, He is our only Lord, which means that He is our absolute and final authority in all things. He is also the Source of right and wrong; His will determines and His command constitutes what is right and wrong. There are other authorities in our life, to be sure—parents, teachers, governments—but their authority has limits. God's has none. His commandments govern all areas of our life and supersede any conflicting demands of all these lesser authorities. To Him alone we owe utter loyalty and absolute obedience. Which means, of course—and we must readily admit this to our children—that even governments and parents can be wrong and that when children feel sure that in a given case the parent or the government is wrong, it is God and not the government or parent that should be obeyed! (It is also true that the less mature the child, the more responsible the parent is for making the decision and controlling the behavior!)

If God is truly King, He is also ultimate Judge. Again, there are other judges in our life who call us to account and, within limits, have this right. But it is to the Judge of all earth alone that we are ultimately accountable. Furthermore, He is the only one who really knows, fully and accurately, all our intentions, all our deeds, and also the exact degree of our freedom and the exact measure therefore of our responsibility. Because He is not only all-knowing but incorruptible as well, subject to no bias and no bribe,

His judgment is always just payment in accordance with our just deserts.

For there *is* payment; there *are* consequences of our deeds, and it is God who is the ultimate source of such "reward and punishment." For the most part, it appears, God works indirectly, allowing the consequences of our actions to come about through the operation of various "laws"—physical, psychological, social, moral, historical. (When we neglect or mistreat our bodies, when we let our minds atrophy, when we become habituated to pernicious patterns of behavior, when we mistreat other people, we usually reap the consequences.) With the eyes of faith, however, these "laws" are seen to be the vehicles of God's justice. Not that we can always discern the workings of God's justice; at times—let us admit it readily to and with our children—there seems to be great disparity between what people deserve and what they receive ("They get away with murder!"). The workings of God's justice are discernible only at times and only in part, yet often enough and in sufficient measure for us to be able to reassure our children and ourselves and reaffirm our trust that our King and Judge is indeed the King of justice.

There is, of course, a danger in talking this way with our children. We may dwell so much on God's role as King and Lawgiver and Judge that the picture may become too awesome, too threatening, too frightening, too guilt-producing—to the point of being religiously overwhelming, morally incapacitating, psychologically damaging. Fortunately, however—thanks to God—He has other titles, qualities, faces, and these others may be the ones we'll decide to stress.

God is the Source of all our blessings. Some of them have already been alluded to: the "distant" blessings inherent in the wondrous workings of His vast Creation, the moral blessings of instruction and guidance inherent in His commandments and our capacity to know them and obey them. But there are a host of more immediate, personal blessings: of food and clothing; of health and healing; of growth of body, mind, and character; of warmth; of family and friends; of sex and love and marriage; of beauty that we find in nature and of beauty that we ourselves create. All these and countless other blessings are tokens of God's love.

For above all else, God loves us—like a father, mother, husband or wife, our dearest friend, and even more than they. He knows our weaknesses and limitations and makes allowances for them; not only that, He gives us strength. When we are depressed and "down," He raises us up and comforts us. When we are ignorant, He instructs us. When we feel lost or lonely, He befriends us. When we feel rejected, He accepts us—even if in our own eyes we are unacceptable. When we feel defeated, overburdened, unable to function or accomplish, convinced we can't do it or go it alone, He reminds us that we're not alone.

Not always, of course—perhaps not often—do we pause to take note of these many manifestations and offers of God's love. But that is because we so seldom engage in prayer, in the acknowledgment that we stand in His presence. Most Jewish parents do not attend synagogue services regularly; when we do attend, we seldom find the experience to be a worshipful one. Even when it is inspiring, we may not take the time or make the effort to engage in prayer outside the synagogue, in our home and with our family. We thus manage to shut off our children and ourselves from God's ever-available presence. Instead of developing, deepening, and refining our religious sensitivity, we allow it to languish and to atrophy. If we can make the effort to pray together with our children, using words of traditional Jewish prayer, occasionally supplementing them with words of prayer from other sources, and at times just engaging in informal God talk, we may well become strengthened in our conviction that God hears our prayer and cherishes it and that He responds as well.

We might find that our prayers of praise are not only an acknowledgment of His blessing but a means of deepening our awareness of the myriad instances and multiple dimensions of His blessing. We might find that our prayers of confession serve not only to make acknowledgment of sins committed but serve as well to cleanse us and remove the burden of our accumulated guilt and to disclose new resources of strength to keep from sinning more. We might find that our prayers of petition for whatever we consider our genuine need are indeed answered, but that God answers in a variety of ways: sometimes by giving us what we ask for; sometimes by correcting our sense of values and our evaluation of our needs so that we come to see that what we began by asking for is actually against our own best interests or is unnecessary for us and is against the well-being of our fellows; sometimes by helping us see that what we asked for depends not only on God but on us as well—and then by strengthening our will to perform that which it is within us to do; sometimes by enabling and ennobling us to accept what is not to be changed, thus making our will coincide with His. But always He responds. Always, therefore, we can be confident and hopeful when we turn to Him.

It is the Lord who is our ultimate hope. Upon Him we can always depend. In Him we put our absolute trust. There are others, of course, upon whom we depend and in whom we trust—for one thing or another, at one time or another, to one degree or another. But all of them—parent, child, spouse, leader, or friend—may someday fail: through forgetfulness or neglect, bankruptcy of one sort of another, desertion, or death. God alone is completely dependable, utterly trustworthy.

But once again our children may interrupt such pious talk and challenge us by saying: "If God is so dependable, then why do the righteous sometimes suffer and the wicked go free? How long does it take for God to right what's wrong? Meanwhile, the victims die!" What they are saying, even if they don't yet know the term, is that this world remains unredeemed.

Here we can begin to talk with our children about the coming of the Messiah: when God *will* right all wrongs; will restore Israel's glory and the people Israel to its land; will vindicate all just struggles and all unjust sufferings and defeats; will disclose to us the full meaning of our lives; and will vanquish death forever. How and when this all will be brought about, we do not know and should not pretend to know. (Childlike formulations need not be insisted on; they also need not be rejected and certainly should not be ridiculed.) *That* it will occur, however, in God's own time and way, we can stoutly affirm, for to believe in the Creator God and King, who is wise, powerful, and just, and to believe in the God who loves us is to be sure that the divine promise of redemption will be fulfilled.

One further aspect of redemption should be included in our God talk with our children, however abstract it may seem at first: redemption not only as something that will occur at the end of history but redemption also as a dimension of life here-and-now. This word picture may prove useful: picture an overarching, curved line, stretching above the horizontal line that represents the course of history from beginning to end. Picture an infinite number of tiny windows in that arch, a different window facing each of us at each moment of our lives: whenever you or I look inward-upward, turning to God, the window of that particular moment opens up, enabling us to catch a glimpse of how that moment is seen from His perspective. The true meaning of that moment is revealed; eternity for a moment has entered time; we are redeemed. ("Now everything looks different!")

But how do we know all this to be true? Our children put this challenge to us at one age or another ("How do you *know* that there's really a God? Some of my friends say there isn't!"), and we, of course, ask this question of ourselves. This question actually represents several different questions.

One question is: can all or any of these God affirmations be proved? The answer to that question is, of course, "No." We can cite indications of orderliness and purposefulness in nature; we can point to the presence of a moral and spiritual dimension in every human being and of some form of religious belief and practice in every known society; we can argue that without acceptance of some ultimate power, life would be meaningless and unlivable. All these may constitute evidence for the validity of our religious affirmation, but there is contrary evidence as well: chaotic aspects of nature, barbaric aspects of human behavior; and, in any case, evidence is not the same as proof. We cannot prove, logically or empirically, that God knows or cares about us or promises to redeem us—or even that He exists. Basic religious affirmations, by definition, can never be proved. (Of course, they cannot be disproved either.)

On what basis, then, do we know our belief to be true? On the basis of our Jewish tradition—let us say—the tradition received by us from believing parents and grandparents, whose faith-tradition goes back, in turn, more than three thousand years to our ancestors in the time of Moses. Those were the Jews who were led forth from Egyptian bondage, heard God speak to them as they stood at Sinai, received Torah and commandments there, and became the covenant people Israel. We are their descendants and their heirs; we accept as true what they, on the basis of their own experience, perceived to be true and handed down to us.

This moving answer is a powerful claim on which to base the validity of our belief. But a perceptive mind—and our children's minds are, at times, at least as perceptive as our own—may well press on and ask: "How do we know that what our ancestors heard at Sinai was not an illusion? How do we know that what the Israelites thought to be the voice of God, speaking from within the cloud, was not an imaginary voice, or else the voice of Moses, who either pretended to be God or sincerely but mistakenly believed that he had heard God speak the words that he was now conveying to the people? The Israelites at Sinai were sure that it was God who had spoken to them, and Jews throughout the centuries have been sure, but how can *we* be sure?"

We can have no external proof. But our ancestors, even those who stood at Sinai, had none either. All depends on whether we can individually, existentially, affirm that it was God who brought them—and us along with them—forth from bondage; that it was God who spoke to them—and to us along with them—at Sinai; that it is He who continues to speak through the Torah book and tradition, telling us enough about

Himself and about ourselves that we can live the holy life of the chosen, covenant people Israel.

If we *can* acknowledge that in some sense God did choose our people Israel, redeeming us from bondage and giving us the Torah, does that mean that we must tell our children and ourselves that He cares about other peoples less, that we are more precious in His eyes than they? In our God talk with our children, how shall we deal with this concept of the "chosen people?"

There are a number of aspects of traditional teaching about Israel's chosenness that can relieve some of the moral concerns that trouble sensitive persons, children and adults alike. For one thing, that Israel was chosen to receive the Torah was not due to our own worthiness or righteousness. Scripture makes this clear (even though we cannot deny that there are midrashic passages that state or imply otherwise). Furthermore, the chosenness certainly does not entail lesser demands, lower standards, or greater leniency in judgment; on the contrary, it entails greater obligation. We are obligated to live on such a high moral and spiritual level that we will serve as God's witness people, "a kingdom of priests and a holy nation." (Not that we always do!) And the actual, historical experience of this "chosen people" has frequently, almost regularly, entailed a greater measure of enmity, persecution, and suffering than that of other peoples. (Indeed, sometimes what troubles us and our children about our chosenness is not a feeling of embarrassment but of bitterness and resentment. Who asked to be chosen? Who *wants* to be chosen? Why did *we* have to be chosen?)

Nevertheless, it would not be honest or worthy to deny that in the eyes of the tradition there *are* overtones of privilege, favor, and blessing inherent in belonging to the people Israel. For one thing, the Torah, for the sake of which we came into existence and remain alive, is far too precious for us to deny or minimize the distinction it confers on us. What is also true, however—as we should remind ourselves and our children and non-Jewish friends—is that in the eyes of our tradition, every single human being is equally precious in God's eyes because every single human being is equally created in God's image; that the "pious among the nations," who faithfully keep the commandments that are binding upon non-Jews (the so-called "seven commandments of the children of Noah"), have their share in the world-to-come and therefore have no reason to become Jewish; that those non-Jews who nevertheless desire to convert to Judaism and take upon themselves the additional obligations of a Jew are always welcome, since Israel's chosenness is not in any sense "racial" or closed; and that in any case, Christians (and Moslems as well), by virtue of their worship of the same one God as Israel worships and their acceptance of Israel's sacred Scriptures, in a genuine sense share in God's covenant with Israel.

Many of the issues discussed thus far are not entirely new; they may well have been faced by previous generations of Jewish parents in talking with their children about God. One problem, however, is new—or at least its urgency and intensity are new—the problem of sexist language when referring to God. ("Why is God 'He' and not also 'She'?") Most men, and at least some women, are not yet troubled by this problem. The question has either not yet occurred to them or has been casually dismissed as of no consequence. To a growing number of women, however, and to at least some men—and to a host of children of the "new generation"—this type of sexism is becoming a real problem. And they are not likely to be satisfied with the cold and glib grammatical answer: "Most languages have no convenient way of referring to living beings as other than male or female." True, they may admit, but beside the point: if God must be spoken of, and spoken to, as either male or female, why in Judaism should it always be as male? The religio-historical explanation—that Judaism sought to guard against pagan notions of fertility goddesses and actual fertility rites and sexual orgies—is equally unacceptable. Indeed, such an "explanation" itself reflects a male sexist bias. Why should one assume that masculine locutions and male imagery are inherently less sexual than their counter-parts? Similarly, the explanation that such divine qualities as strength, authority, knowledge, and justice are most "naturally" associated with masculinity is exactly what is meant by sexism!

But what can even the most sensitive parents *do* in the face of the tradition's consistently masculine language in referring to God? Not much, perhaps, but something. In God talk with our children, we can point to the crucial passage in Genesis that "God created humans (*adam*) in His image ... male and female He created them," which, though employing the usual masculine verbs and prepositions, clearly affirms nevertheless the equal likeness to God of man and woman and thus clearly implies the sexlessness (or bisexuality?) and genderlessness of God. We can also point to the few biblical references to divine roles or qualities specifically identified as feminine ("As a man is comforted by his mother, so shall I comfort you") and to the widely accepted derivation of the Hebrew word for compassion (*rahamim*) from the word for womb (*rehem*), keeping in mind that God is often called the Compassionate One. We can point further to the feminine word for God's near presence (*Shekhinah*), so common in talmudic writings and so prominent in Kabbalah. (The Kabbalah is bold enough to speak of male and female aspects of God's "inner life.") Furthermore, we can try the experiment, in our informal prayer conversations with our children and even in our formal prayer, of referring to God as "She," and sometimes adding to our "He" or "She": "Of course, God is not really male *or* female."

Which brings us to a problem that for some parents is the key problem in their whole religious outlook and the greatest single obstacle in talking with their children about God, a problem far greater than the problem of God's sexuality—the problem of God's personality. Throughout the centuries-old tradition, with near unanimity and consistency (except at times by philosophers), God has been spoken of in personal terms—as indeed we ourselves have been speaking of Him throughout this chapter. Yet how can God be a person? Presumably, He doesn't have a body; but what is a bodiless person? Where does a bodiless person live? How does a bodiless person function? How can a modern person not be troubled by the notion of a personal God? (Actually, premoderns too were evidently troubled: medieval thinkers, talmudic sages, and even some of the biblical writers reflect, in various ways, their problems with this notion of a personal God.)

Perhaps we can never believe that God "is a person"; perhaps it was never intended that we should. But surely if God "is not a person" like us human persons, He must be not less personal but more personal than we. Can we imagine God to be less knowing, less concerned about right and wrong, less sensitive and caring, less filled with righteous indignation, less disappointed and hurt, less planful and hopeful than we, who are created in His image, know ourselves to be? Granted, He is not subject to the weaknesses and defects of our human personality, but is He inferior to us in our virtues and our strengths? If we find ourselves unable to say that God "is a person," can we not at least say that He is the living God who personally affects us, personally relates to us, and is personally available to us?

But what of those of us who find ourselves unable to go that far? What if, after appropriate reading, talking with some approachable believers, reexamining and reflecting on our religious situation, even attempting to pray, we still feel dishonest in talking about a living God at all? Is there anything further that we can do?

For one thing, we can make sure not to try, by pressure, argument, or ridicule, to disabuse our children of their "childish notions." After all, they may be open to dimensions of truth and worlds of meaning that are, at least for the present, closed to us. Second, in talking with our children on religious matters, we can substitute other words and images for the traditional ones, "translating" the language of tradition into what we find to be more acceptable language—but still seeking to retain the dimension of the ultimate, the transcendent, and the mysterious. We can express joy and gratitude for our blessings but also—without mentioning a personal, living God—our wonderment that these blessings have "somehow" been given to us, beyond our own doing or our own desert. We can express contrition at what we have done wrong or failed to do right toward both our fellow human beings and whatever "powers that be," and express our resolve to change and then—without so much as mentioning a personal living God—express wonderment at the cleansing and unburdening that comes from our confession and at the resources that are somehow made available for changing our ways.

We can acknowledge our need for help and our dependency on powers that are somehow there. We can express our joy and gratitude for being members of the age-old, worldwide Jewish people, heirs to the Torah tradition. We can express our wonderment that somehow, against all odds, we have survived. We can express our confidence—even when confronted, as Jews or as human beings, by trouble, suffering, defeat, sickness, or death—that life is somehow still worth living, and—without alluding to a living, personal God—we can affirm, in the face of life's impenetrable mysteries, that beyond the mystery there is meaning and that someday the meaning will be revealed.

TAKING THE FIRST STEP OF *TESHUVAH*

A rabbi's lot, so very often, is a frustrating one. The level of *mitzvah* observance among Jews, of regular prayer, of Jewish knowledge and Torah learning, of Jewish interest and involvement, of ethical behavior, of Jewish discipline, is usually so low, and even when present is apparently so lacking in *kavvanah* (the proper intention) and so devoid of *kedushah* (holiness), that as a rabbi I often find myself filled with resentment, self-doubt and a sense of failure, despair and desperation. Then, seeking to suppress all these, I tend to compensate by adopting the stance of disdainful superiority. Why are almost all of "them" so ungrateful for my faithful rabbinic service and fine example, so unresponsive to my sincere and urgent pleas, so resistant to my earnest efforts to have them become good Jews like me? Alas, that is the way I feel much of the time.

And yet, there are some moments, as when the *Yamim Nora'im* (Days of Awe) approach, and at least occasionally between *Yom Kippur* and the next *Rosh Ha-Shanah,* that my righteousness, so sharply contrasted with their unrighteousness, is recognized even by me to be self-righteousness.

Ungrateful? Is it not I who am ungrateful? For is it not an undeserved privilege to be able to study and teach Torah, to be looked up to as authority or at least as guide, to be a source of strength and hope in time of trouble, to lead others in prayer to God, to spend so much of my time in doing *mitzvot?*

Besides, even assuming that the level of my Jewish living is so superior to theirs, was I not reared in a richly Jewish home, given an extended and intensive Jewish training, and then elected to a position that makes it in many ways both more convenient and more mandatory for me to lead a Jewish life? (Said a businessman in my very first congregation, when I was indiscreet enough to bemoan my lot to him: "Why, Rabbi, you are able to do meaningful things during your working hours; I can find meaning in my life only after hours!")

Furthermore, even if quantitatively my observance of *mitzvot* is greater than theirs, can I be so sure that qualitatively this is so as well? Is my own *daven*ing (praying) really so fully characterized by *kavvanah,* so free of *mahashavot zarot* (distracting thoughts), so untainted, when in the presence of others, by self-display? As to my Torah learning and Torah teaching—how much of it is solid, authoritative, thorough, profound, and reverent, and how much is superficial, distorted, careless, biased, show-offy, even fake? And isn't my observance of the various "ritual" *mitzvot* often automatic, perfunctory, hurried, or calculated to impress? And when it comes to taking a stand on sensitive public issues, speaking out on morally outrageous acts committed by Jews or non-Jews, avoiding the use of stereotypes and slogans in my public pronouncements and private conversation, how courageous, or even honest, have I been?

And with regard to my personal behavior, toward my neighbors, toward unkempt beggars who approach me on the street, toward the bosses and braggarts and bores I encounter, toward the troubled and lonely and bereaved, toward the fellow passengers on bus and train, toward members of my extended family, and even toward members of my immediate family, is such behavior really of superior moral quality? What if the true motives behind even my "good deeds" were to be examined closely?

Is this an ideal model of a Rabbi, of a Jewish leader, of a Torah-teaching, Torah-loving, Torah-living Jew? How urgently I need to say—and mean—the yearly *al het....* (for the sin....) *selah lanu* (forgive us) and the year-round *selah lanu ... ki hata'nu* (forgive us ... for we have sinned). How urgently I need to do *teshuvah*.

I need to do *teshuvah*. But can I? Even if I have not remained completely unrepentant since the *al het* of last *Yom Kippur,* even if I have at least occasionally really meant the *selah lanu* of my regular weekday prayer, still, the accumulated load of unacknowledged unrepented sins is large and heavy. To undo all those sins of commission, to make up for all those sins of omission, seems impossibly difficult. It is just too much; I just can't do it. I cannot do it all alone.

But I'm not alone; God is present; God is with me. Therefore, matching my need to do *teshuvah* are the means to do *teshuvah;* what I need to do I'm able to do. What a blessing, what a miracle, that *teshuvah* is available.

The only problem, and the mystery, lies in beginning: who is to take the initiative in *teshuvah*? Surely it is God, who calls to me, as to each one of us, "Turn back to Me." Or is it rather I who must go first, uttering the first word, taking the first step; and only then will come forth divine assistance, the helping hand? But then again, what is that first word of mine as I *hozer bi-teshuvah* (return in repentance)? Is it not: *Hahazirenu,* "Turn us"? "You, O God, must help me, enable me, to turn." But once again—we have come full circle—God says to me: "First *you* must turn, even a little, and then I'll turn, immediately."

We cannot solve the mystery of "who goes first" in *teshuvah*. But then we need not solve it. It's enough to know that the possibility and reality of *teshuvah* are there. Or rather, here.

NOT EVERY MYSTICISM IS A JEWISH MYSTICISM

I speak as one whose early Jewish training was received from teachers who for the most part ignored and disdained Jewish mysticism, but as one whose further study brought a belated awareness of the powerful role that mysticism has played in the Judaism of many countries over many centuries. I speak as one whose personal religious development has made him open to the mystical dimension of life, but closed to many of the particular forms of traditional Jewish mystical expression. And I speak as one whose considered conclusion is that mysticism can be either essential or incidental or heretical to authentic Judaism—depending on how "mysticism" is understood.

In seeking to correct the bias and even the distortion that characterized much of the approach of *Wissenschaft des Judentums* to Jewish mysticism, and to affirm the authenticity and importance of the latter within Judaism, the revisionists have usually pointed to a) the deep influence and broad diffusion of Hasidism, Lurianic Kabbalah, the *Zohar,* and earlier expressions of Jewish mysticism; b) numerous mystical passages in rabbinic literature that had been previously unrecognized, unacknowledged, or minimized; and c) a few biblical passages like Genesis 1, Ezekiel 1, and some of the psalms. Most of these revisionists, however, in the very act of defending Jewish mysticism, have made themselves vulnerable to attack. They have implied that the validity of Jewish belief or behavior derives simply from antiquity of occurrence or extensiveness of diffusion.

A much sounder basis for Jewish mysticism is the *centrality of numerous biblical passages that are permeated with mysticism.* Consider, for example, the Covenant of the Pieces, the Burning Bush, the Splitting and Crossing of the Sea, the Giving of the Torah, the Encounter at the Cleft of the Rock, the Tabernacle, Elijah at Horeb and Carmel, and the various calls to prophecy. These passages are almost universally seen to be characteristic, crucial, and formative. Some of them indeed are archetypal; they are intended to be repeatedly experienced through the ages in personal-yet-shared reenactment and existential appropriation.

These "moments" constitute the paradigm of authentic Jewish mysticism. Drawing upon these moments (and upon others in Scripture), I offer a formulation of what constitutes essential biblical mysticism: it is the *intense awareness* a) of belonging to the holy community of the covenanted and redeemed people Israel; b) of thereby becoming heir to the

Torah, which contains the record (revealed-yet-concealed) of God's word; c) of being introduced, through this Torah community, into the awesomely mysterious yet wonderfully precious Presence of *YHVH;* d) of thereby receiving adequate guidance for living worthily in this world-and-age; and e) of being granted access, in the here-and-now, to the ultimate reality of the universe and the ultimate meaning of life. This mysticism, since it is so central to the Bible, is essential to any authentic Judaism.

But Jewish mysticism in its postbiblical development has produced a vast body of further teaching (at times guarded from the uninitiated and at times made available to all). This teaching includes a yearning for the experience of God's presence; the technique and discipline for attaining, retaining, and regaining that experience; a way of thinking, speaking, and behaving as a result of the above; and a formulation of doctrine concerning the above. This teaching also includes a host of symbols, images, terms, formulations (e.g., tree, *sefirot, adam kadmon,* eye, hand, heart, light, breath, letters, numbers, sexual organs and powers, circles, wheels) and a host of patterns, actions, gestures, and melodies.

Is this body of postbiblical mysticism also essential to Judaism? And is all of it authentic?

In response to the first of these two questions, one must acknowledge that the rich elaboration of postbiblical mysticism has served with remarkable effectiveness as a means for enabling various Jewish communities and individuals to express their mystical awareness. The acceptance of past forms and formulations, however, depends upon the particular temperament, personality, intellect, insight, or mood of the individual; or upon his particular age, environment, background, or situation. No one form or formulation has been—or can be expected to be—accepted by all Jews. The particulars of Jewish mystical expression are thus variable.

In response to the second question, not all of postbiblical Jewish mysticism is authentic. Wherever it denies or contradicts any central biblical affirmation, it is prima facie inauthentic. A few examples must suffice. Where mysticism speaks of human beings as *merged* with God, the universe, or fellow human beings, it becomes Jewishly inauthentic—since the essential biblical teaching, although affirming an ideal unity and harmony among these three, insists upon the uniqueness and integrity of each.

Where mysticism speaks of divinity as power, spirit, light, "stuff," emanation, etc. to such an extent that this "divinity" displaces the Living

God who wills, creates, decides, acts, speaks, commands, judges, loves, forgives, responds—it again becomes Jewishly inauthentic.

Where mysticism affirms a sharp dichotomy of body and soul, of material and spiritual, of this-worldly and otherworldly—and denies the reality, importance, or worth of the former—it becomes Jewishly inauthentic, since the essential biblical teaching affirms the interpenetration of both, as aspects of the Creation which is good.

Where mysticism affirms transmigration or reincarnation, it becomes Jewishly inauthentic—since the essential biblical teaching affirms that each *person* (the whole person, a psycho-physical unity) is created in God's image, that this age provides the sole arena for fulfilling one's task, and that death is real and final (until the coming of the Final Day, when the full consequences of life in this age will be made known).

Where mysticism affirms the power of any being—human or superhuman—to control, coerce, guarantee, or prevent any divine action, intention, or decision, it becomes Jewishly inauthentic—since essential biblical Judaism affirms God to be the one absolute Sovereign, subject to no other power (except insofar as He chooses to grant a measure of freedom to human beings).

The perils of any postbiblical mysticism—whether stemming from foreign influences without or from "alien thoughts" within, whether ancient, medieval, or contemporary—are real and great; but so too are the blessings. Since we live in the world, the perils are unavoidable; since we live in God's presence, the blessings are available. Drawing from the wells of His living presence, we can hope to receive the necessary strength and wisdom to withstand the peril and imbibe the blessing.

FADING IMAGE OF GOD?
THEOLOGICAL REFLECTIONS
OF A NURSING-HOME CHAPLAIN

1

The creation of human beings in the divine image constitutes, as is well known, a primary affirmation of Jewish faith. It is primary in two senses: occurring as it does in the Torah's account of Creation, it is one of the very first affirmations; and alluding as it does to the essential nature of human beings, it is one of the most basic. Volumes could be, and in fact have been, written seeking to explore the manifold implications of this fundamental doctrine. Indeed, it would be no exaggeration to say that creation-in-the-image could form the basis for an entire theology of Judaism.

Many of the implications are familiar: the potential awareness, by every normal human being, of having been created in God's image; the further awareness that all others have been so created—with each one nevertheless being unique; the ability to distinguish between good and evil, between the permitted and the forbidden; the freedom and obligation to decide between right and wrong in any given situation, and to act on the basis of such decision; responsibility and accountability for the actions taken; the capacity, when one has chosen to do wrong, to repent and seek forgiveness and reconciliation; and the awareness of ever standing in the presence of the One in whose image we have been created and whose likeness we bear.

Less obvious, perhaps, are several other implications which have only recently become apparent to me—or at least apparent in their full force—as a result of my service as chaplain in various hospitals, nursing homes, and geriatric facilities. These implications are both striking and troubling.

2

One implication involves the relation between the image of God and our own body.

Normally, when we think of creation-in-the-image we assume—and when questioned, insist—that this refers not to any physical characteristics but rather, to our intellectual, rational, psychological, or spiritual faculties. Surely God has no body, we say; our likeness to God, therefore, cannot possibly reside in our body. And yet, even if we follow Maimonides, who included among his Thirteen Root-Principles of Jewish Faith the affirmation that God has no body,[81] it seems clear that there is strong support in the tradition for affirming a bodily dimension to the image of God in *us*. After all, the very scriptural passage concerning creation-in-the-image declares: "God created *adam* in His image; in God's image He created him; male and female He created them" (Genesis 1:27). Surely sexuality involves body!

The famous rabbinic tale about Hillel the Elder is also à propos:

> When he had finished the lesson with his pupils, he accompanied them part of the way. They said to him, "Master, where are you going?" He replied, "To perform a *mitzvah.*" They asked, "Which *mitzvah*?" He replied, "To bathe in the bathhouse." They asked, "Is that a *mitzvah*?!" He answered them, "If someone is appointed to scrape and clean the statues of the king that are set up in theaters and circuses, and is paid to do the work,... how much more should I, who am created in the divine image, take care of my body!" (*Va-Yikra Rabbah* 84:3)

The Talmud similarly declares: "One should wash the face, hands and feet every day out of respect to one's Maker" (*Shabbat* 50b). For these rabbis, evidently, to envisage the human body as being or bearing the likeness of God, far from being either unthinkable or blasphemous, was entirely appropriate, perhaps even necessary.

Why necessary? Because the link between the "soul" (spirit, mind, will, psyche, conscience?) and the body is so close and intimate, and their interdependence and interweaving so complete, that without the body, the image of God could hardly be discerned or even function, could hardly exist or even be conceived of. The use of the word "soul" in common parlance is instructive; when we admiringly speak of people as "beautiful souls," their saintliness surely expresses itself in the mouths that utter their kindly words, the smiles with which they comfort and reassure, the hands

81. As is well known, *Rabad,* Rabbi Abraham ben David of Posquieres, challenged *Rambam* on this: "There are many people greater and superior to him who adhere to such a belief" (*Hassagot* on *Mishneh Torah, Teshuvah* 3:7). We cannot be sure, of course, how literally even these "other authorities" took God's corporeality; in any case, *Rabad* himself does not state that he agrees with them. Perhaps their primary concern in affirming corporeality was to safeguard belief in *YHVH* as a Living God in the face of those philosophers whose God seemed too abstract, impersonal, distant, uninvolved in the affairs of the world, and unconcerned with human beings.

and feet that perform their loving deeds. In an age that speaks so readily of "psychosomatic illness" and "holistic medicine" surely we should be able to understand what the ancients already sensed: that the image of God involves the whole person, body no less than soul.

3

But to what extent does the divine image endure when there is serious weakening, malfunctioning, and deterioration of the body?

A nursing home provides numerous examples of such bodily impairment. I think of the completely deaf and even the "merely" hard-of-hearing (whose hearing aids constantly get lost or broken or seldom seem to work): they plead with me to speak louder, ever louder, and to repeat my words over and over. And the blind: they never can read a book or newspaper, watch TV, behold any of the beauty of God's creation, see another human face or even their own, or communicate with their eyes. Then there are the stroke victims: they often cannot speak at all; or when they finally manage to utter something, it is unintelligibly garbled; or they must spell out, on a special machine, every single letter. I think of those who, by reason of stroke or accident, are paralyzed; they cannot stand or walk or lift or move or feed themselves or perform any bodily act unaided. And then too, there is that vast number of nursing-home residents—some authorities put the number at sixty percent or more—who are incontinent of bowel or bladder or both, and must therefore wear diapers; aside from the resultant discomfort to themselves and annoyance to others, they often feel desperately humiliated.

If "image" involves "body," such drastically reduced functioning of the latter would surely seem to affect the state and status of the former. Do not continuing and increasing dependence, frustration, infantilization, embarrassment, and self-disgust somehow diminish human dignity and mar the divine image?

One might argue, nevertheless, that in spite of the above-mentioned psycho-physical unity of the human personality, there is a hierarchy of status within each of us, that mind and spirit are superior to body, and that through the strength of will with which we are endowed we are, in principle, able to transcend physical handicap, disability and impaired functioning. From personal experience I can testify that numerous patients actually do summon up unsuspected resources and perform remarkable feats of spiritual strength, providing awesome examples of the triumph of unimpaired mind over seriously impaired body.[82] Never will I forget the nursing-home resident who had soiled himself and was being cleaned and changed by a female nurse; when for the moment he had to be restrained from lowering his gown to cover his genitals, he raised the gown to cover his eyes! Where mind retains its power, "image" retains its glory.

4

What can be said, however, when mind itself falters and regresses, and when such mental capacities as reason, logic, memory, recognition, response, imagination, anticipation—all of them surely aspects of the "image"—begin to deteriorate and function only feebly or intermittently?[83]

Many examples from my hospital and nursing-home experience come to mind. There are the men and women who have lost all ability to read but remember that "a book is for reading"—and who therefore during the worship service, hold prayerbook in hand (even if upside down) and feign that they are reading; they chime in with the word just uttered by the other worshipers, or join in by chanting "la-la-la," or simply turn pages while staring at them blankly. There is the woman who sits through the entire service, to all appearances completely "out of it"—but who suddenly, when *Shema Yisra'el* or *Ein Keloheinu* is sung, is drawn out of her blankness by momentary recognition of a word, a phrase, a melody that had been implanted "centuries ago" and has been retained deep in the recesses of blocked-out memory. Another woman no longer recognizes husband or children and when they visit her keeps asking them, "Who are you?" Still another woman keeps shouting, literally hundreds of times: "Nurse! Nurse!" or screams out nonsense syllables. I think of an observant man who cannot remember whether he has put on *tefillin* that morning, but, seeing the marks of the *tefillin* strap still visible on his arm, realizes that

82. Did I say mind *over* body? But mind *involves* body: the bodily brain, though brain itself, is more than mere body. How easily we fall into the dubious dichotomy of body and mind, and the dubious identity of body and brain!

83. With some nursing-home residents, of course, such mental deterioration never occurs; they live to advanced age with physical capacities reduced but with mind functioning perfectly.

he must have. Deterioration of memory and mind proceeds apace.

If mind is a crucial aspect of image, when mind becomes so seriously impaired, image, it would seem, must surely be diminished. Or shall we rather say that the examples given above reflect a precious vestige of memory, the tribute paid to memory by loss of memory—and that to the extent that mind still functions at all, such functioning, however faint, constitutes striking testimony to the continued presence of "image"?

5

But what shall we say when deterioration has progressed to the point that the mind has *entirely* ceased to function, and such bodily functions as respiration, circulation, heartbeat, ingestion, digestion and elimination are sustained entirely through artificial means; when the patient, if disconnected, would immediately die? (I think of the handsome young man in his early twenties whom I visited occasionally and whose mother visited daily, over a two-year period—while he remained in irreversible coma.) It almost seems that a human being, so completely dependent on machines, so fully interconnected, by pipes and tubes and wires, to multiple machines, has *become* a machine; that this "shell of a person," this "vegetable of a person"—what horrible expressions!—is no longer a person; that the image of God in this person has by now become so defaced that it has been effaced.

Even in such a case, however, the aura of image persists. Our tradition, therefore, which requires us to show *kavod* (honor, respect, reverence) even for a corpse, would surely insist that greater *kavod* be shown to one who, however tenuously, still clings to life, to whom life still clings. Why is this so? Because however minimal the present level of functioning, this still-surviving human life can serve as a continuing, triple reminder: a reminder of this particular, formerly conscious and flourishing image of God;[84] a reminder that in God's eyes the worth of a person *does not* depend—and in our eyes *should not* depend—on efficiency and utility or "quality" and normality; and a reminder of the abiding mystery of life, which extends from the very moment of its beginning (however indeter-

---

84. Cf. the talmudic admonishment: "Be scrupulous with [honoring] an old person who has forgotten his learning through no fault of his own, for we are told: 'Both the [whole] tablets and the broken ones were kept in the Ark'" (*Berakhot* 8b).

minable that exact moment is), when image is as yet only potentiality and anticipation, to the very moment of its ending (however indeterminable that exact moment is), when image now lies in retrospect and consummation.

6

But even if there is debate, because there is uncertainty, as to when the exact moment of death occurs, one thing is certain: that moment eventually and inevitably arrives. Indeed, the very notion of life involves the notion of death (except, of course, for the eternally Living God): on the objective level, once life has begun, it has already begun moving toward its end; on the subjective level, once we become aware of the reality of any other person's death, we become aware of the possibility of our own—and, as we mature, aware also of its inevitability. Indeed, this capacity to be aware of our own death is inherent in our very humanity: creation-in-the-image implies awareness of eventual extinction of the image!

If this is true of life in general, it is especially true of life in a hospital or nursing home, where the awareness of death and the prospect of death—with all the ambivalences surrounding death—are intensely, almost palpably, present. I think of the reluctance of most elderly people to move into a nursing home and the reluctance of their families to arrange for their admission—and thereafter even to visit them there—knowing, as they do, that this home is to be their last home. I remember the man who, each time he learned of the death of a fellow resident, expressed his own envy: "He's much better off." And the numerous patients who, upon hearing the traditional blessing "May you live to be a hundred and twenty!," respond in vehement protest, "Don't wish such a curse upon me; the sooner I die, the better!"—and who nevertheless express in various ways their fear of death. Then there is the man who said to me more than once: "I would readily commit suicide, except that I know that according to the *halakhah* it's forbidden"—and who constantly feared, when his family went on vacation, that there would be no one to arrange for his funeral. Then too, there are the numerous attempts and the varying ways of denying, masking, or concealing the reality of death: through euphemism and circumlocution (such as "passed on," "no longer here," "gone away"); through lowering the voice to a whisper, as if death were an indecency; through avoiding all mention of any resident who had died. (I remember the wise advice of a staff member who encouraged me to make a point of referring to recently deceased residents, and to recite the *kaddish* and the memorial prayer for them—thereby reassuring the other residents that when *their* turn would come to die, they would not be forgotten nor their name go unmentioned.)

Yes, the prospect of death, the eagerness for death, the fear of death, the denial of death—and, above all, the reality of death—are all present with special intensity in nursing home and hospital. Whether readily or reluctantly, whether immediately or only gradually, the realization comes that life has ceased to be; that creation has ended in destruction; that this particular image of God has completely faded out and disappeared.

7

Disappeared forever? An ever-recurring, often troubling, sometimes haunting and desperate question—and one to which Judaism, in the vast breadth of its Torah tradition and the vast length of its history, has offered a variety of answers. Which can we personally accept? Which answers should a Jewish chaplain give to sick, ailing, and aging Jews—and their families—who face the prospect and then the presence of death?

That death is real, that the body has ceased to function, that it then decomposes—is obvious; and however much we are tempted to avoid, suppress, and deny this inevitable, stark, and even gruesome reality, Judaism bids us face it squarely. "Dust you are, and to dust you shall return" (Genesis 3:19). "Know.... where you are going: to a place of dust, maggot, and worm" (*Avot* 3:1).

But though our body dies, is there not something about us—pleadingly we ask—that survives? Is there not some way in which the divine image in each of us lives on?

Biologically speaking, of course, we live on in our progeny, and this can be a source of comfort. That kind of survival, however, is for some of us too vague and impersonal, too "chemical"; besides, not all of us leave progeny. Whether or not we leave children behind, however, we all leave memories behind; in that sense, at least, we all live on—and this too can be a source of comfort. And yet our survivors' memories of us are almost sure to fade as time goes on; in any case, their memories of us will obviously die when they themselves die. Perhaps some of us can find some comfort in knowing that the influence of our words and deeds will continue on, directly or indirectly, even if we are no longer remembered or acknowledged as their source. For most of us, however, such survival is once again too general and diffuse to satisfy us. Is there not some aspect of our being, less material and less perishable than our body, yet more specific and personal than vague memory or influence, whose survival we can count on?

8

What about our soul, our *neshamah*?

That our tradition includes references to a soul or spirit that survives the body cannot be denied. In the Bible itself, however, such references are few and indecisive.[85] The predominant view in the Bible is rather that death truly marks the end of life, including the cessation of the ability to speak, even to God.[86] In rabbinic and medieval literature references to the survival of the soul are, of course, much more frequent—so much so, indeed, that in popular impression and scholarly opinion alike the view that "immortality of the soul" is the authentic Jewish doctrine has become the dominant view.

But however widespread this view and however attractive this doctrine, "immortality of the soul" is inadequate and potentially misleading. If it implies that the soul, upon leaving the body, merges with, and is absorbed by, the divine All-Soul, then the identity and unique personalty of this particular person who has died are thereby compromised, diminished, even dissolved. If it implies that the soul alone is *worthy* of survival, it thereby disparages the body, which, no less than the "breath of life," went into the formation of Adam, pinnacle of God's good creation and paradigm for all of Adam's descendants. If it implies that no one has the power or right to terminate a human life, it constitutes a denial of God's sovereignty. In any case, the very dichotomy between "body" and "soul" impugns the integrity of the "whole person," which, as we have seen from the very outset, is crucial to the Torah's primary affirmation of creation-in-the-image.

9

Is there no firm ground, then, in traditional Jewish teaching, for

85. Even Kohelet, who in one verse refers to "the spirit that returns to God who gave it" (Ecclesiastes 12:7), in another verse merely raises the question: "Who knows whether the spirit of a human being goes upward?" (Ecclesiastes 3:21).

86. "Can the dust praise You? Can it declare Your faithfulness?" (Psalms 30:10). "The dead do not praise God, nor any who go down into silence" (Psalms 115:17).

ultimate hope beyond the grave? There is. That hope lies in a double assurance: the assurance that each one of us lives on, even after death, in the enduring, caring memory of *YHVH,* who lives forever; and the assurance that *YHVH,* keeping faith with those who sleep in the dust, can be depended upon to restore us to life, body-soul life, in the Final Day— for judgment, reward and punishment, mending and purification, and life eternal.[87]

The famous verse in the Book of Daniel concerning those who sleep in the dust is one of the rare biblical passages to refer unequivocally to this promised resurrection.[88] The well-known talmudic parable of the blind and lame guardians of the garden illustrates the resurrection graphically.[89] The traditional Nineteen-fold Prayer (*Tefillah, Amidah*), recited thrice daily, affirms it emphatically (six references in one single *berakhah!*).[90] And

87. For further discussion of this subject see above, "An Outline of Jewish Eschatology."

88. "Many of those who sleep in the dust of the earth will awake: some to everlasting life, and some to shame and everlasting contempt. The enlightened will shine like the radiance of the sky; and those who turn many to righteousness, like the stars forever and ever" (Daniel 12:2-3).

89. "R. Ishmael said that the matter resembles a king who had a garden with fine early figs. He put two keepers in it; one was blind, and one was lame, and he bade them to look well after the figs. After a time the lame man said to the blind man, 'I see some fine figs in the garden.' The blind man said, 'Bring me to them, and we will eat.' The lame man said, 'I cannot walk.' The blind man said, 'I cannot see.' Then the lame man got on the shoulders of the blind man, and they went and ate the figs. After a time the king came to the garden, and he asked, 'Where are the figs?' The blind man said, 'Can I see?' The lame man said, 'Can I walk?' But the king was clever; he set the lame man on the shoulders of the blind man, and made them walk a little, and he said, 'Even so have you managed, and you have eaten the figs.' So, in the world-to-come, God says to the soul, 'Wherefore have you sinned before me?' The soul replies, 'I have not sinned; the body has sinned. Since I have come out of the body, I have flown around like an innocent bird in the air. What is my sin?' Then God says to the body, 'Why have you sinned before me?' The body replies, 'I have not sinned; it is the soul that has sinned. From the hour that the soul went out of me, I lie prone like a stone cast upon the ground. How can I have sinned against thee?' What does God do? He brings the soul and casts it into the body, and judges the two together" (*Va-Yikra Rabbah* 4:5).

90. "You are mighty forever, *YHVH.* You revive the dead, are abundant in saving. You sustain the living with lovingkindness and revive the dead with great compassion. You support the falling, heal the sick, release the bound, and keep faith with those who sleep in the dust. Who is like You, master of might? Who is comparable to You, O King, who

even the daily morning *Elohai Neshamah* blessing, which deals entirely with the "soul" (actually, "breath of life"), can be seen, upon careful reading, to be affirming not the continuation of the soul but rather, its *restoration* to the body.[91]

In this life-and-eon we are unable, of course, to understand the when and how of such an act of resurrection or the nature of such a resurrected life—or even how literally or figuratively the whole notion is to be taken. But at moments of deepest faith and trust we rest secure in the divine assurance that the One who brought us into life by creating us in the divine image, who sustains us in life and eventually takes our life away, is not defeated by death but overcomes death in the Final Day. Then will the full measure of *YHVH*'s power and justice and love be made manifest; each ailing, fading, disappearing image of God will then be healed, renewed, restored.

takes life and restores life, and causes salvation to sprout. You are dependable for reviving the dead. Blessed are You, *YHVH*, who revives the dead."

91. "My God, the soul that You have planted within me is pure. You created it, You formed it, You breathed it into me, and You guard it within me. In the future You are to take it from me and are to restore it to me in the time-to-come. As long as the soul is within me, I give thanks before You, my God and God of my ancestors, master of all creatures, sovereign of all souls. Blessed are You, *YHVH*, who restores souls to dead corpses."

MIRACLE AND *BERAKHAH*: HOW SHALL WE APPROACH THE MIRACLES OF THE BIBLE?

As Jews, we love and honor the Torah. We wish to be intimately familiar with its teachings, guided by its standards, shaped by its outlook, and accepting of its truth. On the other hand, we are children of the modern age, open to its influences, shaped by its science, touched by its philosophy, acccustomed and encouraged to ask and to challenge, to wonder and to doubt. Science is not our god, of course; its claims are to be examined and its spokesmen cross-examined. But the Torah too, though containing God's word and therefore holy and precious to us, is not so sacrosanct that it is beyond question and investigation. The truth of the Torah and the truth of modern knowledge must be brought into some genuine relationship with each other. If their two truths are not identical, if they are not saying the same thing, they must at least be compatible. For if the "seal of the Holy One, blessed be He, is truth," that truth cannot be split into two contradictory parts. We, in any case, cannot and are not willing to live with compartmentalized minds.

We find ourselves troubled by many things in the Torah: some of its law, some of its heroes, some of its accounts of actions by men and women, and some of its accounts of actions by God. But especially are we bothered by its miracles. There are so many miracles in the Bible, and they are so important to the biblical story: Creation itself, the Flood, the saving of Lot, the birth of Isaac, the burning bush, the plague in Egypt, the splitting of the Sea of Reeds, the provision of the quail and of the manna, the Giving of the Torah, water from the rock, the punishment of Korah, the fall of Jericho, the feats of Samson, Elijah at Carmel, Elisha, and Daniel, etc. The Bible, through and through, seems to involve miracles.

Can we believe all of them? We are children of the modern age. Some of these tales sound like fairy tales. Our Torah is the holy Torah, the Torah of truth. And we want to be good and faithful Jews. Yet we have doubts about the biblical miracles. Let us examine our doubts.

The first kind of doubt that plagues us is the most serious. We find ourselves asking, at some moment at least, whether the miracles recorded in the Torah *could* have really happened. How could even God have performed such miracles? They seem to be against the laws of nature and to contradict the evidence of science. For a woman to conceive and bear a child at ninety—this contradicts the very facts of life! For two million people in the desert to live for forty years on seeds that appear with the dew—impossible! For the sun and moon to stand still (or was it the earth?) for a whole day—the universe could not endure! Such claims seem to fly in the face of all that science tells us. The world could not possibly operate this way! What shall we say when such doubts arise? What answer can there be for us—who are committed to the truth of the Torah and yet are committed also to the truth of science!

As children of the Torah, let us understand that if God were not *able* to have performed such miracles, He simply would not be God! For a moment we may doubt, but after even the slightest reflection, we realize that He who could *create* the world would remain its Master. Even Abraham doubted for a moment: "A child when Sarah is ninety and Abraham one hundred?" How laughable! So Abraham and Sarah laughed. But the answer came: *Ha-yippale me-adonai davar?* "Is anything too wondrous for *YHVH?*" Even Moses doubted: "Meat for all this people in the wilderness?" But the answer came: *Ha-yad adonai tiktzar?* "Is the power of *YHVH* so limited?" Laws of nature? A God who could establish the laws could alter them! The rules? A God who could make the rules could make exceptions to the rules! A God who could create the world normally to work with regularity, in set patterns and rhythms, could intervene, call a halt, make a change, innovate; otherwise He would be not God! This is the Torah's assurance—and through the ages Jews have been thus reassured.

But can *we* be thus reassured? Or does the modern scientific outlook require us to reject the miracles of the Bible as impossible? Does science prove that these could not have happened? Many people today, moved by the currents of scientific thought around them, take for granted that science disproves miracles. Many people claim with certainty that science has demonstrated miracles to be impossible. But some who know science best and understand it most profoundly make no such claims. These scientists and philosophers of science point out that science does not and cannot disprove (or prove) the possibility of miracles; science does not deal with miracles. Science takes what can be demonstrated to have happened, it tests and checks and experiments, and then formulates laws to describe what has happened and to explain how it happened. Science then proceeds, on the *assumption* of the uniformity of nature, to predict what will happen under the same circumstances. But note, science merely *assumes* that the laws of nature that it has formulated have always operated in the past and will continue to operate in the future. Whether there have been or will be exceptions to these rules, whether (in other words) the biblical miracles *could have happened,* science cannot and does not presume to say.

Our first doubts have now perhaps been satisfied. The claim that God *can* perform miracles, so basic to the text and tradition of the Torah, is not contradicted by modern science and can never be so contradicted. As modern Jews we can say with no less certainty than our ancestors: God could have certainly performed any and all miracles mentioned in the Torah.

But did He?

A second kind of doubt now pressures upon us: the miracles are all possible, but are they true? They could have happened, but did they really? We often feel we have grounds for doubt. Some accounts in the Bible seem so exaggerated and so fanciful. Did people in the early days really live for hundreds of years? Did Creation, from the very beginning to Adam and Eve, really take only six days? Did Jericho really fall when the Israelites marched around its walls seven times on the seventh day? Some of the stories in the Torah have such striking parallels in the literature of other ancient peoples and cultures, dating from prebiblical time. There are stories of creation and stories of floods. Is it not possible that some of the accounts of miracles in the Bible are merely legends, borrowed from other peoples or made up by the Jewish folk imagination? Can we accept them all as true? In order to be "good Jews," faithful children of Israel, must we believe *all* the miracles in the Bible? Or are there perhaps some particular miracles that are more important than the rest? Of the vast number recorded in the Bible, are there any central, crucial miracles, which simply must be true, without which our life makes no sense at all?

There are. One crucial area of miracle we have already dealt with earlier (however briefly): the area of Creation. We said then that if God *could not* have created the world, He would not be God. Now we must add: the miracle did occur, the world did come into being and God created it. If He did not create, no one did create. And if there is no creator, we have no assurance that the world is under God's control, nor that life has any plan or purpose, any goal or any meaning. The biblical details of *how* God created the world—when he did so, how long it took and in what order— are *not* essential for a believing Jew to accept. Perhaps they were never meant to be taken literally. But that God created the world, miraculously, out of nothing—in such a way as to allow for both its regularity of operation and its apparent irregularities—is surely necessary for a Torah-true Jew to affirm. God may indeed have made provision from the very beginning of Creation for the exceptions that were later to occur—but He was the One who did it.

There is another area of miracle that is crucial: the complex of miracles known in the tradition as *yetzi'at mitzrayim,* the Exodus from Egypt, the redemption of Israel from slavery. This includes the selection of Israel by God as His special people (going back to Abraham), the miraculous deliverance from the hand of Pharaoh in Egypt, the dividing of the Sea of Reeds so that Israel might pass through in safety, God's sustenance of Israel in the wilderness, the promise of the land of Canaan, and the entrance into that land. Without the miracles, there is no accounting for the rise of the people Israel, there is no explanation for how we came to be or how we have survived. Again, this or that detail of the miracle may involve exaggeration or imagination or may never have been meant to be taken literally; but that God miraculously called a special people, and miraculously delivered and redeemed them from oppression in Egypt, is crucial to our very existence. Just as without Creation there is no meaning to our life as human beings, so without the Redemption from Egypt there is no meaning to our life as Jews.

There is still another miracle so crucial that without it Israel's life is meaningless: the miracle of *mattan torah,* the Giving of the Torah. The Lord who had created the world and brought Israel forth from Egypt now spoke to Israel from Heaven, came down on Mount Sinai, told Israel that it was *He* who was their redeemer, gave commandments to Israel and was accepted by Israel. Without this *mattan torah* there is no Torah; and without Torah, Israel makes no sense and has no purpose. Once again, there may be question and doubt and denial of this or that detail of what happened at Sinai; perhaps what cannot be taken literally by us was never meant to be taken literally; but that God spoke to Israel there, revealing both what He had done for Israel, what He offers Israel and what He demands from Israel—this is essential to the faith of every believing Jew.

These miracles, then, are the basic miracles, which we realize must have happened and which in faith we know did happen. As for all the other biblical miracles, one could say that they are not *necessary,* since what God has performed in these basic miracles is enough—*dayyenu.* Or one may say that the rest of the miracles present no problem; the Lord who performed these basic miracles performed all the others as well. Or one can say: we believe He performed some of the many miracles; we have our doubts about the others.

What does science have to say about these basic miracles, which are crucial to the Torah tradition and crucial to those who seek to be faithful heirs of that tradition? How does science deal with the basic religious affirmation that God *did* miraculously create the world, redeem Israel from Egypt, and give the Torah? Simple enough. Science says: "We do not think in terms of miracles; we deal with facts—the world is here, Israel is here, the Torah is here. The world had some beginning; it came into being either suddenly, like an explosion, or gradually. Israel entered history, left Egypt, entered Canaan. The Torah was composed somehow and then was written down. As scientists, we do our best to explain what these phenomena are like; how, when and where they came about; what caused them to arise and how they operate. What you consider to be miracles we consider facts. What you think of as the mighty acts of God, we think are events that have taken place. What you see as the workings of God's plan and purpose, we see as the laws of nature and the laws of history. Any report of anything that has happened, once it has been properly authenticated, is incorporated into the laws with which we deal. Religion may speak of miracles performed by God if it so desires; a living God who performs miracles is beyond *our* ken."

Our second question has, perhaps, been answered. Our second kind of doubt has been removed, or at least allayed. In faith we now know that God not only *could* have performed *any* miracle, but that He *has* performed at least the mightiest ones, the crucial ones—and science offers no proof to the contrary.

There is a third kind of doubt about the biblical miracles that closes in upon us: no longer a doubt about their possibility and no longer a doubt about their actuality (concerning at least the crucial ones), but rather, a doubt about their relevance. Let us grant that God not only *could* have performed but that He *did* perform miracles in the *past.* Why does He no longer perform miracles? Why did He stop? Is He no longer God? Are we no longer Israel? Why no miracles today?

The response of science to this third doubt about miracles is perhaps obvious. We have shown that science does not deal with the miracles of the past as miracles. Rather, once they have been authenticated, it finds explanations to account for them, fitting them into previous or newly revised "laws." The same is true of whatever may happen today. If anything "new" happens, anything that runs counter to the previously accepted laws of science, the scientist (if he remains a true scientist), does not get angry; he does not argue or despair. He simply revises his previous formulation of the "laws of nature" and incorporates the new data, however radical or revolutionary, into a new formulation. Indeed, if the scientist (as scientist) is allowed to feel any emotion, he feels a certain joy that more of the working of the universe can now be explained and understood!

How does a believing Jew respond to the doubt about miracles today? He looks at the new data, the newly discovered phenomena, and sees them as new evidence of God's work. They are new miracles no less miraculous than the miracles of old. He calls these new miracles by the same names as the old; he calls them *nes,* he calls them *ot,* he calls them *mofet,* he calls them *pele.* He experiences the same sense of wonderment, awe, and grateful amazement in the presence of the newly disclosed miracles as in the presence of the miracles of old.

In fact, for the faithful Jew, the miracles of old are constantly renewed. The mighty miraculous act of creation is renewed by God each day when the sun rises: *ha-mehaddesh be-tuvo be-khol yom tamid ma'aseh vereshit.* Were God to remove His sustaining finger for even one moment, the world would instantly relapse into nothingness. The mighty miraculous redemption from bondage is renewed by God each *Pesah,* each *Shabbat,* indeed each day whenever one prays. The giving of the Torah is renewed by God at *Shavu'ot,* and on each day whenever one studies Torah—*ke-illu ha-yom nittenu,* "as if Torah were given today." Thus, for the faithful Jew it makes no difference that the biblical miracles happened long ago; for him these same miracles happen again and again. The miraculous past becomes contemporaneous.

Just as there is no real difference between present and past, so there is, for the faithful Jew, no real difference, as far as miracle is concerned, between the exceptional event and the regular, ordinary event. Both kinds of events are equally miraculous; both are from God—performed by His will, accomplished by His power, provided by His love; different, miraculous aspects of one miraculous whole. Miracles are happening all the time. A child is born; the sun sets; our body functions; the mind thinks; the rain falls. True, some miracles are more dramatic or come at what seem to be more crucial moments in the life of the individual person or in the life of the whole people and therefore appear to be more decisive. The splitting of the Sea of Reeds is often spoken of in the tradition as the miracle par excellence, the greatest miracle ever. True. And yet that very same tradition declares that the provision of our daily food and sustenance is no less miraculous than the splitting of that sea! Some say it is more miraculous. The miracle wrought in a sick person's recovery is greater than the miracle of the deliverance of Hananiah, Mishael, and Azariah from the fiery furnace. And the falling of the rain is comparable to the resurrection of the dead!

Now at last we are able to see what a miracle is. *A miracle is any event in which one sees the power and love of God.* Thus, every miracle depends upon God; it is *His* power and *His* love that create the miracle. But every miracle depends also upon *us: we* are the ones who with God's help must see.

So often our eyes remain closed to the miracles that God seeks to disclose. We pass through a world of miracles, but allow the miracles to pass us by. When we come upon miracles we reduce them to laws and explain them—and explain them away! Any miracle can be explained *after* it has happened, when it is past. But any miracle can also be relived, making it present again. All we need is: a *berakhah.*

The purpose of a *berakhah* is to help us recapture the miracle, to open our inner eye, to show us the way across the threshold of the world of miracles. It reminds us that we have been there all the time, in God's great House of Miracles, without our even having known it! With the aid of a *berakhah,* uttered with true *kavvanah,* the momentary can become momentous, and the ordinary can become holy. The mighty moments of the past can become present, when we say *yotzer or* or *go'el yisra'el* or *noten ha-torah.* Everyday moments like rising from sleep, eating a meal, or beholding the weather can through the appropriate *berakhah* become special moments. The facts of life and the laws of nature, without being denied, can be seen as "the work of God's creation"; they can suddenly become transparent, and the loving power of God shines through.

When we first began to speak of miracles in the Bible, it seemed that we were speaking of believing with a blind faith. And in a sense we were, for in one sense miracles cannot be seen. But in another sense, as we have now discovered, this faith is not really blind at all. Quite the contrary; this faith is seeing! With our vision not denied or dimmed or distorted by the science of our age—in some ways indeed sharpened by the science of the age—we can behold a world of miracles. In the light of the Torah we can see! *Torah or.*

ACKNOWLEDGING THE KING:
THE YOU AND HE,
THE THEY AND WE, OF *ALEINU*
In memory of Joel Abba Bernards

1

Of all the prayers that constitute the order *(seder, siddur)* of the traditional Jewish liturgy, the prayer known (from its opening Hebrew word) as *Aleinu* is surely one of the most important and fascinating.

The *Aleinu* is recited three times a day each day of the year. It serves as climax and conclusion of every service—and on *Rosh Ha-Shanah* it also introduces *malkhuyot,* first of the three sections into which the *musaf* service is divided and at the end of each of which the *shofar* is sounded. It is the only prayer—except for the cantor's reenactment of the service of the high priest on *Yom Kippur*—that is marked, on the High Holy Days, by the kneeling and full prostration of the cantor and in many congregations of congregants as well. The *Aleinu* is chanted on these same Days of Awe to a centuries-old melody of haunting awesomeness. Historically it evokes memories of Jewish defiance, martyrdom, loyalty, and hope in the face of Christian persecution and pogroms. It contains the basic Jewish affirmation of the kingship and oneness of God, putting it almost in the class of the *Shema,* to which it has a striking affinity. Small wonder, then, that the *Aleinu* constitutes one of our major prayers.

2

But the *Aleinu* also presents a major problem, for in addition to affirming the kingship and oneness of God, it also affirms the uniqueness of Israel. It not only declares that *YHVH* "is in truth our King with none beside Him," but also praises Him for not having "made us like the nations of the lands nor placed us like the families of the earth; for not having set our portion like theirs, nor our lot like all their multitude." And it furthermore asserts—implicitly in the Ashkenazic version and explicitly in the Sephardic—that the distinction between "us" and "them" involves not merely difference but superiority. The Sephardic version, which preserves the original wording, states that "they prostrate themselves to vanity and emptiness, and pray to a god who does not save"—in contrast to us, who (according to both versions) "bend the knee, prostrate ourselves, and make acknowledgment before the King of Kings,[92] the Holy One, blessed be He."

It is hardly surprising that those Christians who learned about the *Aleinu*—whether by chance or upon deliberate examination often occasioned by reports from hostile Jewish apostates to Christianity—felt offended, insulted and embittered. In vain did Jewish scholars point out that some of the most "offensive" passages (such as "vanity and emptiness" or "pray to a god who does not save") are taken from the Book of Isaiah and were thus written centuries before Christianity came into existence. In vain did Jewish teachers explain that the prayer itself was composed (according to some) in a period before the birth of Christianity or (according to others) in a place—third-century Babylonia—where Christianity was not widespread or firmly established. The repeated declaration of the rabbis that "non-Jews in this age are not idol worshipers" was to no avail. In spite of all such explanations and disclaimers Christians continued to be offended and provoked, and Jews were often required to make some accommodation. Sometimes the synagogue simply changed the phrase "they worship" to the past tense: "they used to worship"; sometimes it removed one or both of the phrases deemed objectionable, or sought to circumvent the prohibition against inclusion of the "objectionable" phrases by omitting them from the written text but continuing to recite them, aloud or in an undertone. (When the non-Jewish authorities became aware of the subterfuge, they would sometimes station inspector-observers in the synagogue to detect and prevent the recitation—whether pronounced aloud, mumbled or whispered!)

It is clear, therefore, why the *Aleinu* frequently posed a problem for Jews in their relations with Christians once the latter knew about the prayer, or lest they come to know about it.

3

For many modern Jews, however, the *Aleinu* has become a problem in itself and for themselves, entirely aside from potential or actual non-Jewish reaction. Many Jews today feel awkward in voicing such a

92. The Hebrew actually says "King of Kings of Kings," usually explained as pointing to the Persian-Babylonian locale of the prayer's origin, since Persian kings sometimes bore the title King of Kings, and *YHVH* is here affirmed to be King even over such a King. Cf. Daniel 2:37: "O King, King of Kings, unto whom the God of heaven has given the kingdom, the power, and the strength, and the glory...."

particularistic claim of utter distinctiveness, especially when such distinctiveness involves superiority. And though the attribution of the responsibility for Israel's difference-and-superiority to *God* may have saved premodern Jews from feeling arrogant about their special role and status, for many modern Jews such attribution is in itself a source of painful embarrassment. The notion that the God of the universe chose our people Israel—whether because of our supposed innate religious insight and awareness or, arbitrarily, simply because He loved us—is for many Jews totally unacceptable.

In many modern editions of the Siddur, therefore, various changes—some radical, some minor and subtle—have been introduced. The Reform, Liberal, and Reconstructionist editions tend to solve the problem in two ways: first, by omitting all phrases that are negative or are disparaging of other people and faiths; second, by introducing phrases, often drawn from traditional Jewish sources, that are affirmative and that stress the universalistic aspects of God's intention and Israel's mission (e.g., "who gave us the Torah of truth and planted eternal life within us"; "He chose us to make known His unity and called us to proclaim Him King"; "who gives life to the nations that dwell upon the earth and breath to them that walk thereon"). Conservative editions retain the Hebrew (Ashkenazic) text intact, but in their translation tend either to soften the starkness of the contrast alluded to in the Hebrew or to explicitly limit the "they" to the heathens of the world (e.g., "He made our lot unlike that of other peoples, He assigned to us a unique destiny"; "He hath not made us like the pagans of the world, nor placed us like the heathen tribes of the earth"). As for the Ashkenazic Orthodox, although they of course do not emend the Hebrew text and do not usually resort to deliberate revision-through-translation (except occasionally, as in one edition that reads "who has not made us as worldly nations, nor set us up as earthly people"), they nevertheless almost always refrain from voluntarily reintroducing those phrases that Jews in earlier centuries had been compelled to omit, except occasionally in Israel.

Evidently large numbers in all of the movements in contemporary Judaism feel ill-at-ease about the particularistic aspects of the *Aleinu*.

4

But is such a sense of awkwardness and embarrassment really called for? Must any of the affirmations of the traditional *Aleinu*—including those of the censored verse—be deemed unacceptable? The answer to this question depends on our answers to four other questions concerning the *Aleinu:* What does it mean to say that God is "King of Kings and Lord of all"? How does one go about worshiping Him alone, in contrast to worshiping other gods who are "vanity and emptiness"? Who exactly are the "we" and the "they" who are said to engage in the contrasting kinds of worship? Must this contrast continue forever, and if not, when will it come to an end?

What does it mean to say, as we do in the *Aleinu,* that *YHVH* is "Lord of all ... Creator of the beginning.... King of Kings.... who stretches forth the heavens and lays the foundations of the earth.... God in the heavens above and on earth beneath; there is none else"? It means that *YHVH* is the ultimate and absolute One, in every sense.

He is absolute Creator, in that everything in the universe came into being entirely by His will, through His wisdom and power, and according to His plan and purpose. He is absolute Master of the Universe, for He retains control of it, maintaining and sustaining its operation in accordance with the laws and patterns that He set for it and which are therefore dependable.

Not only is He absolute ruler of nature; He is also absolute ruler of humanity: He has set the rules and laws for human conduct and is thus the ultimate source of absolute standards of right and wrong. But His rulership over humanity differs from His rulership over nature, for the latter involves causation, inevitability, and determinism, whereas the former allows for a significant measure of choice and freedom, responsibility and obligation.[93] As our absolute sovereign, He is also our absolute judge: there are many authorities to whom we owe respect, obedience, loyalty, and love, but He alone deserves these in the ultimate degree.

He deserves them, but He cannot coerce them, although He does set limits to our freedom: the limitations posed by our natural environment and endowments as well as those of human action—both the actions of other human beings and our own past actions. In these and other ways He can bring us to recognize the emptiness and inadequacy of the many false gods around us and within us that we are tempted to serve. Nevertheless, because in creating us in His image He chose to limit His own freedom, even He—absolute sovereign though He be—cannot compel us against our will to acknowledge His kingship. Such acknowledgment must be our own free and personal decision.

93. For an elaboration of this theme see above, "Human Choice and God's Design."

An absolute Creator, Master, Ruler and Judge would seem to be remote and stern and awesome. Indeed He is. Yet He is also near and compassionate, loving and forgiving; He is a God who not only knows but cares. (In this sense, at least, He is a "personal," living God.) He is *YHVH:* the ever-present One, the Merciful One, the One who can be depended on to keep His promises; the zealous and passionate God who is angry, sad and disappointed when we turn away from Him, and who rejoices when we turn back to Him—for our own well-being and for the advancement of His kingship through our decisions and our actions.

Indeed, so significant is our act of decision that unless and until we decide to acknowledge God's kingship, in one sense He is not King! For "king" is one of those terms that depend for their actuality upon the existence of a correlative. Just as there can be no parent without a child (and vice versa) and no teacher without a pupil, so there is no king without subjects who acknowledge and accept his kingship. ("Until Abraham, I was King only on high; with Abraham, I became King also below." "If you are My witnesses, I am God; if not, I am—as it were—not God.")

5

These, then, are some of the implications of acknowledging that *YHVH* alone is our King. But how exactly does one make such acknowledgment? Of what does the acknowledgment actually consist?[94]

Words of prayer, worshipful words, are an important element: words of trust, of praise, commitment, and loyalty; words of petition, confession, and sometimes even words of challenge and complaint. For in words we attempt to articulate our most profound thoughts, our most heartfelt feelings, our deepest loyalties to the Ultimate One.

But words themselves are often insufficient, for they are sometimes "mere words," empty words, false and deceptive words—not revealing but concealing our actual thoughts, feelings and loyalties. Besides, even when our words are sincere, the situation often calls for more than words.

Similarly with other forms of worship: ritual acts and gestures, participation in public worship, use of sacred objects and the accoutrements of worship. Like words, they are meant to be vehicles for the expression of our deepest needs and hopes, our innermost convictions and commitments, which are both profoundly personal and also shared with

94. For a further elaboration of this theme see above, "What Does It Mean to Believe in God?"

all other heirs and participants in the same tradition and way of life. But—again like words—these actions, occasions and objects can at times be so routinized and externalized that they become not aids but obstacles to true acknowledgment of the kingship of the King, not means but substitutes for serving Him. ("Even if you multiply prayers, I am not listening. When you spread your hands to Me, I shut My eyes to you.") Much more is required than ritual words or ritual acts, even in combination.

The "much more" consists of an inner attitude and relationship to God, of love and awe, of gratitude and wonder, of obedience and trust and hope; it consists of reverent behavior toward all of God's Creation, and of righteous conduct, acts of justice and compassion, toward fellow human beings. For can we ever claim truly to be children of the Father and servants of the King if we needlessly neglect or hurt His other children and servants? ("Have we not all one Father? Has not one God created us? Why then do we deal treacherously, one against the other—profaning thus the covenant of our fathers?") To the extent that I neglect a fellow human being's creation in God's image, her or his divine parentage; to the extent that I act toward my fellow in less than complete justice, reverence, and love, or approach my fellow as an "it" rather than as a "thou"—to that very extent I deny the supremacy of the Eternal Thou and the kingship of the King. I set someone or something else as the ultimate authority in my life and the ultimate object of my loyalty; I worship another god than *YHVH*. And often I do make nature or some part of nature, my family or my friend, my party or my government or my cause, or most often myself, into an idol.

6

How can I—knowing how often I am less than fully faithful in the service of the King—claim in the thrice-daily recitation of the *Aleinu* that I am one of those who "bend the knee, prostrate themselves, and make acknowledgment before the King of Kings"? And how can I further claim that it is all my fellow Jews along with me—and we alone—who constitute His true worshipers? Is it not an act of colossal *chutzpah* to affirm that all of us Jews and none of those non-Jews are the loyal servants of the Holy One, blessed be He? Dare I, dare we, continue to make such a sweepingly self-righteous and self-evidently false affirmation?

But perhaps the *Aleinu* does not, and never did, require us to do so. Even in ancient times, when Israel alone amidst a pagan world had received through Abraham and subsequently with Moses at Sinai the Torah revelation that *YHVH* alone is King, and that besides Him all powers and persons, all forces and objects that are worshiped as gods are false gods, even then there was a recognition as part of that selfsame revelation, that not all of Israel were always faithful, that often many and at times most of Israel were faithless. ("You have been rebellious against *YHVH* from the day I knew you"; "Run to and fro ... and see ... if there be any who does justly, who seeks the truth—and I will forgive.") And sometimes there was a further recognition that in their very worship of false gods, pagans were nevertheless striving—however inadequately, dimly, "impurely"— toward the one true God. There was even occasionally the recognition that among the pagan nations there were at least some scattered individuals ("the pious and righteous among the peoples of the world") who, rising above their heathen environment, not only sought but actually found, and were found by, Him.

What then did the Torah-tradition mean when it affirmed that Israel alone was a kingdom of priests, a holy nation, firstborn son, the people whom He chose as His inheritance, witness people, servant of *YHVH*? If some within Israel were not faithful servants of the King and if some outside Israel were, wherein lay Israel's distinction—and chosenness?

7

The chosenness lay, first of all, in the establishment by the Lord of all peoples, for the enrichment and blessing of all peoples, of a special covenant relationship with a *particular people*—the people descended from Abraham, who were enslaved and then redeemed from slavery, to whom the Torah-and-commandments were given at Sinai, and to whom the land of Canaan was promised as the prime locale for living out the covenant way of life. "You shall be My people, and I shall be your God." This covenant involved a promise of eternal fidelity, an unbreakable oath, on *YHVH*'s part, and thus an assurance of never-ending covenant love toward this people.

The chosenness lay furthermore in the special measure of guidance and instruction, command and demand, that is involved in a complete life of holiness—including both ultimacy of degree and all-inclusiveness. "You shall be holy, for I, *YHVH* your God, am holy." "Walk before Me, and be of perfect integrity." "You shall love *YHVH* your God with all your heart, with all your soul, and with all your might." "In all your ways know Him." The potentiality for holiness and obedience, which all human beings were affirmed to have by virtue of their creation-in-the-image, and the basic standards of piety and justice, which all human societies were therefore

154

assumed to be aware of and bound by, were now supplemented, extended, and spelled out in far greater measure and detail in the Torah-revelation to Israel. The chosenness thus involved a much higher degree of responsibility and accountability. "You only have I known-in-love from among all the families of the earth; therefore will I hold you strictly accountable for all your iniquities." And it involved a much more explicit statement of the blessing and the curse that would be the consequence of obedience and disobedience, faithfulness and unfaithfulness, to the covenant standard.

There was yet another dimension: Israel's separation-in-holiness from the nations of the world by means of a regimen of distinctive "ritual holiness." (The Hebrew word *kadosh* means, as is well-known, both "holy" and "set apart.") This regimen would serve the triple function of preservation of identity, protection from the immoralities of paganism, and cultivation of that reverence and awe, that joy and purity, that are the fruit of an ever-renewed awareness of living in the presence of *YHVH*. All areas and aspects of life were affected: worship and celebration (daily, weekly and seasonal); diet, sex, clothing, work, and home; birth, puberty, marriage, sickness, death; child-rearing and lifelong study. Unlike the basic moral law, which was binding upon all of the "children of Noah," these aspects of separation-in-holiness were considered obligatory for Israel alone.

The apartness-and-separation that is part of Israel's chosenness has often called forth from the "peoples of the world" a sense of puzzlement and annoyance with Israel. It sometimes developed into suspicion, mistrust, and hostility, then persecution, exile, and even attempted extermination. Many factors have entered into this anti-Semitism through the ages; they are too numerous and too complex to be analyzed or even summarized here. But on one level, at least, such negative feelings are a peril that is almost inherent in the very notion of an Israel covenanted to the Lord. As the talmudic rabbis put it—playing on two Hebrew words— "when Sinai came into the world, *sin'ah* (hatred) came into the world." For although Sinai's covenant-and-Torah involve love, they also involve law; though they express compassion and forgiveness, they also dictate "thou shalt" and "thou shalt not." No wonder that the pagan-within-the-human wishes to cast off the yoke of the Torah. And since Israel is associated with God and His Torah, the resentment and rebellion against God-and-Torah can be expected to be directed against the Torah-people—whether they actually live up to the Torah-standards or not. One who has been called to be the "servant of *YHVH*" is likely to be made into a "suffering servant."

8

But for how long? Will most of humanity reject *YHVH* and His Torah forever? Will idolatry and paganism never cease?

In striking counterpoint to the markedly particularistic tone of the first half of the *Aleinu,* the second half is a firm and explicit promise, striking in its universalistic tone, that the One who at first singled out Israel by revealing to them His word and way, the One who had first been acknowledged by Israel, will eventually be recognized and acknowledged by all humanity. All will then put aside their evil ways and thoughts, their idolatrous abominations; all will recognize in every human being the image of God; and all will worship *YHVH* alone, in purity and love. As a result of human deeds of utter justice and love, completed, corrected and perfected by divine action, the world will at last be mended and perfected, transformed into the Kingdom of the Almighty, established as the Kingship of the Almighty. Then at last "*YHVH* will be King over all the earth. In that day"—the messianic day—"*YHVH* will be One and His name One."

9

From the time of Israel's coming upon the stage of history until the coming of "that day," Israel's role remains the same: to live as God's witness, to live the holy life of the covenant people—whether in the Holy Land or in Diaspora—no matter what the cost, and to continue to be nourished by sure hope and confidence in God's messianic promise.

But is Israel's situation and outlook in any way changed once Christianity comes upon the scene? Are the affirmations of the *Aleinu* at all affected by the presence in the world of Christianity?

In one sense, the answer must of course be "no." For since Christianity has no inherent identification with any particular people—and indeed stresses that "in Christ there is neither Jew nor gentile.... but all are one in Christ Jesus"—the claim of the *Aleinu* that Israel is the only people who as a people acknowledges *YHVH* as the One and only God, remains as valid as in pre-Christian times. But in another sense the significance of the *Aleinu,* or at least its frame of reference, changes radically once Christianity (and later Islam) is on the scene. For Christianity derives from Judaism both historically and—in spite of the very basic differences involved in its Christology—in most of its teaching, including the acceptance from Judaism of *YHVH* as Creator and King, and the content and confidence of the *Aleinu* concerning the messianic day.[95] How then can Jews continue to recite the *Aleinu* without unjustly ignoring or—what is worse—maligning the multitude of Christians (and Mohammedans) who daily acknowledge Israel's *YHVH* and reject all other gods as emptiness and vanity, gods who cannot save?

10

Continued deletion of the formerly censored phrases is no solution to the problem, because even with such deletion the contrast between Israel as *YHVH* worshipers and all other inhabitants of the earth as idol worshipers is still clearly evident. The only adequate and appropriate solution is a threefold, paradoxical one:

First, we should *restore the deleted verse,* to make clear that to be of Israel still involves the crucial obligation of resistance to idolatry, which remains an ever-present snare and danger: there are still in the world those "who prostrate themselves to vanity and emptiness, and pray to a god who does not save."

Second, as we recite the *Aleinu,* restored to its original "exclusivist" wording, we should at the same time adopt and extend the talmudic statement that "he who repudiates idolatry is called a Jew," and thus broaden the "we" and "us" of the *Aleinu* to include all Christians, Mohammedans, and others who acknowledge *YHVH* as the only God.

Third, even as the "we" is broadened, let us affirm that within the larger, extended "Israel" we Jews remain the *people* Israel, in our continuing distinctiveness and separation. For until the actual coming of the Messiah—what Christians call the "Second Coming"—the people Israel is still needed in the world, because whenever Christianity (or Islam) becomes too established, too comfortable, and too much at ease, the paganism that is ever present may well erupt and bring about the demise of genuine Christianity (or Islam) in that time and place. (We Jews have often, alas, been victims of such eruption.) When this occurs, those of us who are members of the people Israel serve as reminder of *YHVH* and His Torah by our very existence, by our presence as Jews—even when we may have been neglectful of, and unfaithful to, Israel's way of "Torah, worship, and deeds of love."

---

95. For an elaboration of the relation between the two faiths see above, "How Shall a Believing Jew View Christianity?"

How great a privilege to belong to the covenant people Israel, the channel through which the message of *YHVH* is carried, to be God's witness and agent in the world, to be "God's stake in history." But how sad it is to be an agent almost unconsciously; to be a witness almost unawares; to be a messenger who has all but forgotten the name of the One who sends him; to be a Jew who doesn't know or doesn't say—or who knows and says but doesn't take to heart—the words of the *Aleinu.*

THE GOALS OF TEACHING JEWISH PRAYER

1

Since our topic is "The Goals of Teaching Jewish Prayer," we shall not here attempt to deal with the *methods* of teaching prayer. (There is a legitimate question indeed whether there can be such a thing as methods of teaching prayer.) We shall likewise not attempt to deal with the *reasons* for teaching prayer; let us rather take the reasons for granted (e.g., that prayer is essential to the full flowering of the human personality, to the full development of the image of God in which we are created, to the full functioning of the people Israel.) We shall also not deal with the *byproducts* of teaching prayer—even such worthy byproducts as the maintenance of Jewish identity, the survival of synagogues, the ability to lead in public worship, etc. We shall confine ourselves rather to the *goals* of teaching prayer, that which we aim after in our teaching: those skills and patterns of behavior, those attitudes and affirmations, that we want our students to acquire and to incorporate into their own lives. If this is what is meant by goals in teaching, then perhaps with regard to prayer, we must change the plural to the singular and speak of goal rather than goals, for in truth there is but one fully valid goal in teaching prayer: praying. The only goal we should aim for and strive for in teaching prayer is that our students will pray: regularly, voluntarily, Jewishly, with *kavvanah*. Any other goal would be desecration or, at best, trivialization.

In a sense, that is all we have to say about the goals of teaching prayer—and theoretically that is all one needs to say. The only reason that anything further needs to be said is that one can no longer take for granted a common understanding of what is meant by "prayer."

2

What is prayer? What does it mean to pray? What is the nature and content of this uniquely human pursuit called "prayer," which we strive to teach to our students?

Once again, before proceeding to the positive, let us begin with the negative, and first indicate what prayer is not. Prayer is not mainly self-expression, the pouring out of feelings and the display of emotions, self-inducement of a state of mind and getting one's self into a mood, "getting high" or "turning on." Prayer is not principally the utterance of prescribed words at a prescribed pace and in a prescribed manner. Prayer is not essentially meditating upon one's self, looking inward—or contemplating other persons or the phenomena of nature, looking outward. Prayer is not necessarily engaging in group singing and chanting, group reading and responding, group sitting or standing or kneeling, or group listening in silence. Prayer is not giving to one's self or to other selves a pep talk about what to do for the public welfare. Prayer is not even theologizing, talking *about* God. Any or many or all of these *may be* present in prayer, but even all of them together do not constitute prayer—for prayer is the personal, existential acknowledgment that one stands in the presence of God. Jewish prayer is the personal acknowledgment that one stands as a *Jew* in the presence of the God of *Israel.* The one goal in teaching prayer is to awaken and stir, to encourage and strengthen, to nourish and sustain the capacity to make such acknowledgment.

3

There are various kinds and types of prayer, various moments and moods, various situations and occasions. Let us examine the main types, familiar to all.

The first and perhaps most familiar type of Jewish prayer is the *berakhah.* The word *berakhah,* of course, means "blessing," and we have no difficulty in using the word to refer to the blessing of God bestowed upon humanity. But how can we account for the use of the word *berakhah* to refer also to what we bestow upon God? And yet that is what we are clearly invited and asked and urged to do when the *sheliah tzibbur* says *barekhu et adonai,* and that is what we presume to do each time we utter a *berakhah.* It does seem strange and presumptuous, indeed close to blasphemous, to imagine that we can bless *God*—until we realize that the whole point of this double use of the word *berakhah* is to indicate that the *berakhah* type of prayer is an acknowledgment by us of God's blessing to us. A *berakhah* is our acknowledgment that something preciously good and infinitely valuable has been received by us from God: a wonder, a marvel, a miracle; something that is a priceless boon, beyond our capacity to create, beyond our right to waste, beyond our desert—something that has come to us though it was not "coming" to us. The blessing of which we have now become aware may be a rare, once-in-a-lifetime phenomenon or a common, ordinary occurrence. In either case it is experienced as a miracle and calls forth a sense of wonder and awe, Heschel's "radical amazement," Buber's "abiding astonishment." A *berakhah* of favor has come from God to me, and a *berakhah* of acknowledgment comes forth from me to God.

This *berakhah* type of prayer makes a world of difference. It makes a difference to me because through it I am able to express the incomparable experience of gratitude at being the beneficiary of God's love. It makes a difference to my fellow human being because I am moved to share with him what I have undeservedly received—so that he, created no less than I in God's image, may enjoy, no less than I, the riches of God's blessing. And to God as well it makes a difference, because the one thing that even God cannot by Himself accomplish is my acknowledgment of *His* blessing through *my* blessing.

4

The second type of prayer is the *viddui* prayer of confession—known to most Jews today only in its *Yom Kippur* version. Sadly, most of our students and their parents are unaware of the traditional recitation of the *viddui* by one who is about to die or by bride and groom on their wedding day. Far sadder, and indeed tragic, is the fact that so very many Jews are unaware of the inclusion of prayers of confession among the prayers of every weekday! Indeed, even teachers, educators, and rabbis have been known to minimize the importance of this kind of prayer and to label it *"un-Jewish"*—despite its daily recurrence in *ve-hu rahum,* in *tahanun,* and especially in the *amidah.* Yet the *viddui* is surely an essential element in our worship. *Viddui* is a pained and shamed acknowledgment that I have sinned against God's will, have violated His command, have failed to live up to His standard for me as human being and Jew, have delayed the fulfillment of His plan, have disappointed Him, and have worked against my own true welfare. A *viddui* prayer is all of this and more: It is an acknowledgment that having become aware of my sin, I now crave His forgiveness, that I seek eagerly to return to Him and to His way, and that I need His help in so returning.

The *viddui,* no less than the *berakhah,* makes a world of difference. To me it makes a world of difference because the burden of my previously unacknowledged, unrepented guilt has been removed; my strength has been replenished and new resources have been released. I now know the joy of having been forgiven, reaccepted, loved again by the One whose forgiveness, acceptance, and love are most crucial to my life. To my fellow human being the *viddui* makes a difference because if it is sincere—and sincere *viddui* is of course the only *viddui* worthy of the name—I am moved to right the wrongs committed against him or in complicity with him, and to become more forgiving and less self-righteous toward those who have sinned against me. And even to God my *viddui* makes a difference and must indeed be precious—for, once again, my confession to Him is the one thing He cannot Himself accomplish. He can punish me; He can hide His face from me; He can make me desperate—but then He must wait for me to supply what He is eager for: my heart's true confession.

5

A third type of prayer is *bakkashah,* the prayer of request and petition. This kind of prayer is the one most associated with the word "prayer" and the one that comes forth most spontaneously from the heart, at least in time of trouble. Yet *bakkashah* is the kind of prayer that we try hardest to avoid in our teaching, that presents the most serious problems in our thinking, and that constitutes the greatest obstacle to our praying. Sometimes we claim that *bakkashot* are presumptuous and superfluous, since God does not need to be instructed concerning our needs; sometimes we claim that *bakkashot* are unavailing, since God cannot—or cannot be expected to—alter the facts of life and laws of nature merely to supply our needs; sometimes we claim that *bakkashot* are too selfish or too petty, too material or too mundane. But whatever the specifics of our objection or of our reluctance, the fact is that we shy away from prayers of *bakkashah* and feel awkward about uttering them.

Perhaps the true reason for our reluctance goes much deeper. Perhaps we are unwilling to make the triple acknowledgment involved in *bakkashah:* the acknowledgment that we are in genuine need, that what we lack cannot be supplied by us but only by God, and that He can be depended upon always to respond to our petition.

In moments of breakthrough, however, I can make this acknowledgment. When I am able to pause from both worthy rationality and unworthy rationalizing, I come to know that in spite of all objections and obstacles, my prayers of petition, if genuine, are genuinely worthy. (They are worthy as long as what I have requested is what I truly feel I need and lack, what I deem essential for my true well-being—and as long as I add, implicitly or explicitly, *ken ye-hi ratzon,* "Thy will be done." In the absence of such a proviso, my request is not request but demand, and demand is not prayer.) I also come to know that God always responds, but in a variety of ways. Sometimes He responds by giving us what we ask for. Sometimes He responds by correcting our sense of values and our evaluation of our needs—so that we come to see that what we began by asking for is not really in our own best interest, or is not necessary for our own well-being and is against the well-being of others. Sometimes He responds by showing us that what we asked for depends not only upon Him but also upon us—and then by strengthening our will to perform our task, fulfill our role. Sometimes He responds by giving us courage and strength to accept what is not to be changed, thus "making our will coincide with His." Sometimes He responds by enabling us to discover blessing and joy in what we already have. But always He responds.

These prayers of *bakkashah* thus make a world of difference. They make a difference to us by enabling us to bring our needs to the concern of God, the only one besides ourselves whose concern is ultimately crucial. They make a difference to our fellow human beings by sensitizing us to see our needs in relation to theirs, by inspiring us to work for the fulfillment of the needs of those whose needs are equal to or greater than our own, and perhaps also by stirring others to bring their needs to God. And finally, prayers of *bakkashah* make a difference even to God, for (once again) there is one crucial aspect of my need that even the All-Knowing One cannot by Himself know until I tell Him, that even the Divine Provider cannot by Himself provide—that is, my acknowledgment that I depend upon Him for the fulfillment of my needs. Yes, for this acknowledgment that I depend upon Him, He depends upon me!

6

Of the various types of prayer, almost all can be subsumed under one or another of the three types already discussed: *berakhah, viddui, bakkashah.* There is one other type, however, that deserves to be considered as a fourth major type: *talmud torah.*

To those engaged professionally in Jewish education it is of course a familiar notion, perhaps a commonplace, that *talmud torah* is a form of Jewish worship. For most other Jews in our generation, it is alas, a most unfamiliar—perhaps an inconceivable—notion. But even for those of us who take this notion almost for granted, it may still be fruitful to ask ourselves: "How can it be that to study Torah is to worship God?" After all, to study and to learn may be important for exercising our mind, increasing our knowledge, appreciating our past, coping with our present, planning our future, transmitting our heritage, preserving our people, refining our ideas, clarifying our thinking, understanding ourselves—and much more; but how is study prayer? If prayer is the personal acknowledgment that one stands in the presence of God, and if Jewish prayer is the acknowledgment that one stands as a Jew in the presence of the God of Israel, how is *talmud torah* a form of prayer?

Talmud torah is a form of Jewish prayer if—and only if—it involves a personal acknowledgment that the Torah that we study and teach contains God's word to Israel, that through that Torah God has spoken to Israel, that from out of that Torah God still speaks to you and me as children of Israel. It may well be that aspects of the Torah, having come to us through human beings, are affected by human limitations and inadequacies, representing less than high-fidelity reception and recording of God's voice. But only when we can affirm that nevertheless God still speaks to us through the Torah—providing us with His light and guidance and instruction, with a proclamation of what He has done for us and demands from us, with His work and way of justice and forgiveness and covenant love, with His promise and assurance and hope—only then can *talmud torah* be a form of prayer. Indeed, of all the kinds of prayer *talmud torah* is in a way the most crucial; finding ourselves addressed by God's voice in the Torah, we are moved to respond to Him in prayers of *berakhah, viddui,* and *bakkashah.*

7

If what has been said thus far has any measure of validity as a characterization of true Jewish prayer, it is apparent that Jewish educators face two formidable problems: the problem that genuine prayer is a rarity in our day and the problem that teaching Jewish prayer is a near-impossibility. The two problems are of course intertwined; indeed the two are almost one: for if true prayer were a common reality in the life of our community, we would find ourselves less at a loss in knowing how to go about teaching prayer. Granted that in one sense, there is no such thing as a guaranteed method of teaching prayer—for if there were any technique or device or prescription or procedure or book or machine that could *guarantee* the learning of prayer, such prayer would not be true prayer, since true prayer must by definition be the *free* and existential acknowledgment we have been discussing. And yet, in another sense, there is one method of teaching prayer that is most likely—or in any event, least unlikely—to succeed: that is the exposure of our children to praying parents, praying neighbors, praying teachers, educators, and rabbis. We should begin with the parents—but even more, we should begin with ourselves, and our problems in prayer.

One of our problems in praying may be called a literary problem. Somehow, in approaching any other work of literature we are fully aware of the difference between prose and poetry, but in approaching the *siddur* we seldom even pause to consider that prayer may be poetry rather than prose. In reading or listening to poetry, we are aided in finding beauty and enrichment, aesthetic pleasure, meaning, and intelligibility through many stylistic features such as alliteration, repetition of words and phrases, multiplication of images, personification, hyperbole, synecdoche, simile and metaphor, and all manner of figurative expression. When any of these occurs in the liturgy, however, we find ourselves disconcerted and our prayer impeded. We tend to be overly troubled by the multiplication of words of praise in *kaddish, ashrei, yishtabah,* or *yotzer or;* disturbed by *serafim, ofanim,* and *mesharetim;* affronted by mention of God's eyes, ears, hand, and arm; self-conscious at the attribution of natural phenomena to divine actions (bringing on the evening, ordering the stars, bringing forth the sun, causing sleep to fall upon, or be removed from, our eyes). Becoming rigidly literalist and unimaginatively prosaic, we blind ourselves to the deeper level of truth in our prayers and are overwhelmed with embarrassment.

But perhaps the problem of our embarrassment is deeper than mere lack of literary appreciation and sensitivity. Perhaps we hesitate to approach prayer poetically because we hesitate to approach prayer at all. Afflicted with what Abraham Heschel *z"l* has termed "religious bashfulness," we are ashamed to be seen or caught praying. The causes of this affliction are no doubt many: the mechanization of work, the atomization of society, the worship of science and technology, the exaltation of reason, the combination of excessive self-confidence and excessive despair, and the erosion of community. The causes are many, but the result is clear: the near-disappearance of communal worship. What was in earlier ages able to be shared publicly is now relegated to the private domain, where, cut off from communal nourishment and replenishment, it atrophies and shrivels. Thus it has come to pass that we are embarrassed to pray not only in the presence of others but even alone, in the presence of God. Indeed, we have difficulty in acknowledging the reality of His presence at all. And if God's presence cannot be affirmed, prayer cannot be attempted.

Which leads us to the heart of prayer—and the heart of our problem of prayer: the awareness of the presence of the Living God. Whether or not we follow those scholars who maintain that "the Present One" is the literal denotation of the name *YHVH,* it surely is almost incontestable that this has become its connotation. What is repeatedly affirmed in the *Shema Yisra'el,* therefore, is not simply that we believe in one God but that we believe in the right one! Not simply that only one God exists, but that this One God is a living God, ever present, encountered again and again in personal relationship. God is not a person just like us, but He is surely not less of a person than each of us; rather He is more than a person. He makes Himself known to us in countless ways—*eheyeh asher eheyeh*—but in all His ways He is One. He meets us in countless ways but in all the ways He meets us, He meets us personally—calling us to be, enabling us to be our most human, living, loving, sensitive, responsive, responsible, personal selves.

To be sure, God is never fully known to us; indeed, we find Him to be at many moments strange, mysterious, silent, distant, unknown, hiding His face. But if at such moments we find it difficult, almost impossible, to address Him by name and call Him "Thou"—even then we need not despair nor feel ourselves completely, utterly cut off. For even at such moments we can look about us or look within us—and if we find ourselves truly, humbly grateful to an ultimate source beyond ourselves for blessing received but undeserved; or if we find ourselves truly heartbroken over sin committed, standing in judgment before an ultimate court above ourselves, and then know ourselves to be forgiven; if we find ourselves in need, dependent for the fulfillment of our need upon an ultimate source beyond ourselves, yet assured that our true need will be fulfilled; if we find ourselves truly guided, disciplined, enlightened, renewed by a voice within and yet from beyond the Torah, then surely we are at last at the threshold of the House of Prayer, approaching the presence of the Living God. Now, at last, are we able to teach our students to pray, because now we ourselves have begun—or begun again—truly to pray. And "God is near to all who call upon Him truly."

KASHRUT IN CONSERVATIVE JUDAISM

1

The time has come for rethinking the Conservative approach to *kashrut*.

There is almost universal agreement among Conservative leaders, rabbinic and lay, that *kashrut* is one of the key elements of Judaism, essential to any proper pattern of the Jewish way of life. (In this regard, certainly, Conservative Judaism differs from Reform.) There is far from universal agreement, however, as to the exact manner, form, and degree of *kashrut* that is necessary and proper for the faithful Jew. (In this regard, certainly, Conservative Judaism differs from Orthodoxy.) As in so many other regards, this insistence that something is essential to Judaism, combined with a lack of agreement on exactly what it is that is essential, leads to confusion from without and from within.

From the left and from the right there come honest questioning and sharp accusation, puzzled searching and impatient dismissal before the phenomenon of a Conservative movement that is united on the importance of *kashrut* observance in general but divided on *kashrut* observance in particular. "Do it right or not at all," we are told; "make up your mind," we are urged. "Where do you get the authority to change and to choose, to omit and to select? If God ordained *kashrut,* how dare you deviate? And if He did not, why do you insist on holding on to what is only of human origin? If *kashrut* is needed to bind together the people Israel, spread through the world and across the ages, then how dare you divide the people and disturb the pattern, thus weakening the bond?"

"And what is more," the challenge continues, "where do you draw the line? How far do you go? How long do you wait, for instance, after a meat meal before drinking milk? How much of a nonkosher ingredient is your food permitted to contain? Do you require separation of utensils? If you do, then how can you eat out in restaurants?"

"And further," it is urged, "what of the diversity of practice within Conservatism—don't you have any rules or standards? Are there any requirements for Conservative Jews, or may each do as he wills? And anyhow, are not half of you practically Orthodox? And the other half practically Reform? Are you a single movement at all?"

In the face of these challenges the Conservative movement has an obligation to its fellow Jews, brotherly critics on the right and left, to answer and explain, to clarify its stand. Even more it owes this obligation to itself. For the Conservative movement has not articulated how it stands on *kashrut*, and its own adherents are uncomfortable, embarrassed, and confused. They waver between a feeling of superiority to Reform on the part of some (as those who have strayed outside the fold of kosher Jews) and a sense of inferiority to Reform on the part of others (as those who have had the courage to make a break with what moderns cannot accept but what Conservatives have not dared yet to reject). They waver too between a sense of superiority to the Orthodox on the part of some (as those who are old-fashioned, rigid children of a bygone age) and a feeling of guilt towards the Orthodox on the part of others (as those who have the courage to live unflinchingly by principles that Conservatives have been too weak still to uphold). And though Conservatives sometimes boast of taking their stand bravely at the middle point of moderation, avoiding all extremes, there is too often a haunting sense of trying unsuccessfully and unworthily to be all things to all.

For the sake of all concerned, the time has come for rethinking the Conservative approach to *kashrut*.

But *kashrut* is a matter of *halakhah*. To solve the Conservative problem of *kashrut,* even to move in the direction of a solution, requires first a clarification of the Conservative understanding of *halakhah*.

2

There is near-unanimity of conviction within the Conservative movement that without *halakhah,* there is no Judaism worthy of the name. But how is *halakhah* to be understood? At first glance the range of halakhic practice within Conservatism would seem to be so broad and so varied—even among its rabbis and its teachers—as to be almost chaotic. Any observer of the American Jewish scene can testify to the almost unbelievable variations among Conservative rabbis and congregations in such areas of *halakhah* as marriage and divorce, order of service, Sabbath observance, funeral practices, etc.[96] And yet, although there is certainly no single Conservative position on halakhic principle or practice, it is not true that there is complete chaos. Properly understood, all the differences and variations can be reduced to two basic approaches to *halakhah*.

---

96. There is, of course, a not dissimilar range of variation within Orthodoxy and Reform; but with the Orthodox it cannot be justified, and with Reform it need not be.

Where do the two Conservative approaches differ in their understanding of *halakhah*? In this: the one thinks in terms of *the halakhah;* the other in terms of *a halakhah.* The one considers the whole traditional pattern as binding, in all detail; the other considers the main outlines of the pattern as binding, with a requirement for detail—one cannot live in outline—but with permission to fill in with one's own selection and creation of detail. The one glories in the Pharisaic achievement as the near-final form of Judaism; the other glories in that same achievement as a model framework. The one thus conceives itself as a pale and unworthy successor of the masters; the other sees itself as privileged and obliged to stand almost in the masters' shoes. The one is sure that God ordained, whether directly or indirectly through the holy chain, the whole traditional pattern—commanding not only that each area of life be hallowed but commanding in detail each rule of hallowing. The other, though sure that God commands the hallowing of all of life and sure that Israel's hallowing boundaries and signposts are from God as well,[97] is not so sure that God has fixed each step along the way—in fact, is rather sure God leaves much freedom to each individual traveler (who of course must not lose contact with the other travelers in his band.) The one fears that without uniformity of practice the bond of Israel's holy fellowship will be broken; the other feels assured that bound by a bond of holy commitment and guided by the signs and boundary marks, the individual children of the covenant are guarded in their holy unity, as they use their God-given freedom to weave the holy pattern.

3

The confusion between these two diverse approaches to *halakhah* within the Conservative movement accounts for the present confused situation of *kashrut.* The situation seems chaotic only so long as the two

---

97. To what extent the "boundaries and signposts" (e.g., the particular animals that are forbidden, the spilling of the blood, etc.) are God's words, and to what extent they are Israel's, is impossible to know. In the divine-human encounter at Sinai there were both a giving and a receiving of Torah; the human element thus inevitably enters in. But if God's intention is to be carried out—that Israel be bound together and guided by the signs—there can be only one set of boundaries and signposts. Hence we can say what in faith we know to be true: whether God-spoken or God-approved, these specific boundaries and signposts, and not only the general command to hallow our partaking of food, are from God as well.

approaches are not recognized and articulated. Once the two are clearly set forth, the picture becomes clear.

To those who understand *halakhah* in the first sense and accept it as a legal system, binding in its entirety upon every Jew, the problem is not what or how to observe; for *kashrut* is to be completely practiced, exactly as tradition has developed and expounded it. The *Shulhan Arukh* and the other codes provide the only proper guidance, and give all the answers to all questions of the diet of holiness for the Jew. New foods and new methods of preparing them may seem to raise new problems; but when analyzed into their component parts, the problems are reduced to earlier problems, which can then be readily answered with the earlier answers. The one problem for these Jews is to be careful, conscientious, and courageously sacrificial in observing the *mitzvah* of *kashrut*.

For those who understand *halakhah* in the other sense—there are two special problems: The first problem is to identify what are the fixed requirements and what the areas open for individual patterning; the second problem is to proceed and work out in detail one's personal pattern.

What are the essentials of *kashrut*? What are those essential requirements, of which all the other regulations are extensions and refinements? Are they not these?—

1. Some creatures are inherently forbidden to be eaten.

2. Animals that are permitted must be properly slaughtered—with the blood, certain fat, and the "sinew of the thigh" removed.

3. The meat of animals properly slaughtered must be kept separate from milk.

These form the main outline of *kashrut* obligation, in the home and out, for those Conservative Jews who understand *halakhah* as *a halakhah,* rather than as *the halakhah.* The one further *kashrut* obligation they accept is the obligation to fill in the outline with a personal patterning woven partly through conscious selection and evaluation, partly through childhood upbringing and habituation, partly through psychological preference and inner need. Each person's pattern will differ from his fellow's; all will share in accepting both the three fundamentals and a holy concern to spell them out in concrete detail.

For example: In carrying out the command to abstain from the forbidden animals or seafood, one Conservative Jew may see himself commanded to abstain from such nonkosher foods themselves but not necessarily from using utensils that have previously contained such nonkosher food. A second Conservative Jew may feel unconcerned (and may feel that God is unconcerned) about minor quantities of nonkosher ingredients; when he avoids forbidden foods he may avoid only a sizeable quantity, identifiable by taste or sight or smell or name.

Another example: In observing the *mitzvah* of *melihah,* one Conservative Jew may see himself required to salt and soak according to traditional rule; a second Jew may feel his religious conscience satisfied with a token momentary rinsing; a third Jew may be satisfied with the draining of the blood at the time of slaughtering.

Another example: In carrying out the *mitzvah* of separating meat and dairy, one Conservative Jew may wait the traditional length of time between eating meat and drinking milk (though the length of time varies even among strict traditionalists) but may not be strict about the separation of utensils—especially outside his home. A second Jew may never ask how many minutes or hours have elapsed between meat and milk but may merely not eat them at the same meal—defining the "same meal" not in terms of lapse of time but rather, in terms of change of place or psychological awareness. The third and fourth Jews may differ on how strict they are to be that no drop of milk or butter is contained in the bread or cracker or cake or pie they eat with their meat meal.

Faithful Conservative Jews of this persuasion do not glory in their "leniencies," vaunting their "liberalism" over their more strictly practicing brothers; nor do they on the other hand feel guilty or inferior for their "leniencies." In fact, they do not think so much in terms of leniency; they do not seek the easy way out. They are concerned to carry out the *mitzvah* of *kashrut* in a manner that they can honestly defend, explain, and justify to others and to themselves—and in a manner that they can pass on to their children and their pupils. For, to repeat, they feel sure that God has commanded Israel to hallow its food life as part of Israel's holy way and yet they feel sure as well that within the main lines set down there is more than one path along that holy way. They seek to walk with *kavvanah,* knowing that within the prescribed limits each person must follow his own heart's direction as he walks.

4

The two approaches to *halakhah,* however much they differ, share much in common: They agree that the faith of Israel is not a set of abstract principles or religious doctrines but is a *halakhah,* a way of life, in which faith is acted out in a pattern of concrete ways. They agree that the *halakhah* is a holy discipline commanded by God to set Israel apart for the sanctification of all of life, including the sustenance of life by food. They agree that the halakhic pattern of *mitzvot* has had a growth and a development, changing through the ages, with some original elements being transformed and occasionally dying out, some foreign elements becoming incorporated. They agree too that despite all change and growth, despite the grafting on and withering away, the halakhic pattern has remained and must remain sufficiently fixed and stable to unite *kelal yisra'el* in any age and through the ages. This much—and this is much—the two approaches to *halakhah* within the Conservative movement share in common, marking the movement off from much of Reform and Orthodoxy.

It may seem at times, however, that what the two wings have in common is not quite enough to keep them bound together, that in spite of what they share in common they ought yet to split. It seems at times that the "left Conservative" should merge with Reform. (Are there not stirrings within Reform for some modified form of *kashrut*?). And the "right Conservative" might merge with Orthodoxy. (Does not the "right Conservative" accept the official decisions and certifications only of the Orthodox?). When such doubts arise about the viability of the Conservative movement, as judged by its position on *kashrut* and *halakhah,* there is perhaps this crucial test: The two wings of Conservatism belong together, form one movement, if each can say of both—and only as long as each can honestly say of both—*ellu va-ellu diverei elohim hayyim.* "Both these and those are the words of the living God."

COVERING MY JEWISH HEAD

Why do I wear a *kippah* when I do? Ought I wear it at other times as well—as many Jews do and I do not? Must I wear it even at the times I do—since many other Jews do not? And what difference does it make—to others, to me, to God, to anyone—whether I do or do not wear a *kippah*?

When I cover my head for particular occasions—for public Jewish worship or private prayer, for study of Torah—I am following what has become a distinctive Jewish way of performing a ritual act, of showing reverence, of acknowledging that I stand in the presence of the Holy One.

But since there are numerous occasions throughout the day when pronouncing a *berakhah* is in order (upon washing the hands, for example; upon eating a meal or even a morsel, taking a drink, beholding a natural wonder or an exceptional person), and since there are innumerable moments when God's presence should be acknowledged and responded to ("there is no moment or place entirely devoid of His presence"), should I perhaps keep my head covered all the time, as indeed many Jews do, and as I myself usually do on *Shabbat* and on *Yom Tov*?

Entirely aside from its religious meaning, covering the head is meaningful in another way: not with regard to the particular act that I am doing, or to the particular moment when I am doing it, but with regard to who I am. For going about with covered head—especially with *kippah*-covered head—means that I am wearing a uniform, and thus will be immediately identified: to non-Jews, as a Jew; to Jews, as fellow Jew. (The *kippah* has become far more visible and far more widely recognized as a Jewish uniform than the Torah-commanded "fringes on the corner of the garment.") When I wear a *kippah* in public, therefore, I demonstrate my willingness, perhaps even my eagerness, to be so identified.

But merely to be identified as a Jew involves, paradoxically, more than mere identification. Even if in one's own eyes one is a secular, nonbelieving, nonreligious Jew, in the eyes of almost all others, non-Jew and Jew alike, the very word "Jew" points beyond the merely ethnic and, on some level and at least to some degree, points to Israel as God's covenant people, called to be a "kingdom of priests, a holy nation," involving mysterious chosenness and miraculous survival; revelation of God's word and way; and redemption, performed in the past and promised for the future. Thus when I wear a *kippah* I serve willy-nilly as witness and reminder of the Holy One of Israel.

These, then, are at least some of the reasons, aside from mere habit and the accompanying sense of "just feeling more comfortable this way," that I wear a *kippah* when I do.

In spite of these good reasons, covering my Jewish head poses problems and dilemmas.

For one thing, granted that covering the head can serve as a sign of, and an aid to, reverence in the presence of the holy, and granted also that every moment is potentially holy; is it not also true that wearing a head covering can degenerate into the magical illusion that the mere wearing of a *kippah* guarantees protection, and into the superstitious notion that the mere baring of my head will bring punishment down upon me?

Far more profoundly dangerous is the possibility that wearing a head covering may become so routine and automatic that I become almost oblivious to its intended meaning, thus allowing what is meant to be an act of piety to become utterly ineffective, and allowing what are meant to be moments of holiness to lose their force and even their frequency. Wearing a *kippah* constantly, I run the risk of reducing the distinction between the holy and the profane—and *not* by raising the latter to the former.

In addition to the peril of routine, there is the peril of self-righteous display: of always appearing to say, "Look at me: how pious I am!" It is true, of course, that peril lies also with the onlooker, who may be rationalizing his own lack of piety by projecting it on to the *kippah*-covered Jew; I dare not deny, however, the reality of this peril which accompanies me when I publicly wear a *kippah*. The effort to cultivate consciousness of God's presence, worthy and indeed crucial as this is, is no guarantee against *self*-consciousness, and self-consciousness runs the risk of becoming self-righteousness and self-display.

Even the ready and open acknowledgment of my Jewish identity through wearing a *kippah,* surely an admirable sign of Jewish self-respect and even of defiance in the face of non-Jewish hostility, carries with it some spiritual perils. For just as being identifiable as a Jew makes every worthy word I say and every worthy deed I do into *kiddush ha-shem,* sanctification of the name of God and of His people Israel, so is the converse also true: my every less-than-worthy deed or word calls Israel and Israel's God into disrepute. Besides, is it not permissible, or even preferable, for one person to meet another person, at least sometimes, simply as one human being to another, one image-of-God to another, I to thou—and only thereafter identify oneself as a Jew? In any case, wearing my Jewish identity on my head runs the risk of becoming too strident, too demonstrative, too proclamatory of my Jewishness. It is, of course, possible that my concern over this peril is but a rationalization for my embarrassment or even cowardice at appearing so openly Jewish—and I ought from time to time to reexamine that possibility; but the peril of judgmental, prideful parading ought not to be denied.

If covering the head were clearly commanded in the Torah, or explicitly ordained in the Talmud, or laid down as mandatory law in the classical codes, or if it had been always and everywhere the accepted Jewish practice, I might have no alternative. Since I strive to abide by the basic discipline of the Torah-tradition, I would accept the obligation of covering my head, and then seek God's help in avoiding these spiritual pitfalls. None of the above, however, seems to be the case.

There is no biblical command for anyone except the *kohen* (priest) to cover the head. And in the Talmud, though married women were required to cover their head in public (exposing their hair was considered to be an indecency), the practice of covering the head by men (other than those who were fasting, in mourning, under the ban, or afflicted with leprosy) appears to have been limited to scholars and other dignitaries, and to have been a voluntary act of special piety and humility. Indeed, for an "ordinary" man to cover his head was considered in some circles to be presumptuous. In Palestine it was not required even that *kohanim* cover their heads during their recitation of the priestly blessing, although in Babylonia this was required.

In medieval Europe the practice varied. Some rabbinical authorities considered covering the head even during prayer and Torah study to be optional; and some of them prayed with uncovered head. Even when covering the head became more widely practiced, almost all authorities granted that this was merely custom, and that there was no law against praying with head uncovered. Even when covering the head had become the dominant practice, authorities as eminent as Rabbi Solomon Luria and the author of the *Shulhan Arukh,* though urging its practice, continued to acknowledge this distinction between custom and law. As late as the eighteenth century the famous Elijah of Vilna ("the Vilna Gaon"), though strongly recommending the practice of covering the head in the synagogue as good manners, makes the same theoretical acknowledgment.

True enough, when long practiced and widely observed, custom can come to be considered law, and when subsequently defied, can even override the law. Thus when in the nineteenth century leaders of the Reform movement, basing themselves on this theoretically nonmandatory status of the practice, did away with it, some of them going so far as to make *baring* the head mandatory, Orthodox leaders responded by condemning bareheadedness as a gross violation of "the law," as an outrageous example of the forbidden "walking in the ways of the gentiles," and by pronouncing the practice of covering the head to be absolutely mandatory—some even extending the duty of keeping the head covered to all the time.

In the contemporary period the extent of the practice among traditionally observant Jews has varied. Some keep the head covered at all times; some whenever they are at home or in any Jewish environment, but not otherwise in public; some while studying Torah, praying, or eating. In some circles observant Jews have been known to don a *kippah* (or merely to cover their head with their hand) for the benedictions at the beginning of the meal, to remove it for the balance of the meal, and at the conclusion of the meal to don it once again for the *birkat ha-mazon* (grace after the meal). In other circles the *kippah* has been considered to provide insufficient covering, at least for some prayer situations, and so the *kippah* is replaced or covered by a hat.[98]

In view of this record of varied historical practice and varied halakhic ruling, what are the standards that should guide *me* with regard to covering my Jewish head?

First, I must guard against the double error of either asserting that covering the head has always been the required and only proper Jewish mode—or of denying that in recent centuries it was widely considered to be just that.

---

98. In Orthodox circles the closest parallel among women to the male practice of covering the head is the rule that married women must not appear in public with their hair exposed; unmarried women are spared the problem—and denied the privilege—of deciding whether and when to cover their head as an expression of Jewish piety or identity. Perhaps some Orthodox married women, or some unmarried women stirred by feminism or egalitarianism to cover their Jewish head on certain occasions, will find in this essay a reflection of certain aspects of their own situation.

Secondly, I should normally cover my head for Jewish prayer and Torah study and at least occasionally for other pursuits as well, depending upon the particular situation or company, or even the particular mood, that I am in. And I should not be apologetic to others or to myself for having such personal preferences.

I should be sensitive, however, to the feelings of other Jews who, because of difference in background and experience, in temperament and personality, in present environment or circumstance, have preferences and principles different from mine, and who therefore cover their head more frequently or consistently, or less consistently or frequently, than I do. I should therefore not try to coerce or pressure others to follow my preferences and principles rather than their own. Nor should I insist upon always following my own, if doing so will greatly offend or pain those in whose company I am, unless I find their insistence on my compliance to be so coercive and intrusive, or so self-righteous, that it becomes for me an intolerable burden.

Finally, I should acknowledge the possibility that my present views and feelings on this subject, my present understanding, and even my present principles, however deeply held, may some day change. I should not necessarily fear the prospect of such change, nor feel obliged to resist it if and when it comes, for change sometimes betokens spiritual growth.

With regard to covering my head, the only kind of change that I should fear and, with God's help, should endeavor to resist, is any change that involves the loss or diminution of this crucial double awareness: that I am a Jew, party to God's covenant with my people Israel, and that as a Jew I stand at every moment before the One whose hallowed and hallowing presence is above my covered (or uncovered) head.

SYNAGOGUE AND COVENANT PEOPLE

1

One of the preoccupations of modern Jews—indeed one of the hallmarks of the modern Jewish situation—has been the continuing quest for an adequate definition of the Jewish group. But the search has been constantly frustrating and the debate inconclusive; for the search and debate have almost always been conducted on a sociological level, and the group known as "the Jews" has been found to fit into none, absolutely none, of the available sociological categories. Race, state, nation, nationality, ethnic group, culture, and even religion—whatever element of validity may attach to any of these terms as applied to "the Jews," no one of them, nor any combination of them, is adequate to describe the Jewish group; none suffices as a definition that will include all members of this group and will exclude all nonmembers. (Resort is sometimes had to terms like "people" or "community," but these are so vague as to be useless; they are really tautologies for the word "group," and as such simply beg the question.)

For those Jews who consider themselves nonreligious, the frustration has been both real and intense. Willingly acknowledging themselves to be Jews, but unwilling to acknowledge themselves to be religious, they have taken for granted that their Jewishness could be affirmed on nonreligious terms and in nonreligious categories; when these terms and categories are called into question, their whole Jewish affirmation becomes problematic. The frustration of many Jews who consider themselves religious has similarly been real and intense. By the admission, indeed by the insistence, of their own religious teaching, every person born of a Jewish mother is Jewish, regardless of personal religious belief or practice. The greater measure of their own religious belief and observance does not make religious Jews any more Jewish, as regards Jewish identity, than their nonbelieving, nonobserving fellow Jews.

And yet, though religion is not the basis of Jewish identity, it supplies the basis for understanding that identity. It supplies the key concept of *berit,* the covenant between God and the people Israel: the covenant that was established with the very first Jew, Abraham, and with his seed after him; the covenant that was confirmed with the whole people at Sinai with the giving-and-accepting of the Torah; the covenant that has continued through the ages and has always been understood to be an everlasting covenant. Thus religion *is* not the definition but *provides* the definition of the Jews: Jews are those who, normally by descent and occasionally by conversion, are within the covenant. Sociologically, the Jews remain a puzzle; psychologically, they are a problem; theologically (in conception) and religiously (in existential affirmation) they become a mystery and a miracle: the unique and supernatural—but very real—covenant people Israel.

2

This concept of covenant and covenant people is the central, crucial concept of Jewish religion and of its sacred Torah-tradition. Obviously, then, this concept should be the leitmotif of the synagogue, which has ever been the teacher of the religion and expounder of the tradition; and indeed such was the case as long as people and synagogue were one. (Not that the people was ever the synagogue in the sense of a church, a religious institution; and not that affirmation of religious faith or adherence to religious practice was ever a condition for membership in the people; but until the modern period the vast majority of the Jewish people appears to have been aware that its Jewishness was rooted in the covenant, whose standards and obligations, Torah-and-*mitzvot,* were always accepted as binding in principle even when violated in practice.) From the onset of the modern period, however, there has been an increasing separation of people and synagogue, with an accompanying waning among the people of covenant-consciousness and covenant-commitment. The synagogue, alas, has failed to acknowledge this momentous separation forthrightly and to come to grips with it squarely; the guardian of the covenant concept has failed to clarify its relationship with that large portion of the covenant people that is now almost unaware of the covenant. It is a reality of Jewish life today that multitudes of Jews are outside the synagogue and multitudes of those nominally inside the synagogue consider themselves to be outside its authority and discipline; the synagogue, however, has refused to come to terms with this reality. It is this failure that constitutes the chief cause of the pathetically slight impact of the contemporary synagogue upon the life of the Jewish people and of its minimal effectiveness even in the lives of its own members. It is this failure that has led the synagogue into several costly temptations.

For one thing, the synagogue has been tempted into thinking that it can properly speak in the name of all Jews, when in fact it has neither the authority nor the power to do so.

Furthermore, the synagogue has allowed itself to be filled with resentment at the activity and sometimes at the very existence of the so-called secular organizations. When these organizations engage in Jewish educational, cultural, religious, or interfaith programs, the synagogue resents them as illegitimate competitors; when they engage in general cultural, recreational, health and welfare, or social activities, the synagogue often resents them as perverters of the name "Jewish" and diverters from proper Jewish concerns; when they act or speak in the name of the "Jewish community," the synagogue resents them as usurpers; and even when they engage in Jewish philanthropic work and in fund raising on behalf of Israel, which the synagogue itself encourages and supports as a prime *mitzvah,* the synagogue tends to resent the priority in time, energy, and manpower that these efforts command and perhaps even the successful response that they elicit. And when all the various "secular" organizations unite to form a Council or Conference or Congress or Assembly or umbrella committee—in which synagogues are included—the synagogue resents being only one among the many.

Feeding upon these resentments, the synagogue often falls into the costly temptation of seeking to incorporate into its own program the whole gamut of activities offered by the various secular organizations. The synagogue-center is the epitome of this tendency, but most synagogues are synagogue-centers, in fact or aspiration, even if not always in name. Synagogues provide, to be sure, services of worship, religious classes, and a smattering of adult education; but in addition—and often with greater effort, emphasis, and publicity—they offer almost everything else. Gyms and swimming pools, bowling teams and bridge groups, basketball leagues and ballet dancing, theater parties and game nights, stamp clubs and scout troops, fashion shows and dances, sports nights and picnics, speakers on subjects like the stock market, flower arrangement, interior decorating, foreign policy, the theater today—these are typical of countless synagogue-sponsored programs. Almost anything that is calculated to draw attention and attendance is acceptable; almost anything that may attract new members and retain old ones is suitable; almost anything that will enable the institution to grow in numbers and expand in size—and provide something for everyone—is considered appropriate for the contemporary synagogue. To become the largest, most popular, most successful, most important Jewish organization; to become the center of the Jewish community; indeed to become the Jewish community—is the implicit goal of almost every synagogue.

No wonder, then, that almost no synagogues have standards or requirements for membership. If the goal is to attract members, why set requirements that will deter prospective members from joining? Besides, what standards or requirements could in conscience be set by those who themselves have joined the synagogue on the basis of "something for everyone"? Thus it has come to pass that to become a synagogue member today—and to remain a member in good standing—one need merely be Jewish by the accident of birth (more rarely by conversion)—and pay dues! To learn that a particular Jew is a synagogue member, even an active member, that he is on the synagogue board or even an officer—tells us nothing, absolutely nothing, about whether he knows or cares about such crucial *mitzvot* as worship of God, study of Torah, observance of *Shabbat,* or practice of *kashrut.* His synagogue affiliation tells us nothing, absolutely nothing, about the level of his business ethics, the quality of his family life, or the measure of his charitableness. To be a synagogue member in good standing in our day, a Jew need not observe any of these commandments, nor accept even the theoretical obligation to do so. He need not even believe in God. The illusion that the synagogue includes all Jews and is thus identical with the Jewish people has kept the synagogue from being even the synagogue; seeking to be what in this age it cannot be, the synagogue has become less than it still can be; aspiring to be more than itself, it has become less than itself.

3

To become itself the synagogue must set as its chief task the revival, among its own members, of covenant-consciousness and the covenant-outlook, and must reaffirm as its primary purpose the cultivation of the covenant way of life. This task-and-purpose may be formulated in various ways. It may be formulated in terms of the general obligation to apply the Word of God contained in the Torah-tradition to the personal and communal situations of modern life. Or it may be formulated in terms of living by the traditional five loves: love of God, love of Torah, love of Israel, love of fellow human being, and love of Zion. Or it may be formulated in terms of areas of holy concern and effort: regular study of Torah; regular worship of God in synagogue and home; the celebration, in the Jewish mode, of prescribed moments in the day, week, month, year, and in the life cycle; continuing involvement in work on behalf of the people Israel, both in the land of Israel and throughout the Diaspora; regular practice of justice and love in personal relations; involvement in work for the alleviation of suffering and the establishment of an equitable society; ever-renewed awareness of standing constantly in God's presence; ever-renewed trust in the coming of the Messiah. Or it may be formulated in terms of the forthright acceptance and faithful adherence to the whole table of *mitzvot* that constitutes the traditional *halakhah.*

Whichever formulation of covenant-task-and-purpose is adopted by the synagogue must then become the basis for synagogue affiliation. The synagogue must have the courage to require of its members, as a condition of membership, an acceptance of such a task-and-purpose and a commitment to strive conscientiously to live by it. All other Jews should be invited to attend the synagogue, join in its worship, utilize its facilities, participate in its program, avail themselves of the services of its staff—and share in its support—for all Jews are full-fledged children of the covenant and full-fledged members of the House of Israel, and as such should always be genuinely and warmly welcomed. Official membership in the synagogue, however—involving the right to vote and the privilege of setting synagogue program and policy—should be open only to Jews who find themselves able to make the personal covenant-commitment and to accept the personal covenant-obligation. This is not a question of invidious distinctions or of first- and second-class citizenship. The worth and importance of the unsynagogued—whether active in secular organizations or totally unaffiliated—may well be as great as, or even greater than, that of the synagogued, and their task and contribution may often be more weighty and more crucial; indeed their position outside the synagogue may often constitute a reflection and a judgment upon the failure, degeneracy and self-righteousness of the synagogue itself. But if the synagogue is to make its own crucial contribution and fulfill its unique role for the welfare of the people, it can do so only when the basis for synagogue affiliation has been clarified and revised.

Such a revision and clarification of the meaning and purpose of synagogue membership would enable and require each Jew to determine, before he joins a synagogue, whether in truth he desires to join; and it would enable all Jews who have decided in the affirmative to pursue with holy vigor and holy joy the goals they have accepted—without being obliged, as at present, constantly to buck, and frequently to capitulate to, the large number of synagogue members who are indifferent or even hostile to the proper tasks and purposes of the synagogue. To those who opt for synagogue membership, as well as to those who decide to remain unaffiliated, the meaning and implications of such membership would now be clear.

4

A further clarification, however, would now become necessary. A Jew has decided to join the synagogue; but which synagogue shall he join? (If only one synagogue is available, he is of course denied—and spared—this choice.) A local synagogue has decided to join a national movement, but which movement shall it join? The present denominational division on the American Jewish scene makes so little sense that the labels "Orthodox," "Conservative," and "Reform" provide little guidance as to the actual theological position or the actual pattern of practice of any particular synagogue. This is partly due, of course, to the aforementioned lack of commitment on the part of individual members and to the consequently nondescript character of any particular congregation. (Nonobservant Orthodox, nonobservant Conservative, and nonobservant Reform present, after all, a marked similarity.) It is equally due, however, to the amazing range of difference in belief and practice within almost any particular congregation and within each of the national movements as well.

Within the Conservative movement the range of religious practice is notoriously wide. Regarding forms of worship: some Conservative synagogues conduct their service almost entirely in Hebrew, some almost entirely in English, some in the two languages more-or-less in equal measure; some regularly use the organ, some never use it, and some use it at certain services only; some abbreviate the Reading of the Torah (in various arrangements and degrees of abbreviation), some allow no abbreviation; some practice segregation of the sexes, others call women to the Torah; some have discontinued calling the *kohen* as first to the Torah, whereas others have maintained or even reintroduced the holiday recitation of the priestly blessing by the *kohen*. As regards *Shabbat*—excluding from consideration the majority of members who observe it hardly at all—the pattern of the Rabbi and Cantor, and of those leaders and members who do observe, varies greatly: many use electricity on the Sabbath, many do not; some travel to synagogue, some for other purposes, some do not; most carry small objects, some do not; some engage in swimming or other forms of recreation, some do not. The range in *kashrut* is similarly wide: some eat only in strictly kosher homes and restaurants, others visit nonkosher places but eat only cold foods, still others eat cooked foods but merely abstain from meat or forbidden seafood; some wait six hours after meat before eating dairy products, others wait five or four or three or two hours, or even one. As regards remarriage after divorce, many require the issuance of a *get* (a Jewish divorce), some do not, and some usually do—but do not when it is difficult or impossible to obtain. Conversion procedures also vary: some require immersion, some do not; most require circumcision, some do not; in the case of one previously circumcised, some require the token "letting of a drop of blood of the covenant," many do not.

With such a variety of practice, the Conservative movement often comes under harsh criticism from both Orthodoxy on the right and Reform on the left: from the former for claiming to be traditional, from the latter for claiming to be modern, and from both for what is termed inconsistency, cowardice, or even duplicity. Whatever the degree of validity in this criticism of motives, and whatever the motives of the critics, the fact cannot be denied: Conservative Judaism does indeed display a remarkably—and confusingly—wide range of religious practice.

But so does Reform. Many Reform temples do not have *bar mitzvah,* do not call individual worshipers to the Torah, do not have men cover their heads during worship, do not use much Hebrew in the service, do not use the *tallit*—but many temples do all of these; most do not observe *kashrut,* do not urge or expect observance of the twenty-four-hour fast on *Yom Kippur,* do not have an outdoor *sukkah*—but some do all of these; most require conversion of the non-Jewish party before sanctioning a marriage, some do not.

Even in Orthodoxy, where one might expect a near-uniformity of practice, the range is wide. Most Orthodox synagogues require segregation of sexes at least during worship, some do not; many use almost no English in the service, some use a great deal; many require at least their officers to observe *Shabbat* and *kashrut,* many do not; some rabbis will accept almost no converts at all, others accept converts after minimal instruction and almost no commitment; most rabbis collaborate with Conservative and Reform colleagues and participate with them in rabbinical and synagogal organizations, others do not even acknowledge them to be rabbis; as regards *kashrut,* not only are there varying degrees of strictness in interpretation and observance, but many rabbis do not honor the *kashrut* certification—or indeed the rabbinic ordination—of fellow Orthodox rabbis.

Whether the range of diversity is as wide in Orthodoxy and Reform as it is in Conservatism is difficult to assess, but surely it is as real and as noticeable in these movements on the right and on the left—neither of which has the "excuse" of being the middle group!

As with behavior, so with belief: within each of the three movements there can be found a wide range of theological views. As regards belief in God, there are within both Reform and Conservative ranks theists who believe in a personal God with anthropopathic qualities; deists whose God is impersonal and whose prime function is "simply" to have started the whole enterprise of the universe; pantheists, whose God is spread through the universe, identical with it as principle or process; agnostics, "ignostics," and even atheists, who nevertheless find themselves able to use traditional theistic language as either literary symbolism aesthetically and intellectually acceptable to themselves, or as a necessary device with which they make their compromise for the sake of communication with less sophisticated congregants. Within Orthodoxy, of course, the range is much narrower, but it is still marked—not only on the level of vocabulary, style, and intellectual sophistication, but also on the level of actual doctrine, where the philosophic and mystical traditions have made possible a striking variety of "traditional" formulations—and where even secularism has made subtle but marked inroads.

The range of biblical interpretation within Conservatism and Reform extends through nearly the whole possible spectrum: a few who come close to viewing the Bible as literally the Word of God; many who prefer the more liberal (and less specific) phrase "divinely inspired"; many who look upon Scripture as the Word-of-God-in-human-formulation; and many who think of it merely as a great, or the greatest, work of the human spirit. Once again, in Orthodoxy the range is much narrower, but a close reading of such intellectually sophisticated thinkers as the participants in the *Commentary* symposium on "The Condition of Jewish Belief" or the contributors to *Tradition* clearly indicates the wide divergence among these writers and the great distance separating them from most of their forebears and many of their Orthodox contemporaries. Indeed, the scholarly work of some of these Orthodox thinkers and of scholars within other camps is slowly leading to a realization that the classical tradition itself (even concerning many of the fundamentals of Jewish belief, such as the manner and content of revelation) was far less monolithic than is often claimed.

To be sure, there are no fundamentalists among the Reform; and presumably there are no humanists among the Orthodox. Nevertheless, the diversity in belief and in practice which characterizes each of the three major movements on the American Jewish religious scene is so broad that the differences within each of them appear at times to be as great as the differences between them. Indeed, rabbis within each of the three movements are occasionally heard to remark that they have more in common with some colleagues in the other two movements than with some in their own ranks.

5

To some extent, of course, dissatisfaction with the present division is inevitable, because no set of boundary lines is ever likely to win universal assent and because no group of people, even a homogeneous one, is likely to agree on all issues. But the present three-way division makes so little sense, is so confusing and unsatisfying that some sort of realignment is indicated. Perhaps several splits and mergers would give rise to a new picture that would be less frustrating and compromising, more satisfying and fruitful, and more understandable to all.

The rightists within the Conservative movement and the leftists within Orthodoxy have so much in common that they belong together, and would surely have long since merged—were it not for the presence of the leftists within Conservatism and the extreme rightists within Orthodoxy! And the rightists within Reform have so much in common with the leftists in the Conservative movement that they too belong together, and would long since have merged—were it not for the presence of the rightists within Conservatism and the extreme leftists within Reform! A realignment is accordingly very much in order, whereby the present tripartite structure would give way to a new four-way division—with an Extreme Right and an Extreme Left, a Right Center and a Left Center.

In such a realignment, what would be the differentiae of the four denominations?

Theologically, the Right Center and Left Center would be in agreement on their acceptance of the Living God of the Tradition—Creator, Revealer and Lawgiver, and Redeemer. But whereas the Right Center would view the Torah as the Word of God in all detail, written by human hand in human words but protected by divine guidance from all error and imperfection, the Left Center would view the Torah as *containing* the Word of God but not *constituting* the Word of God—and subject, therefore, in its human aspect, to error, inadequacy, and obsolescence. The Right Center would differ from the Extreme Right in its less literalist interpretation of the traditional descriptions of God's attributes; of God's relationship to the world, to humanity, and to Israel; and of the respective human and divine roles in the revelatory process. The Left Center would differ from the Extreme Left in its acceptance of a theistic position and its acknowledgment of a supernatural aspect to Torah.

The differences among the various groups with regard to Jewish practice flow naturally from their respective theological positions. The Right Center would be united in its acceptance of *halakhah,* the whole body of traditional Jewish law explicated in the Talmud, codified in the *Shulhan Arukh* and other codes, and applied to new problems and situations in the continuing stream of *Responsa.* It would consider this whole traditional pattern as binding in all detail, since it is in all detail God-ordained—whether directly, or indirectly through divine guidance of the holy chain of rabbinic explication—and commands not only that each area of life be hallowed but provides in detail each hallowed step along the way. (It would differ from the Extreme Right in its acceptance of a historical approach to the development of *halakhah,* in its greater acknowledgment of the realities and needs posed by the contemporary situation, and in its greater flexibility and creative application of halakhic norms in facing these realities and answering to these needs.) The position of the Left Center too would be based on *halakhah,* but in terms of *a halakhah* rather than *the halakhah.* That is, it would see itself bound by the main outlines of the traditional halakhic pattern, and further bound to live a Jewish life in full detail (one cannot live in outline), but with permission granted to reweave the traditional pattern, to select, adapt, and thus create a personal pattern. Though certain that God commands the hallowing of all of life, and that the main boundaries and signposts of life are set by God as well, the Left Center is not so sure that God has designated each step along the way. Rather, it believes that God allows a significant measure of freedom to each individual traveler along the way—who, to be sure, must not lose contact with the other travelers in the covenant band.[99] (The Left Center

99. Because of this element of voluntarism, the range of difference within the Left Center would of course be much greater than within the Right Center, but the range

would differ from the Extreme Left in its greater acceptance of both the binding character of the halakhic outlines and the larger number of traditional details; in the greater weight it would attach to matters involving personal status and acceptability to *kelal yisra'el;* and in its greater emphasis on the peoplehood aspect of *kelal yisra'el.*)[100]

Such a realignment into four rather than three denominations would be rational, intelligible, liberating, and fruitful. Is it at all likely?

Given the realities of the American Jewish religious establishment, with its varied vested interests—psychological, sociological, academic, political, and financial—the likelihood of such a realignment is minimal. The factions within Orthodoxy and within Reform, which fulfill a valuable internal function, would produce—if the bonds should be severed—mere proliferation. Only a split within Conservatism could open up realistic possibilities for a general thaw, which might, in turn, bring about a more fluid situation. Such a split, however, is hardly probable, although several halakhic decisions recently announced or under active consideration—in such areas as marriage and divorce, conversion, and the second day of the Festivals—make it remotely possible. An extreme formulation by the Conservatives, or an extreme reaction by the Orthodox, or some chance extraneous factor, might conceivably become the spark that could ignite the long-smothered impatience of the Conservative Left or the long-smoldering resentment of the Conservative Right, forces kept in check these many years largely through the astuteness and charisma of [Louis Finkelstein,] the Chancellor of the Jewish Theological Seminary.

But even if the proposed realignment is not likely to occur on the national level in the foreseeable future, the crucial issue remains, and can be faced, on the local level now: the issue of the covenant. Each local

would now be understandable and legitimate. It is also possible that a "Center-Center" group might emerge, which would normally accept the *halakhah* but would depart from it in rare instances where the resources within the halakhic system appeared inadequate to deal with a particularly urgent or crucial problem. But such an alignment would really not be necessary. The Right Center itself allows for emergency enactments and exceptions on the ground of *she'at ha-dehak, hora'at sha'ah,* and *et la-'asot la-shem.*

100. How the Reconstructionist movement would fit into this general picture is not easy to determine, since most of its spokesmen have articulated (as have many secularists) a strongly naturalist-humanist position on God, along with a strongly people-centered position on Israel. Its more theistically-inclined members would belong in the Left Center.

synagogue would do well to engage in serious soul-searching and self-analysis regarding the relation of the synagogue to the covenant people and the relation of the synagogue to the uncommitted within its own ranks. For until synagogue and people are again at one—which may well not occur until the messianic day—it is the synagogue that must guard the covenant vision, teach the covenant task, and live the covenant way. It would be tragic indeed if the synagogue, through misconceived expansionism and continued loss of identity, would blur that vision, neglect that task, and forsake that way. For granted that the synagogue, even by being true to itself, cannot bring the Messiah; nevertheless, by not being true to itself, it can delay the day and obscure the promise of his coming.

PRINCIPLES AND POLICIES
FOR THE IDEAL CONGREGATION

The ideal congregation, by definition, does not exist in the "real world." A description of an ideal congregation, however, has great relevance for "real" congregations, in at least three ways: (a) it reminds them of the goal toward which they should at all times be striving; (b) it helps them to assess the quality of their present congregational program; and (c) it helps them make the best (or the "least worst") choice among the options that are available at any given moment. What follows is a description of an ideal congregation as I envisage it.

I. THE CONGREGATIONAL PROGRAM

A. Guiding Principles

1. The Jewish tradition rooted in the Bible, explicated and expanded in the Talmud, and developed through the ages—should be the main source and framework for congregational policy and program, for synagogue practice, and for public and private Jewish living.

2. All programs, services, facilities, and activities provided or sponsored by the Congregation, or by any of its affiliates, should be directly related to the specific purposes and standards of the Congregation and to the content and spirit of the Jewish tradition.

3. The varying backgrounds, present situation, and acknowledged needs of the members, however, should be given weighty consideration in determining which of the vast resources of traditional Jewish teaching and practice are most relevant, applicable, feasible, and accessible to the particular group of Jews who are members of a particular congregation.

4. The Rabbi of the Congregation should be the acknowledged authority within the Congregation on all matters of Jewish teaching and practice, including those aspects of congregational management, administration, and programming upon which Jewish tradition has some bearing.

B. Basic Policies

1. The approval of the Rabbi shall be required for all projects, programs, services, and activities of the Congregation and its affiliates, and for the engagement and retention of all personnel.

2. As regards the ritual practice of the Congregation, policy shall be set by the Rabbi, after consultation with members and appropriate officers.

3. The study-and-teaching of Torah (interpreted broadly) shall be considered as one of the principal functions of the Congregation, and adequate provision—in terms of budget, staff, scheduling, publicity, etc.—shall be made for it, under the supervision of the Rabbi.

4. The Congregation shall, under the guidance of the Rabbi, lay stress upon the importance of striving to live a life of holiness on a personal, family, and communal level—and shall encourage its members to participate in efforts for community betterment, social justice, and reconciliation among the various divisions in the community. When deemed appropriate, it shall as a Congregation engage in such efforts.

5. The development of a sense of holy fellowship shall be considered as one of the main purposes of congregational life. Rather than seeking such fellowship too directly, however, the Congregation shall aim for the realization of such fellowship through the shared efforts and experiences of members who work together in worthwhile congregational pursuits.

6. Special attention shall be given to the needs of specific categories of members—such as children (preschool and school age), youth, young marrieds, parents of school children, men as men and women as women, the aged, etc.—but care shall be taken not to overstructure, oversegregate, or overemphasize artificial or irrelevant divisions among members.

7. If the Rabbi ceases to be acknowledged by the Congregation as its authority on Jewish teaching and practice, he shall not seek to remain in his position, nor shall his services as Rabbi be retained.

II. CONGREGATIONAL MEMBERSHIP AND LEADERSHIP

A. Guiding Principles

1. Membership in any organization or institution should presuppose an acceptance of the purposes of that organization or institution.

2. A congregation is intended to be a holy fellowship of Jews who accept for their own personal lives the basic purposes of a synagogue: the regular study-and-teaching of Torah; the regular worship of God in the Jewish mode, and the celebration of prescribed moments in the day, week, month, year, and life cycle; the regular practice of justice and love; and the regular sharing of concern and effort on behalf of the covenant people Israel.

3. Membership in a synagogue should therefore involve an acceptance of these purposes, standards, and goals and a commitment to strive to live by them.

4. Leadership of a synagogue should presuppose a higher-than-average degree of commitment: the higher the position of leadership, the higher the degree of commitment.

B. Basic Policies

1. Charter members shall adopt a statement of congregational purposes and standards for Jewish living that will serve as a general guide (with specific illustrations) for themselves and for future members in making their membership commitment.

2. Membership shall be open to all Jews who acknowledge these purposes, accept these standards, and undertake this commitment—if not as present accomplishment, then as firm intention and resolve.

3. There shall be no discrimination, whether in membership status or ritual privilege-and-obligation, on grounds of financial means or support, longtime residence, past service, sex, or age above thirteen.

4. Those who are not ready to acknowledge these purposes, accept these standards, or undertake this commitment—and who thus do not qualify for membership—shall nevertheless be welcome, at

all times and at no charge, to participate fully in all services, programs, and activities, and to avail themselves freely of staff and facilities, except that where not all can be accommodated, preference shall be given to members.

5. Membership enrollment efforts shall include periodic invitation to both new and longtime residents of the community to consider affiliation, and shall also include periodic self-review by presently affiliated members as to their qualification for continued membership.

6. Positions of leadership shall be offered only to those who signify their acceptance of a higher standard of commitment than is expected of the average member.

7. The statement of purposes and standards, and the guide for membership commitment, shall be periodically reviewed and, if necessary, be reformulated—with an eye both to raising standards and commitment and to encouraging new affiliations.

III. CONGREGATIONAL FINANCING

A. Guiding Principles

1. Financial support of a synagogue is primarily the obligation of those who accept the commitment of membership.

2. Secondarily, it is the obligation of those who, whether members or nonmembers, avail themselves of its services, program, staff, and facilities.

3. Thirdly, it is the obligation of those who, while neither accepting the commitment of membership nor availing themselves directly of its program or facilities, nevertheless acknowledge the validity of its purposes, the importance of its availability, or the significance of its existence.

4. The measure of financial support should depend upon such factors as one's means, the intensity of one's participation in its program, and the degree of importance one attaches to its purposes.

5. Since these factors vary greatly from one person to another (and indeed even for the same person, from one time to another), and since they cannot easily be measured, and since the responsibility of synagogue support is a very personal responsibility, a synagogue should neither impose uniform financial obligations, nor assign members to varying categories of financial obligation, but should depend exclusively upon voluntary support for meeting all of its financial needs.

B. Basic Policies

1. There shall be no required dues, tuitions, assessments, fees, charges, etc. except perhaps a token membership registration fee.

2. All income shall be derived from voluntary pledges of support (in specific amounts) for the next fiscal year, and from any additional contributions and freewill donations that are forthcoming—with no public announcement or other publicity of the names of any supporters or contributors.

3. There shall be no financial campaigns, drives, or appeals—except for the calm, reasoned, and dignified presentation of the needs of the present and proposals for the future, and an invitation for support of these by those who acknowledge their validity and importance.

4. There shall be no sales, raffles, benefits, journals, or profit-making dances, parties, events, affairs, etc.—in a word, no fund raising.

5. Only those congregational programs shall be undertaken, and only those congregational financial commitments shall be made, as shall be covered by advance pledges and likely contribution—in a word, no deficit financing.

HOW SHALL A BELIEVING JEW
VIEW CHRISTIANITY?

1

The relationship between Judaism and Christianity is, on a theological level, essentially ambiguous. The relationship between individual Jews and Christians is, on a psychological level, almost inevitably ambivalent. And the relationship between the Jewish and Christian communities has been, on the historical level, so frequently marked by Christian persecution, by Jewish fear, and by mutual hostility, suspicion, and mistrust that it is inherently problematical. No wonder, then, that through the ages Jews and Christians have almost never been in a position to confront squarely or explore fruitfully the true nature of their relationship. Indeed, our own age may be the very first in which such confrontation and exploration are possible. And even for us, any chance that the problems can be solved and the ambivalence resolved depends on whether the basic ambiguity can be clarified.

2

The heart of the ambiguity in the relationship between Judaism and Christianity is the dual reality of their similarity and difference.

The similarities are numerous and basic, flowing from the common acceptance of the Hebrew Scriptures as Holy Scriptures: e.g., the common affirmation of the Creator God who formed the universe by His will and the human being in His image; who established His covenant with the children of Israel and redeemed them from bondage; who revealed His word and will at Sinai; who gives commands to human beings, judges, rewards and punishes them, and forgives them when they truly repent; who hears their prayers and responds; and who promises a messianic era of judgment and redemption.

In the face of such mighty similarities, shall we say perhaps that the two religions are really but variants of one religion, and that any differences between them are but minor? But how can we possibly say so, once we even begin to set forth the differences: on the one hand, Christ and his Universal Church; on the other hand, the people Israel and the Law? Surely, the inherent duality of relationship between Judaism and Christianity—however puzzling it is—must be maintained: the two faiths are at once fundamentally similar and fundamentally different!

3

Were we dealing with an exclusively historical phenomenon or an entirely theoretical issue, this duality of relationship, though it might intrigue us, would not trouble us. What makes us troubled—religiously disturbed and psychologically ambivalent—is that issues of existential truth are at stake. As a believing Jew, I know that God, through the covenant that He has made with my people Israel and through the Torah-of-truth that He has given us, has revealed all that human beings need to know about Him and about our relationship to Him and to each other. Why, then, should there be another covenant and another revelation? Even assuming that somehow I could come to terms with such duplication, what if that second covenant, that second revelation, affirms something that is *not* included in my original covenant (e.g., that God was in Christ, that the Messiah has come) and denies something that *is* included (e.g., that Israel's Law is still binding, that it is a fully adequate channel of God's word and of His love)? How can such a second covenant be equally valid? Yet Christianity claims its covenant with the same one God to be of equal—indeed of superior—validity with Israel's own covenant!

Must I, therefore, as a believing Jew, deny the Christian claim and impugn the full validity of Christianity, granting only its partial validity? ("What is true in Christianity is not new, and what is new is not true.") Or is there another possible approach to the two faiths, whereby their respective claims to full validity can both be accommodated?

Let us explore the rationale for each of the covenants—and see.

4

Why the covenant with Israel?

God's original hope—it is clear from the Torah—was that through creation-in-His-image all human beings would not only know right from wrong but would consistently choose the right, simultaneously advancing God's purpose and promoting their own true well-being. The biblical stories of the Garden of Eden and of Cain and Abel are parables of the frustration of God's hope; hence, the Flood and the subsequent establishment of the covenant with Noah and the new humankind. But human beings again showed themselves to be sinful (witness the story of the Tower of Babel), too unaccepting of God's authority, too unmindful of His word, too ready to deface the image in which they were created.

It is at this point that God establishes His covenant with Abraham—singling out one person and his descendants; concentrating, as it were, upon one family of humankind; providing the seed of Abraham with a fuller measure of instruction and guidance, demands and discipline ("to keep the way of *YHVH*, doing righteousness and justice")—not to the detriment or neglect of the rest of humanity, however, but to their greater benefit ("through you shall all the nations of the world be blessed"). At Sinai, the covenant was renewed and confirmed with the entire people Israel, called to be a "kingdom of priests and a holy nation," to serve—as later prophets declared—as God's light and witness to the nations, until the day when all would acknowledge the one true God.

5

But what of those individuals among the nations who, drawn by that light and example, wished immediately to cast off the idolatries and immoralities of paganism and to take upon themselves immediately "the yoke of the kingship of heaven" and "to keep the way of *YHVH*"? Was such a course possible, was such a step permissible? There are clear indications—in the Hebrew Scriptures to some extent, in the New Testament and contemporary writings to a greater extent—that not only was it possible and permissible for non-Israelites to join the covenant community of Israel, but that many actually did so. (There is some evidence that on occasion, there were even missionary efforts on the part of Jews.) Indeed, according to the estimates—perhaps exaggerated—of some historians, at one point as many as ten percent of the inhabitants of the Roman Empire were Jewish!

To convert to Judaism, however, meant not only to affirm one's personal faith in *YHVH,* the one true God of Israel, but to become part of the *people* Israel and to accept the discipline of Israel's entire regimen of holy living—including circumcision, *kashrut, Shabbat,* etc. Not all who were attracted by the light of the Torah found themselves able to make such a complete commitment. It thus came about, around the turn of our era, that in addition to those who actually became full-fledged members of the House of Israel, there were countless others who surrendered their pagan ways and became "fearers of *YHVH*." But, although those who came near in these two ways—either through full conversion or through acceptance of something less—numbered in the hundreds of thousands, they obviously constituted but a small fraction of humankind.

The Christian claim is that at this juncture in history—about two thousand years ago—the same one true God who had long before revealed Himself to the people Israel then decided to reveal Himself—or perhaps had decided long before to reveal Himself at that time—in the Christ Event, establishing the new covenant. Through this new covenant in Christ—so Christianity claims—God has now made available to all humankind His word and way, His love and forgiveness, true salvation and redemption.

6

How shall a believing Jew respond to this central Christian claim?

It would seem apparent that as a Jew, he cannot acknowledge its truth. From the Torah text-and-tradition he knows that God's covenant with Israel is forever valid; from his personal appropriation of the central events of his people's past—again and again being redeemed from bondage, again and again receiving the Torah—he knows that this covenant is real; from his daily personal experience he knows that this covenant is adequate. Whatever is claimed by the Christian to be provided through Christ, the Jew had already received a thousand years and more before the Christ of Christians ever appeared. Christ fulfills no need for the Jew and offers him nothing new. How, then, *could* a Jew possibly acknowledge the validity of the Christian claim?

And yet, cannot a believing Jew grant the possibility that what is not new to the Jew—or even addressed to him—might yet involve something new when addressed to others? Can a Jew not grant the possibility (as Rosenzweig and Herberg have taught) that an alternate form of God's covenant with Israel was now being made available to the rest of humanity?[101] This new (form of the) covenant would be with the same one-and-only God of Israel; those who would enter it through accepting Christ (the one-man embodiment of Israel) would thereby become linked to the people Israel—but as a denationalized, de-ethnicized, de-particularized form of Israel. (Christians sometimes speak of themselves as the "New Israel" or "Spiritual Israel.") The role of this new (branch of) Israel would be to go forth to the ends of the earth and seek to spread the new

---

101. See Will Herberg, "Christianity and Judaism: Their Unity and Difference," *Journal of Bible and Religion* 21:2 (April 1953) for an incisive analysis and creative extension of Rosenzweig's seminal thinking on this whole subject. I am deeply indebted to, and have borrowed from, Herberg's presentation.

(form of the) covenant—the denationalized Torah way of the Lord—and thus through Christ, bring all humankind to the God of Israel. The role of the original people Israel ("Israel of the flesh") would be to remain identifiably apart in holy separation—continuing to be faithful to the original (form of the) covenant, continuing to serve as a living model of holy community: a community of true righteousness and justice, true love and compassion.

7

Herein lies the key to the mysterious phenomenon of the basic similarity-and-difference between Christianity and Judaism. All of the genuine differences between them—major and minor, obvious and subtle—can be seen, upon careful examination, to stem from this fundamental difference of role in the divine purpose and of situation in the world.

One crucial set of differences stems directly from the differing nature of the two *vehicles* of revelation: in the one case, the *people* Israel, bearers of the Torah; in the other case, the *person* of Christ, one-man embodiment of Israel and the Torah. Through their respective vehicles, Judaism and Christianity affirm, God makes known His word and will and way, His resources and even His indwelling presence. ("I shall dwell in the midst of Israel"; "God was in Christ.") In both cases the recipients of the revelation are, through that very revelation, constituted into a community. Yet the nature of the community and the manner of entering are significantly different. In the case of Judaism the members are normally *born into* the covenant community (except for occasional converts), as are also therefore their brothers and sisters and cousins. The Jewish community thus has an ethnic base; the intense we-feeling is almost familial; the pattern of Jewish holiness has a group reference and dimension. In the case of Christianity, since the members of the covenant community identify with each other and with God through the person of Christ, their religious identity, though not lacking a group dimension, tends to be more individualized and privatized—and so too, their life of prayer, their sense of sin, their yearning for forgiveness, their awareness of God's judgment and love, and their vision of salvation. Similarly even with the hope for life after death. For the Jew, the grounds for that hope are through the Torah granted to the people Israel; fulfillment of that hope is envisioned as a function of the vindication and redemption of Israel; and the locale of that fulfillment is identified as the (perhaps expanded) land of Israel. (The vision of the dry bones in Ezekiel is extremely apt in its portrayal of the resurrection of individuals as an expression of the revival of the people.) For the Christian, that hope—grounded as it is in the resurrection of the person of Christ—tends to highlight his own individual resurrection.

8

A second set of differences relates to "the Law." Law has various meanings, and in assessing the alleged differences between Judaism and Christianity with regard to the Law, it is important to distinguish among them.

Law in the sense of "ritual law"—*kashrut,* circumcision, and *Shabbat,* for example—which serves as a constant reminder of God's covenant with the people Israel and as a means for distinguishing that people from the other peoples of the world, would obviously not be appropriate for the New Israel, which was meant to encompass all peoples. (The word *ot,* sign, when used in connection with circumcision and *Shabbat,* and the word *kadosh,* set-apart-as-holy, when used in connection with *Shabbat* and *kashrut,* both involve consecration, not only in the usual meanings of holiness but also in the sense of separation and distinctiveness.) In this first usage of the term "law," therefore, it is correct to say that the Law constitutes a significant difference between Judaism and Christianity. (Christianity, of course, gradually developed its own body of ritual law, which serves to distinguish Christians from non-Christians.)

With regard to law in the sense of "moral law," the two faiths agree that it is essential to the life of holiness. Yet the claim is often made that in their approaches to the moral law the two faiths are radically different. Judaism—it is claimed—is characterized by a stress upon divine sternness of command and human dread of punishment for the constant failure to fulfill the ever-present "thou shalts" and "thou shalt nots"—and that Judaism is therefore plagued with a grim preoccupation with a "bookkeeping morality" of debits and credits, and casuistic concern with the technicalities of the forbidden and the permitted. In sharp contrast—it is claimed—is the Christian emphasis on love: God's love for humanity, human love of God, and the love of human beings for one another. Is there anything to this claim? For the most part, such a contrast is ridiculously (and unlovingly!) false. On the one hand, the Hebrew Scriptures—which are presumably the source of this supposed Jewish overemphasis on strict moral law—are also filled with passages about this very threefold love! (Indeed, the original source of Christian teaching about love is in those very Jewish Scriptures!) On the other hand, the New Testament places great emphasis on certain "thou shalts" and "thou shalt nots," stressing, at least as strongly as does Judaism, their absoluteness and bindingness, and the dire consequences of their violation or inadequate fulfillment. Furthermore, a major branch of Christianity has been characterized by a highly developed body of canon law and a whole tradition of casuistic interpretation. Nevertheless, there is perhaps a grain of truth in the alleged difference between the two faiths regarding the moral law. In the Christian situation, partly because of the keen expectation among the earliest Christians of the imminent return of Christ and partly because of the emphasis on conversion through the personal acceptance of Christ as lord and savior, the stance has tended to be "charismatic"; in the Jewish situation, partly because of the group dimension of the holy life and partly because of the assumption that life in the present world-and-age would continue indefinitely, the stance tended to be halakhic[102]—and in the halakhic perspective each act *does* have definite social obligations, and each particular situation *does* call for careful scrutiny before a decision is made and for genuine accountability afterward.

With regard to law in the sense of "legalism," it is sometimes claimed that Judaism urges—regarding both ritual and moral law—strict adherence merely to the letter of the law, punctilious observance solely of externals, mechanical performance by rote—in contrast to a Christian emphasis upon the spirit of the law and upon reverent inwardness. This supposed difference, like the previous one, is basically false; indeed it constitutes more of a caricature than a characterization of Judaism. On the level of general principle, Judaism urges the importance of *kavvanah,* direction of the heart to the loving fulfillment of the divine command and the joyful performance of God's will. On the level of actual practice, Christians—no less than Jews—must be assumed to be subject to the peril of rote prayer and routinized ritual, of grudging performance of moral obligations, and of hypocritical words and deeds. It may well be, however—because of the larger scope of Jewish ritual and the greater emphasis on the group dimension of life—that there is greater *resort* to law in Judaism and, hence, greater *risk* that law may degenerate into legalism.

---

102. See Monford Harris, "*Halakhah* and Charisma," *Judaism* 1:1 (January 1952) for the very suggestive use and development of these terms. See also his two further articles, "The Bifurcated Life," *Judaism* 8:2 (Spring 1957) and "Interim Theology," *Judaism* 7:4 (Fall 1958).

There is still another sense of "law" wherein Judaism and Christianity are said to differ: law in the sense of "social justice," "law and order." Is there any basis for the widespread view that Judaism sees the stability and viability of any social order as dependent upon just law, whereas Christianity sees as sufficient the simple practice of love among its members? As regards Christianity, it is true, once again, that because the earliest Christians felt sure of Christ's imminent return, with its messianic dissolution of human government, that they could afford, in the short run, to "render unto Caesar that which is Caesar's," could preoccupy themselves with the spread of the Gospel, and could depend upon the resources of the loving community. As the hope for an early return diminished, however, Christianity came to accept the need for government and enforceable justice on a continuing basis. (Through the centuries Christians have had to face—but perhaps have never fully resolved—the question of how great should be their involvement as Christians in the governance of society, and how great their responsibility.) As regards Judaism, it is true that whenever Jews have lived in their own land, or in other lands where they had a large degree of autonomy, they have recognized as central to their task of holy living the establishment of a just social order in accordance with Torah law. (When under the jurisdiction of non-Jewish governments, Jews have had to face the question of whether and to what extent they were still bound by the civil and criminal laws of the Torah; often the "law of the land" has come to displace—or, more exactly, to suspend—the laws of the Torah.) In this sense alone one can say that Judaism has stressed justice over love. It has recognized that although ideally, love transcends justice, in the absence of a just government that protects basic rights and imposes basic obligations, complete dependence upon personal love will almost inevitably result in tyrannical subjugation of the weak by the strong—for the temptation to sin is ever present.

9

Another issue that is often said to constitute a crucial difference between Judaism and Christianity is the belief in original sin. Christianity is inherently pessimistic about human beings—it is claimed—because it recognizes, even emphasizes, that all human beings are under the burden and taint of the original sin of Adam and Eve, and are therefore bound to sin. Judaism—it is claimed—by not accepting this doctrine remains inherently optimistic.

To what extent is this contrast valid? It cannot be denied that certain Christian formulations of the doctrine of original sin do insist that every human being must inevitably sin. Other Christian formulations, however, make a significant distinction: in theory, no human being needs to sin; in practice, all human beings known to us actually do. Each moment in life presents one with the theoretical possibility of avoiding sin; the possibility turns out, however, to be an "impossible possibility." In any case, whether or not authentic Christianity draws such a distinction, authentic Judaism does: since every human being bears the image of God, every one is endowed with genuine freedom to choose between right and wrong—and thus to avoid sin; in actuality, however, "there is no righteous person upon the face of the earth who lives and does not sin," and "the inclination of the human heart is evil from his youth, only evil all day long [or, every day]." As Buber puts it, every person sins "not *because,* but *as,* Adam sinned."

The emphasis upon this "inclination to evil" *(yetzer ha-ra)*—its power, its constancy, its universality and ubiquity, its insidiousness—has been very great in the Jewish tradition, even though in contemporary Jewish teaching it is often slighted and, consciously or subconsciously, largely censored out. And yet, with all of its stress on the *yetzer ha-ra,* Judaism has not succumbed to despair about humanity—because it has insisted that humanity need not succumb to the *yetzer ha-ra*! Judaism has taught that the same God who created in humankind the temptation to evil has provided Israel with the antidote to that temptation: the Torah. Through the Torah the human inclination to good *(yetzer ha-tov)* can be nourished and strengthened; through the Torah not only can a person learn the good but can be fortified to do it. The life of holiness and righteousness—good deeds performed with pure intention—although not *guaranteed* by study of Torah remains, in principle, a genuine possibility. Through the Torah, which not only contains God's word but harbors God's presence and conveys God-given strength, human beings can be delivered from the power of the sinful inclination. And even when one momentarily succumbs to the *yetzer ha-ra,* he can—by availing himself of the resources available in the Torah—turn back to God in repentance *(teshuvah);* and having truly repented, he is purified from sin and is granted atonement.

10

"Purification," "atonement," and "deliverance from sin" lead us to another alleged contrast between the two traditions: the contrast between faith and works. In Christianity—it is argued—the sole basis for hope, the sole key to salvation, is belief in Jesus Christ ("believe and you shall be saved"); the basis for hope in Judaism—it is argued—is the individual's own record of righteous deeds, his faithful fulfillment of God's commandments ("behave and you shall be saved"). This contrast is so widely accepted and so emphatically stated—by Jew and Christian alike—that it would seem to be undeniable; yet it actually represents a distortion of both faiths. On the one hand, Judaism does *not* teach that an individual has a right to count on God's approval and vindication simply on the basis of his own accomplishments, standing on the record of his own achievements. On the other hand, does authentic Christianity really teach—in spite of some of its extreme formulations—that an individual may count on salvation through Christ regardless of whether he *willfully* spurns God's commandments and *regardless of whether he repents?* Indeed, not only do many Christian formulations stress human behavior as the test of true belief, but they often make clear that the very forgiveness of sins made available through the death and resurrection of Christ is intended for *repentant* sinners and is efficacious only upon their contrite acknowledgment of their sin.

11

But even if these alleged contrasts are seen to be grossly exaggerated and largely invalid, is it not true, nevertheless, that in their general perspectives on life and the world Judaism and Christianity are basically different? Is it not true that Judaism is this-worldly and Christianity otherworldly? Does not Judaism stress the bodily and the material, and Christianity the spiritual? Does not Judaism exalt the rational, Christianity the mystical? And don't all of these together constitute a crucial and fundamental difference?

Let it be granted that since Christians in the earliest years—as we have had occasion to note already several times—looked for an early reappearance of Christ and the speedy establishment of the messianic kingdom, many of the above tendencies did indeed characterize early Christianity. What need to be concerned for history (any more than for government), for physical well-being and economic sustenance, for marrying-and-begetting, for the problems of this world—when the end of history and the beginning of a transformed world with a transformed humanity were at hand? (A very similar spirit and outlook has characterized those occasional moments over the course of Jewish history when the coming of the

Messiah was believed to be imminent.) Since that early period of Christianity, however, these alleged contrasts between the two faiths are valid only in the sense that they represent slight differences in emphasis and tones—except with regard to the issue of body vs. soul and material vs. spiritual. For here it is true that Christianity has often been subject to mystical and Greek philosophical influences that have tended to denigrate, deny, and suppress the bodily, the sexual, and the material. Often, however, Christianity remained true to the Hebraic acceptance of body-and-soul—or more correctly, to the Hebraic affirmation of the worth, unity, and potential sacredness of the whole person. (It is also true, however, that foreign influences have similarly crept into Judaism, intro-ducing a tendency—sometimes widespread—toward asceticism, morti-fication of the flesh, and a sharp dichotomy between body and soul.)

As regards this-worldliness vs. otherworldliness, Judaism—though it has, as we have seen, sometimes given more attention than did Christian-ity to the establishment and maintenance of a just social order—has actually been as much concerned, after the biblical period, with the world-to-come as with this world. ("This world is like a vestibule before the world-to-come; prepare yourself in the vestibule, so that you may enter the dining hall.") And Christianity, in spite of its great concern for the "heavenly city," has in most periods also been deeply concerned for the this-worldly condition of individuals and groups. More often than not, both faiths have kept both worlds within the purview of their concern, sharing the conviction that this world is crucial as the time-and-place for striving to live the life of holiness, and that the world-to-come is crucial as the time-and-place for facing the full consequences of the faithfulness and faithlessness of that striving. Both faiths have also affirmed the possibil-ity—and have provided the "means"—of receiving at least a glimpse and foretaste, in this world and in this life, of that which in full measure is reserved for the life of the world-to-come.[103]

As regards "rational vs. mystical," the situation in both faith traditions is almost identical; both include teachings and teachers that are rational-istic and others that are mystical. When they are to be counted within the mainstream of authentic Judaism and Christianity, however, all will be found to make—explicitly or implicitly—this threefold affirmation: a)

---

103. For a summary and interpretation of Jewish teaching on this subject see above, "An Outline of Jewish Eschatology."

that human reason is one of the primary means with which God has endowed humanity for understanding God's teaching and design, and the human role and task in the world; b) that human reason alone, however, can never grasp the vastness of God's creation or the wisdom and greatness of His ways—and certainly not the profundity of His thoughts or the nature of His being; and c) that nevertheless God grants us the ability to perceive—through a dimension of knowledge beyond the rational—a measure of the mystery and miracle of His creation, His revelation, and His redemption.

12

Inclusion of "mystery" and "miracle" as elements common to Judaism and Christianity may come as a surprise to some, for it is often alleged that Judaism, unlike Christianity, places no great stress upon the miraculous. No one, of course, denies that accounts of miracles occur in the Hebrew Scriptures, but—it is argued—miracles play no *central* role in Judaism, and belief in them certainly does not constitute a dogma. In fact—it is claimed—Judaism has no dogmas. In one sense, this is certainly true: the denial of any particular belief, such as the belief in miracles—or even the denial of all belief—does not call into question one's status as a member of the Jewish people, as it does in the case of membership in many Christian churches. In that sense it is correct to say that Judaism, unlike Christianity, is not a dogmatic or creedal religion.[104] In the sense of centrality to the pattern of traditional faith, however, miracle is as important in Judaism as in Christianity! The belief in God as Creator of the universe and humanity, as Redeemer of Israel, as Giver of the Torah-and-*mitzvot*—these are as pivotal and as miraculous in traditional Judaism as are the Incarnation and Resurrection in Christianity. Concerning the other miracles recounted in Scripture and in the postbiblical tradition, varying versions of Judaism (as of Christianity) accept them in varying degrees of literalness and authoritativeness; but that God is in principle *able* to perform—directly, through His own act, or indirectly, through any of His creatures (including humans)—*any* act that He *wills* (except an act involving a genuine self-contradiction) is stoutly affirmed by any authentic version of Judaism. (If He *could* not, He would not be the God of the Torah.)

---

104. For a further discussion of this issue see above, "Dogmas in Judaism."

But note: this means that from the point of view of Judaism even the miracles that in the New Testament are said to have been performed by Jesus—such as curing the "incurable," multiplying quantities of food, walking on water—are theoretically possible. Judaism, far from denying, must insist on affirming that God could perform them!

Whether God not only could but actually did bring about these particular miracles of Jesus is, of course, another question, but even to this question a believing Jew need not, on grounds of Jewish faith, necessarily answer "no." For one thing, there are parallels to these New Testament miracles in the Hebrew Bible, where they are portrayed as brought about by God through human agents such as Moses, Aaron, Elijah, and Elisha. Besides, there are numerous instances through the ages—and even in our own age—where events that had been totally unexpected, previously considered impossible, contrary to what were held to be the immutable "laws of nature"—have nevertheless actually occurred. They are perceived as miracles when the power and wisdom and love of God are seen to be at work on our behalf.[105] That such miracles may have been performed by Jesus *need* not be *denied* by a believing Jew.

13

But a much more fundamental issue now presents itself, one that *would* seem to constitute a crucial difference between Judaism and Christianity: the issue not of miracles performed *by* Jesus but of miracles performed *in* Jesus; not what he is said to have done but what he is said to have been. We speak now of such central and distinctive Christian beliefs as the Virgin Birth, Incarnation, Resurrection, Christ as Savior, and the Trinity. These certainly mark the dividing line between the two faiths. To the vast majority of people—except for occasional Jewish converts to Christianity (who claim that as "Jewish—or Hebrew—Christians" they remain Jewish though having accepted Christ) and except for occasional halakhic theorists (who claim that even a Jew who has sinned through apostasy remains a Jew)—it seems self-evident that no Jew can make such basic Christian affirmations and remain a Jew.

Granted, then, that a Jew cannot affirm such miracles. But need he deny them? We ask now, concerning these miracles that are at the heart of Christian faith, the same question that we have asked twice before: does Jewish nonaffirmation of their truth require affirmation of their falsehood?

105. See above, "Miracle and *Berakhah.*"

As already implied in the preceding discussion of miracles alleged to have been performed *by* Jesus, a believing Jew need not necessarily deny even these miracles alleged to have been performed *in* Christ—at least in their visible, outer form. Surely the theoretical possibility that God could (if He so willed) cause conception to occur without the agency of a human male, or the dead to live again, is not a contradiction but an affirmation of Jewish faith. (Indeed, that God will in the future raise the dead to life is not only affirmed in several passages of the Hebrew Scriptures but in talmudic Judaism is affirmed to be an essential "article of faith": "One who says that the resurrection of the dead is not derived from the Torah has no share in the world-to-come!") But even the historicity of such wonders need not necessarily be denied by a believing Jew. After all, if the dead were revived in the time of Elijah and Elisha, why may the dead not have been revived in the time of Jesus?

This, of course, misses the point of the central Christian miracles. The point is not their mere occurrence but their significance, not their outer manner but their inner meaning, not their empirical verifiability but their religious authenticity. But as soon as we speak of inner meaning and religious authenticity, we are in the realm of personal, existential appropriation: "the knowing in faith." And in this realm the whole notion of affirmation or denial by one person of the faith-knowledge of another is inappropriate, pointless, and even ridiculous. The question of whether "God was in Christ, reconciling the world to Himself," whether God (the Father, First Person of the Trinity) has through Christ (His uniquely born Son, Second Person of the Trinity)—and since Pentecost, through the Holy Spirit (Third Person of the Trinity)—provided love and forgiveness, light and truth, salvation and redemption, the key and way to eternal life—such a question is, for the Jew, not a meaningful question at all, and is therefore not *possible* for a Jew to answer, affirmatively *or* negatively! The most that a Jew can do—and while this "most" is less than some Christians would like, it is more than some Jews would like—is to acknowledge that in the lives of countless men and women who profess Christ the power and presence of God appear to be evident.

14

But doesn't the word "Christ" itself bring us to the point where a Jew must go beyond mere noncommitment concerning the Christian claim? After all, since "christ" means the anointed Messiah, in affirming Christ the Christian affirms that the Messiah has come. The Jew, however, has a vivid picture of what the coming of the Messiah entails: the end of war, poverty, suffering, sin, and death; the resurrection of the dead; the ingathering of scattered Israel to the land of Israel and the rebuilding of the Holy Temple in Jerusalem; the final judgment, involving reward and punishment; the inauguration of the true community of humankind, where perfect justice and love and true fellowship are an enduring reality; in a word, the establishment of the Kingdom and Kingship of God upon earth. In the face of the Christian claim that the Messiah has come, must not the Jew insist that he has not?

How would Christianity respond to this challenge? Not by rejecting as incorrect or irrelevant the above Jewish description of the messianic era, for Christianity shares the same vision. And surely not by claiming that such messianic fulfillment is manifestly here! Rather, by referring the Jewish challenger to the Christian doctrine of the Second Coming—when Christ in all his glory will, at history's culmination, return and visibly usher in that fulfillment. But if the fulfillment must wait until that Second Coming—the Jew will ask—what was the purpose and meaning of that First Coming two thousand years ago The Christian answer is: to mediate to humankind the reality both of God's judgment and His gracious, sacrificial love; to implant in their hearts the vision of the final day; to teach them, by precept and example, how to prepare for that day and how to hasten its coming; and to provide, within believing hearts and faithful communities, a foretaste here-and-now of the love and peace that constitute the messianic reality.

15

This explication of the roles of Christianity and Judaism does not, of course, alter the faith affirmations of either one. It does, however, disclose a striking parallel: not only the messianic vision, but almost all else too that the Christian becomes heir to through the new covenant of Christ, and the community that professes Christ, is—as we have seen—strikingly similar to what the Jew became heir to long before, through God's original covenant with the people Israel when they received the Torah. A host of terms are common to the two traditions, referring in the one case to Israel-and-the-Torah, and in the other case to Christ and the Church: covenant, cornerstone, the word, the way, the truth, the light, firstborn son, witness, chosen one, suffering servant of the Lord, beloved one, anointed, God's dwelling place, key to life eternal. Again, even these breathtaking parallels do not, in the slightest degree, persuade the Jew to "accept Christ" nor the

Christian to "surrender Christ." They can nevertheless remind the Christian that God's covenant with His people Israel abides unbroken, and remind the Jew that God's covenant promise and providence have been opened up to extend beyond the people Israel.[106]

Israel and the Church of Christ: how different they are in role and situation—and yet how similar in their common source, their common teaching, their common commitment, and their common goal. Until the messianic goal is achieved, they must remain separate—to some extent blind to each other's true nature and to the full measure of each other's validity. (The Christian cannot grasp the full adequacy of the old covenant; the Jew cannot grasp the full meaning of the new.) But together they can, and are obliged to, both work and wait for the coming of the promised Messiah. (Each must be careful not to become so preoccupied with the working as to disdain the waiting, nor to become so preoccupied with the waiting as to shirk the working.) And together they can cherish the certainty—since each knows that God has promised but one Messiah—that he whose second coming is awaited by the Christian and he whose (first) coming is awaited by the Jew will be seen, when he comes, to have the same face.

---

106. We must reserve for separate treatment two important related questions: a) whether, in principle, there could be not only a dual form of the covenant but multiple forms; and b) if the answer is "yes," whether—and if so, to what extent—Islam, being the only other religion that is a direct offshoot of Judaism, constitutes a valid third form.

SHOULD CHRISTMAS MEAN
ANYTHING TO JEWS?

Does Christmas mean anything to Jews? Does it involve us or affect us at all? For most Jews, in some obvious senses it does. As Jews living among a Christian majority, we cannot help being aware of Christmas and having reactions to it. For some Jews (as, of course, for many non-Jews) a sizable part of their year's income depends on it. Some Jews resent it—because of its pagan antecedents, traditional theology, or contemporary commercialization. Some Jews rejoice in their Christian neighbors' rejoicing on that day; some Jews are touched by the mood and message of that day; and some Jews, defying both the preachment of their rabbis and the disapproval of their fellow Jews, even observe it!

But *should* Christmas mean anything to Jews, to Jews *as Jews?* Before we can adequately answer this question, we must ask ourselves what Christmas means to Christians. To Christians *as Christians* surely it is more than a day for trees and gifts and parties, songs and Santa Claus. Is it not rather the anniversary of the birth of him who is for them the Christ, the Messiah, the anointed one who has come?

But for us Jews the Messiah has obviously not yet come. In our eyes the coming of the Messiah represents the kind of fulfillment and perfection, the kind of deliverance and salvation, that involves the end of war and suffering, of poverty and illness, of hatred and cruelty; it involves healing and wholeness, absolute justice and love, true fellowship and harmony, true *shalom.* To the Christian, therefore, who asks us how we can *not* accept Christ and Christmas, we Jews must respond by asking how he can. To the Christian who asks: "How can you be so blind as not to say the Messiah has come?" we must reply: "How can you be so blind as to say he has?!"

The truly believing and informed Christian will of course know how to answer our challenging question. He will say: "What you describe as the Coming of the Messiah is what we call his Second Coming, not yet accomplished—promised by God, confidently awaited by us."

What then do Christians mean by the First Coming? What is the significance for them of the one whose birth is observed on Christmas Day? Christians see in the Christ Event—the birth and life and death and resurrection of Jesus—the supreme example of God's mighty acts of salvation, through which and through whom God's power and love and grace and word and way and light and forgiveness have been existentially made known to them. It is through Christ—in his First Coming—that they receive the content and the means, the wherewithal, for living in proper relation to God and human beings; it is through Christ that the Christian is entered into the covenant; it is through the First Coming of Christ that the Christian receives the promise and assurance of the Second Coming.

But such a Christ, even with all that is made available through him to the Christian, is not needed by us Jews; he is not sent to us; he is not addressed to us; he offers us nothing. Not because what is provided through Christ to the non-Jew is not necessary also for us Jews (God forbid!), but because all that is offered through Christ had already long before Christ been made available to us—through the covenant with Abraham, the covenant of Sinai, the covenant of the Torah. (Not that we have always been fully loyal and faithful to that covenant between God and Israel; far from it, alas; but the reality and the riches of the covenant word and way have always been available to us; indeed it is that covenant that made and makes us Jews!) Christ is the way whereby God's covenant with Israel was opened up and made available as the new (form of the) covenant for the non-Jews of the world; that is why the Christian Church can be called the New (form of) Israel; those who accept Christ thereby become Spiritual Israel, descendants-by-faith of Abraham our father.

Should Christmas, then, mean anything to us Jews? On one level, no; Christmas is not meant for us any more than Christ is meant for us. But on another level, yes; for it marks the beginning of the enlargement and the extension of what we stand for and exist for. Through Christ and Christianity, the gift and task and hope of the Jew—our approach to life and our perspective on life, involving the relationship to both God and human beings—are spread through much of the world. Christianity is thus a denationalized, de-particularized form of Judaism: Judaism for the nations of the world.

Jews and Christians—our situations are somewhat different; our roles and tasks are somewhat different; our styles and modes are somewhat different. But we are covenanted to and by the same one God of Israel; our essential teachings are markedly similar; our goals, identical. And the one whose second coming Christians await and whose (first) coming we Jews await—when he comes—will surely turn out to have the same face for all of us.

A JEWISH APPROACH TO SEX EDUCATION

1

Before we can develop a proper approach to sex education, we must first formulate a proper approach to sex. The world in which we and our children are living is a highly sex-saturated world; the age in which we are living is a highly sex-conscious age. Movies, the stage, TV; magazines, newspapers, and books; advertisements at every turn; fashions in dress and undress; everyday conversation, even in mixed company; the actual conduct of the sexes—almost all aspects of our society involve a frankness of sexual expression and openness of sexual behavior that constitute a veritable sexual revolution. There are no doubt many different causes for this revolution, but however many and varied the causes, the revolution is a reality—and a reality so overwhelming and all-encompassing that we as parents are often in a state of utter confusion.

In our confusion, we find ourselves unable with any assurance to answer our children's questions, to meet their challenges, to correct and discipline our children—or even with confidence to guide them. Instead, we find ourselves falling into one or another extreme of reaction: either we overreject, storming and ranting and berating the whole range of sexual behavior among our children and their contemporaries; or we overaccept, smiling and approving or at least condoning whatever is done, since "everybody's doing it"—seeking thus to prove that we are as "modern and advanced" as our children; or we overwithdraw, retreating into noncommittal silence—thus raising even higher the already near-impenetrable barrier between the generations. Almost never, it seems, do we seek to understand what the sexual rebellion is all about; to analyze its various elements; and to evaluate what in that rebellion is good and what is bad—and why.

2

Surely the sexual revolution has brought much that is good. Knowledge is generally recognized to be good—and who can deny that knowledge of sexual matters has vastly increased. Adults know more and children know more; sometimes indeed the children seem to know more than the adults. We know more about what our bodies are like and how they work. We understand where babies come from, and how to delay or prevent their coming; the facts of conception and contraception are ever more widely known; misconceptions are more and more rare. Our knowledge of the harsher realities of sexual behavior has also vastly increased: venereal disease, premarital pregnancy, abortion, illegitimacy, prostitution, promiscuity, adultery, homosexuality—all are matters of common knowledge to adults in all segments of society, to almost all teenagers, and to many preteenagers as well. To the extent that knowledge is a good thing, the sexual revolution has surely been a boon. Awareness also is usually considered to be a benefit—and the sexual revolution, as it has increased our knowledge, has also increased awareness. We have become much more aware of the presence and power of our own sexual needs and desires and drives, of our satisfactions and frustrations—which, we now realize, are those of all normal men and women. We have become more aware also of the reality and significance of our children's sexual curiosity and of their needs and problems and confusions, their fears and fantasies. We have become more aware of how many areas of life and how many aspects of behavior are affected by sex. We have become more aware of how hypocritical we have been in permitting, in encouraging, and in practicing a double standard in various forms—as between men and women, as between the people we are willing to marry and the people we merely go with or go to, as between one group or occasion or circumstance and another. And we have become more aware of our own self-righteousness, whereby we frequently deplored, condemned, ridiculed, exposed, forbade, and punished those whose words and deeds we ourselves were guilty of engaging in.

As the sexual revolution has increased our knowledge and awareness, it has also increased what is widely considered to be a further benefit: matter-of-factness in reaction and frankness in expression. What we now have come to know and be aware of, we find ourselves able more freely to express. We are less secretive and inhibited, with adults and with children, in discussing sexual matters. We no longer feel compelled to resort to vague terms and circumlocutions when referring to parts of our anatomy, functions of our physiology, or articles of our clothing; almost nothing sexual is any longer unmentionable. In private conversation and in the public media, we are able to allow full and frank descriptions and portrayals of sexual matters. And what we see or read or hear presented so frankly in the various media of entertainment and communication, as well as in actual life, no longer angers or disgusts or shocks us; nor do we feel the need to overprotect the public—including the children—by imposing or accepting practically any form of censorship.

214

Furthermore, the sexual revolution, as it has increased our knowledge, awareness, and frankness, has decreased many of our fears. Because of advances in technology, science, and communication, many of the fears that plagued our predecessors have diminished or disappeared: unwanted pregnancies, premarital or postmarital, can usually be avoided—and when they occur, can more safely be terminated; venereal disease can be prevented—or when contracted, can usually be cured; impotence, sterility, and frigidity can often be corrected or cured. Our fears about masturbation have been all but eliminated and even our fears about homosexuality have been markedly reduced. Much of what used to be terrifying because it was called perversion has become less frightening when termed "abnormal," and has tended even to become acceptable, as the term "normality" has come to include an ever-broader range of behavior. All in all, we are less afraid of other people's sexuality and of our own.

3

And yet, in spite of all that is good in the sexual revolution, almost all of us realize that there is also much that is bad. Indeed, we sense that somehow the very things that are good in it are also bad. Or more exactly put, most of the changes wrought by the revolution are inherently neither good nor bad, but neutral—able to lead to good or bad results. Surely neither the increase in knowledge, awareness, and frankness, nor the decrease in fear, has brought about an unmistakable growth of genuine health, happiness, and harmony—for the older generation, between the older and younger generations, or for the younger generation itself. Each gain seems ambiguous. There is much greater knowledge—but is there greater understanding? (Knowledge without understanding may be not a blessing but a curse.) There is greater awareness—but is there greater concern? (Awareness without concern may be not a blessing but a curse.) There is greater frankness—but is there greater compassion? (Frankness without compassion may be not a blessing but a curse.) There is less fear— but is there not also less awe? (Fearlessness without awe may be not a blessing but a curse.)

But curse and blessing, understanding, concern, compassion, awe—all involve values, standards, and faith affirmations! What is at the heart of our confusion concerning the sexual revolution is thus the issue of value and belief. On the one hand, we are products of another world than our children's, heirs to a religious outlook and a moral code that, however much we may have deviated from it in practice, nevertheless enabled us in the past to feel sure of what was right and what was wrong; and to a significant degree we still hold to that outlook and feel bound by that code. On the other hand, we are enough involved in our children's world to share, if not their rejection, then at least their questioning of our previously unquestioned sexual standards; we are no longer sure of the complete validity, adequacy or relevance of these standards. No wonder we are confused. We are torn between two worlds and two world outlooks—and we cannot choose between them.

But perhaps we need not choose between them; perhaps we can choose from both of them. Within the new world outlook perhaps we can distinguish between what is really new and what merely appears to be new. Within the old world outlook perhaps we can distinguish between those elements that are of central importance and of abiding worth, and those elements that are peripheral and of only temporary significance, subject to error and to obsolescence. And perhaps we can even find within the old world outlook that which can serve as criterion for choosing what there is within the new which is not only new but also true.

Where shall we turn for a statement of our previously held standards, and for an indication of their sanction and source? If we consider ourselves to be truly Jewish we must turn to the Torah, for to be truly Jewish is to take seriously the claim that whatever human elements are reflected in the Torah, God's own word is in some genuine sense contained there too—and that that Word is eternally true and eternally relevant: to every aspect of life (certainly to sex) and to every generation (certainly to our own sex-obsessed generation). "One who says that the words of the Torah are one thing and the words of the world another is as if he denies God."

4

What does the Torah say concerning human sexuality?

The Torah says that "God created heaven and earth," the world and all that is in it—which is to say that what is often called "nature" is neither simply necessary nor simply accidental but comes as a result of God's power and wisdom and love, in accordance with His plan, for the fulfillment of His purpose. (Perhaps we should say "creation" rather than "nature.")

The Torah says that God "created *adam* in His own image" and that since among all His other creatures "no fitting helper was to found," "male and female He created them." What a strange paradox! Human beings, men and women both, are unique among God's creatures: they bear a likeness to God, who has personality but no sexuality; and they bear a likeness to animals, who have sexuality but no personality. And both the divine image and the sexuality, each of them present already in the Garden, are essential to our humanity. Furthermore, the two aspects affect each other and limit each other: on the one hand, even when man and woman unite sexually, their sexual union, though natural in the sense of "normal," is not natural in the sense of a mere animal copulation but is a distinctively human relationship—an I-Thou relationship, a relationship of two-persons-in-the-divine image, each of infinite worth, neither one intended to be exploited as an object of the other's aggressiveness or selfish satisfaction; on the other hand, the relation between man and woman, however aesthetic and moral and spiritual, is intended to find sexual expression.

The Torah says that "God saw all that He had made"—including man and woman—"and found it very good." Human sexuality, therefore, far from being unworthy or ugly or "dirty" or obscene, or in any way evil or unpleasing to God, is good.

The Torah says that God's command to man and woman—His very first command—was: "Be fruitful and multiply and fill the earth." Sexual relations and human reproduction are thus a fulfillment of God's will and intention for humanity.

The Torah also says: "The Lord God said: It is not good for man to be alone; I will make a helper fitting for him.... And man said: This one at last is bone of my bone and flesh of my flesh.... Therefore let a man leave his father and his mother, and join himself to his wife, so that they become one flesh." Not only reproduction but also enduring companionship, mutuality, helpfulness—and sexual union as a regularly renewed means for their expression and nurture—are among God's prime purposes for man and woman. Furthermore, when children come of age they must break away from their parents and unite with each other, founding a new family of their own.

The Torah says that after the first man and woman had sinned by disobeying God's command, they sought to "conceal themselves from the presence of the Lord God.... but the Lord God called to man and said: 'Where are you? Did you eat of the tree from which I commanded you not to eat?'" Whatever one does is known to God; wherever one goes, he remains in God's presence.

The Torah says that at first Adam and Eve "were naked, yet they felt no shame" but that later, after they had disobeyed God's command—succumbing to the serpent's temptation to be like God—"the eyes of both of them were opened and they perceived that they were naked—so they sewed fig leaves together and made themselves loincloths," and that still later, when they were driven from the Garden, "the Lord God made garments of skin for the man and his wife, and clothed them." In God's original plan and in the ideal world, human nakedness occasions no shame; in the actual human situation, however, nakedness connotes immodesty.

The Torah says: "Thou shalt not commit adultery.... Do not follow the inclinations of your heart or the allurements of your eyes after which you go wantonly astray.... The inclination of the human heart is evil from his youth, only evil all day long.... Sin couches at the door, its desire is directed toward you, but you can master it."[107] Concerning the immoral sexual practices of the pagans, the Torah admonishes: "You shall not copy their practices, nor shall you follow their laws.... Do not defile yourselves in any of those ways.... nor do any of those abhorrent things.... Behold I set before you this day life and good, and death and evil; choose life." We are endowed with the capacity to distinguish, and the ability to choose, between good and evil; we are tempted again and again to choose the evil; we are able to resist temptation; no one always does. "There is no human on earth so righteous that he does not sin."

The Torah says: "Be sure to reprove your fellow and do not [through your silence] incur sin because of him.... Do not follow the majority to do evil.... Sweep out the evil from your midst." The Torah-tradition says: "Do not judge your fellow until you are in his situation." The Torah says: "Happy is the one who stands in awe of God, who greatly delights in His commandments."

The Torah—both the Torah-book and the Torah-tradition—has many other things to say about human sexuality; about how human beings are meant to act and not to act; about those who live faithfully by God's command and those who live unfaithfully; about the consequences of sexual immorality for the individual and for society. And throughout this literature, which was studied through the ages by old and young, there is almost always a striking degree of frankness and explicitness. It was

107. "Evil" and "sin" do not refer specifically to sexual immorality but to immorality in all its forms—one of which is certainly sexual immorality.

evidently not felt that holiness must involve prudishness or censorship, nor that explicitness of sexual reference constituted a profanation of the sacred. Yet in spite of the frankness and explicitness, the Torah-tradition—both in literature and life—managed to nurture and sustain in sexual matters the quality of *tzeni'ut:* an exquisite mood of delicacy, reserve, and modesty.

Drawing upon the complex of Torah-teachings cited above, one can arrive at the following formulation of a Jewish approach to sex: *Human sexuality, like every human capacity, comes from God and is therefore holy and good—provided that it is exercised in faithful acceptance of God's purpose and in reverent awareness of His presence. The proper sexual relation is that which serves both to express and to further the mutually responsive and responsible love of a man and woman who recognize that each has been created in God's image.*

5

Now that we have explored the Jewish approach to sex, we are in a position to consider what would be a Jewish approach to sex education. To be Jewish, sex education would have to include four aspects: transmitting information, conveying attitudes, training in values and standards, and nurturing faith. All four are important.

Transmitting information is important to Judaism because the human being, created in God's image and therefore able to learn, is intended to learn and should be helped to learn, in accordance with his capacity. What the child is taught about sex (as about all of God's creation) should be true and accurate, clear and adequate. It should come in answer to the child's questions (spoken and unspoken), on the level of his readiness, and in response to his need. It should speak to her present situation and should set the foundation for her future growth and understanding.

Conveying attitudes is even more important than transmitting information, because how one feels about what one learns is more decisive in developing one's personality than is the information itself. Judaism would therefore be concerned that children acquire an attitude toward sex that involves such elements as the following: an acceptance of their own sexuality, masculine or feminine, as a normal and worthy and essential facet of their personality; a respect for the personality and sexuality of others; such a degree of confidence in their capacity for both sexual expression and sexual self-control that would free them from excessive inhibition and excessive exhibitionism; such a degree of readiness for each new phase of their sexual development that their growth need not be arrested at a stage already passed or be accelerated to a stage not yet reached; and such a degree of inner security that they would be able to face any deviant patterns of sexual behavior around them—including sickness and perversions—without being impelled either to emulate such behavior or to ridicule or punish those who engage in it.

Even the conveying of attitudes, however—though of crucial importance—is, from the point of Judaism, not enough. For attitudes, at least in healthy personalities, imply and reflect moral values and standards that are matters for choice and assent and decision. (In sick personalities, attitude may not imply value or reflect freedom, but in that case it is closer to drive, impulse, compulsion, etc.) A Jewish approach to sex education, therefore, would give considerable attention to training in moral values and standards. Such training would involve not only articulation in words but also proper example on the part of the teacher; provision for the making of moral decisions by the children themselves in actual life situations; and opportunity to review and evaluate the decisions that have been made. (In view of the element of privacy that is appropriate for many aspects of sexual relationship, more of the life situations must remain on the level of discussion than would be the case in most other moral issues; the conclusions drawn from these other life situations, however, would often be applicable to problems of sexual morality.)

Some of the moral values and standards involved in the Jewish approach to sex have already been indicated above. They include: self-respect; reciprocal respect; mutuality of concern, help, and fulfillment; nonexploitation; independence from parents upon maturity; modesty and reserve; faithfulness; self-discipline; willingness to give and accept reproof; restrain from judgment—almost all of which are, of course, expressions of love: love of fellow and love of self. In order to make sure, however, that this moral training not be dismissed by the students as overgeneralized, glib, and moralistic—reflecting the adult's distance and noninvolvement, with the accompanying self-righteousness and hypocrisy—this training in moral values would have frankly to acknowledge the moral ambiguities and dilemmas that are involved in life's actual decisions. It would have to be bold enough to reaffirm that the Torah's age-old, absolute standards are relevant to present realities, and yet be humble and honest enough to admit that the issues in actual life are not usually "black and white" but exceedingly complex, with elements of both right and wrong on each side and in every available option, and that the absolute standards can seldom be applied with absolute assurance and seldom to an absolute degree. (Take, for instance, the area of premarital conduct, involving such questions as masturbation—whether, under what circumstances, how often; and dating behavior—"how far to go," with whom, under what circumstances.)

But for sex education to be truly Jewish, it must also include something else, which, though often omitted from discussions of this subject, is most basic of all: nurturing faith. For just as attitudes reflect values, so do values reflect faith; the values we hold stem from the faith affirmations that we make—not necessarily from the faith affirmations that we verbalize, but from those that command our inmost assent. A Jewish program of sex education, therefore, would include a study of those Torah texts that involve the basic faith affirmations relating to sex; a theological analysis of the concepts involved (on the appropriate level of maturity and sophistication); and the provision of actual religious situations such as group and private worship, meditation and reflection, and sharing of religious concern. The faith affirmations to be considered would include those that have been indicated in the previous section, such as affirmations of God's wisdom, power, and love. With the eyes of faith one sees the basic role of sexuality in man-and-woman-created-in-God's-image—and is moved to wonder; one sees the mysterious power and attraction of human sexuality—and is moved to awe; one sees the goodness and joy of human sexuality—and is moved to praise; one sees the intricate and subtle functioning of human sexuality—and is moved to surprise; one sees the human offspring of human sexuality, giving evidence of human partnership with God in the work of Creation—and is moved to amazement; one sees the temptations and perils of human sexuality—and one is moved to confession and to a plea for strength; one sees the manifold blessings of human sexuality—and is moved to gratitude.

6

If all this is involved in sex education, who shall provide it? The school? The synagogue? The mass media? The "gang"? Society in general? The parents? The reality, of course, is that all of these will inevitably play a role—and that some will play their role improperly, some inadequately, and some unwillingly. Much is as yet unclear about who will play which role—or even about who should. But what *is* clear is that it is the parents whose role is greatest and whose responsibility is greatest.

Their responsibility is greatest because it is at once "natural" (in that it is they who have brought the helpless child involuntarily into the world) and God-given (in that God enabled them to bear and rear children, and commanded them to "teach them diligently ... when you sit in your house and walk by the way, when you lie down and rise up").

But even when parents try to avoid accepting the major responsibility, they cannot avoid playing the major role. For no matter how much they depend upon other agencies to provide sex education for their children, and no matter how little effort they make themselves, the most they can keep from conveying is perhaps some of the information; they cannot help conveying attitudes, values, and beliefs. For it is the actual parental attitudes (whether healthy or unhealthy); it is the actual parental values (whether true or false); it is the actual parental beliefs (whether Jewish or secular)—that children inevitably perceive and largely adopt. True, the influences of other agencies are also at work. True, at certain ages and in certain regards, the influence of adults other than parents and the influence of the child's own peers may be most effective. True, the child retains a degree of freedom to rework the various influences and a degree of imperviousness to them all. Nevertheless, because the earliest years are the most formative and because parent-child relationships are the most intensive and intimate, parental influence remains the most crucial.

7

Our conclusion must therefore be that though Judaism has much of importance to say about your child's sex education, Judaism can say it to you only to the extent that its attitudes, values, and beliefs become yours. For with regard to your child's sex education, it is what *you* say—in the various ways of "saying"—that will be of ultimate importance. So if you wish to assess your child's sex education, look inward and ask yourself—concerning this subject of sex—what information you possess, what attitudes you have, what values you hold, what beliefs you accept. The answers to these questions about your own outlook on sex will constitute the stuff of your child's actual sex education.

SIN, CRIME, SICKNESS, OR
ALTERNATIVE LIFE STYLE?
A JEWISH APPROACH TO HOMOSEXUALITY

Homosexuality, which in the general community has for some time been a major issue, has begun to be a matter of concern and controversy in the Jewish community as well. This development has come about for several reasons: partly because Jewish homosexuals are, like non-Jews, increasingly "coming out"; partly because some of them are seeking—even demanding—to be accepted as full-fledged members of the Jewish community and of the synagogue; and partly because Jews and non-Jews alike, both heterosexual and homosexual, are turning to rabbis and scholars for a clarification of what Judaism has to say on the subject.

1

That Judaism must have something to say should be obvious, for the Torah-text-and-tradition, claiming—as it does—to contain the revelation of God's word and will for human life, claims to have something significant—indeed crucial—to say about every important area of life, surely about such a basic dimension of life as sex. "One who says that Torah is one thing and the affairs of the world something entirely different is as if he denies God."[108]

What Judaism has to say about homosexuality would appear to be equally obvious, for all of the relatively few passages in the Torah-text that clearly refer to homosexuality[109] do so in negative terms. The words of the men of Sodom (Genesis 19), who surround Lot's house and say, "Where are the men who came to you tonight? Bring them out to us, that we may know [or, "be intimate with"] them," almost certainly have a homosexual reference. (The usage of the word "sodomy" is thus well-founded.) And the horrible story of the "concubine in Gibeah" (Judges 19), probably

---

108. *Midrash Pinhas* (Warsaw, 1876), 4:34, p. 32.

109 Some biblical passages that are commonly taken to refer to homosexuality are actually in dispute among scholars. The so-called male prostitute *(kadesh),* for example, may possibly not be a homosexual but a pimp or a male who engages in heterosexual prostitution. The love between David and Jonathan ("Your love was for me more wonderful than the love of women" [2 Samuel 1:26]) may possibly refer to normal love between friends of either sex.

related to the Genesis passage, similarly involves the threat of homosexual attack. It is sometimes argued that the horror and condemnation expressed in these two stories are directed not against homosexuality as such but against homosexual rape or against the violation of the sacred obligation of hospitality; it is also argued that the moral abhorrence expressed in the narrative passages does not, in itself, constitute legal prohibition. The two brief passages in the law code of Leviticus (19:22 and 20:13), however, are clear and categorical: "With a male you shall not lie as with a woman; it is an abomination.... If a male lies with a male as one lies with a woman, the two of them have done an abhorrent thing; they shall be put to death."

References in talmudic and posttalmudic sources—likewise relatively few—remain consistent with the biblical prohibition. Whatever the question at issue—whether two men may share the same blanket, or even be together in private; whether two women may sleep in the same room; whether climatic conditions stimulate homosexual temptation; whether Jews are likely to be influenced by the homosexual behavior of non-Jews; whether the age of the homosexual offender should be a factor in determining culpability; what the appropriate punishment is, in theory and in practice; whether the punishment should be the same for male and female offenders; whether rumors concerning a fellow Jew's homosexuality should be given credence; which privileges, communal and synagogal, should be denied to a homosexual—every single decision, pro or con, takes for granted that a homosexual act is a moral perversion, an outrageous and disgusting deed, a serious violation of the Torah's command and therefore a grave sin. It would thus appear absolutely clear that a Jewish approach to homosexuality must end where and as it starts: with utter condemnation and categorical prohibition.

2

Yet such a conclusion, at this point in our discussion, is premature. For if what we seek is a *truly Jewish* approach to a *contemporary* problem, we must not only consult biblical sources and subsequent halakhic decisions, but must do two other things as well: a) determine, as far as we are able, the rationale and presuppositions of the traditional stand; and b) inquire whether there are now any changed circumstances or new data in the light of which the Torah's stand today—though based on the same divine and enduring concerns and purpose—might possibly involve changed formulations or different emphases.

Why does the Torah condemn homosexuality so utterly and consider it to be such an abomination? The reason cannot be simply the abhorrence of the unknown, for a law does not forbid the unknown. Besides, the Torah specifically alludes to, and obviously was familiar with, the practice of homosexuality (along with other sexual offenses, often practiced as part of idolatrous cult worship), by both the Egyptians "in whose midst you dwelt" and the Canaanites "into whose land I am bringing you" (Leviticus 18:3). Nor can the reason be merely "psychological" and "esthetic"—that homosexuality is inherently disgusting—for that would be begging the question: why was it considered disgusting? Nor can the reason be "statistical"—that the majority of men and women did not and do not practice homosexuality—for Torah-law must surely be based on more than statistics and averages; indeed the Torah specifically warns *against* following the majority, when the majority is bent on evil.

The reasons for the Torah's condemnation must be related rather to the will of the Creator for the human male and female whom He created: "God created *adam* in His image ... male and female He created them [Genesis 1:27].... God saw all that He had made and behold it was very good [ibid. 31].... It is not good that man should be alone; I will make a helper for him [as complement and counterpoint to him, his opposite number] [ibid. 2:18].... This one shall be called woman [ibid. 2:23].... Let a man leave his father and his mother, and cling to his wife [his woman], and they shall become one flesh [ibid. 2:24].... Be fruitful and multiply and fill the earth [ibid. 1:28].... The Lord created the earth to be inhabited [Isaiah 45:18].... I will establish My covenant between Me and you [Abraham] and your seed after you, throughout their generations ... as an everlasting covenant [Genesis 17:7]."

In the light of such Scriptural passages, some of the reasons for the Torah's prohibition of homosexuality become discernible. One reason must be that in the order of Creation the sexual "nature" and "structure" of the human male and female—including what we refer to as their anatomy, physiology, and psyche—call for mutual complementation, completion, and fulfillment through a heterosexual relationship. Another implied reason is that only through such a relationship, using the organs of generation in a manner conducive to generation, can a new generation appear to populate the earth. A third reason: only with the appearance of a second and third generation can there be a family in the full sense of the word: one that calls for and allows for caring love and reverent responsibility, not only between spouses but also among parents and children and grandchildren. This points to a fourth reason: homosexuality precludes history, not only individual and family history, but history as such—the stage on which both the divine and human roles in the providential drama are to be acted out. In the case of Jewish homosexuality, one further denial is involved: that of the continued survival of the covenant people Israel, vehicle of God's involvement in the world, "God's stake in history."

It is out of such concerns as these, we must assume, that the Torah-text-and-tradition prohibits homosexuality.

3

But whenever we speak of the Torah's prohibitions we must be mindful of one of the Torah's key presuppositions: the freedom and capacity of the individual human being to obey. Surely the very creation-in-the-image, which is the basic biblical teaching about human beings, male and female, implies such freedom. How else could God hold Adam and Eve responsible for the first violation of the first prohibition? And when, in the very next generation, Cain is distressed at God's acceptance of Abel's offering and the rejection of his own, God tells him: "Sin couches at the door: its urge is toward you; yet you can be its master" (Genesis 4:7). Therefore when Cain proceeds to murder his brother, God "has the right" to confront him with his responsibility for this murder, the first ever committed. In a famous midrash, human moral freedom and responsibility are made even more explicit. Before conception takes place, "the seminal drop is brought before the Holy One; there and then it is decided, concerning this one, whether it will be strong or weak, wise or foolish, rich or poor—but not whether it will be wicked or righteous."[110] Or as the famous talmudic statement puts it, even more succinctly, "All is in the hands of Heaven—except the fear of Heaven."[111] The clear and consistent assumption behind all of the Torah's commands and prohibitions is thus that human beings have the freedom to obey or disobey.[112]

4

But what if one violates the Torah's command involuntarily, due to circumstances beyond one's control, or with no other options available?

---

110. *B. Niddah* 16b.
111. *B. Berakhot* 33b.
112. For a further discussion of the problem of determinism, freedom, judgment, and providence, see above, "Human Choice and God's Design."

Is one still culpable? And is the act still punishable? The Torah-tradition contains numerous examples of such involuntary offenders who have done what was forbidden, or failed to do what was commanded, out of constraint and lack of freedom *(me-ones)*. The cases discussed involve varying degrees and kinds of constraint: threat of torture or death, extreme financial duress, mistaken impression of the facts, forgetfulness, insanity, intoxication, illness, accident, and other factors beyond one's control. Although the halakhic authorities differ as to whether the factor of *ones* should be the governing consideration in any particular case—and whether therefore the offender is to be fully exempt, is to be held fully responsible, or partially both—a frequently invoked principle is that "in cases of *ones* the Merciful One exempts."[113] The underlying principle is apparently that when forbidden acts are performed in the absence of voluntary choice and free decision, or in the absence of other options, the offenders are judged more leniently.

5

The tradition does not appear ever to have looked upon homosexual behavior in such a light. It appears, rather, to have *assumed* that whenever homosexual acts are performed they are engaged in willingly and willfully, through a free choice from among several options. It is only in our own generation that homosexual behavior has been found to involve not merely a single, overt act, or a series of such acts, but often to reflect a profound inner condition and basic psychic orientation, involving the deepest levels of personality. However deep and numerous are the differences among contemporary experts on homosexuality,[114] on one aspect there seems to be near-unanimity: that *for very many homosexuals the prospects of change to heterosexuality are almost nil.*

113. *B. Nedarim* 27a.
114. They differ on the causes (some positing a hormonal or other hereditary factor; some stressing a seriously inadequate or disturbed parental relationship in the earliest years; some pointing to early traumatic sexual experience; some insisting that the causes are thus far simply unknown). They differ on the possibilities for changing to heterosexuality (some insisting that no true homosexual can change; some claiming that all who truly desire to, can be professionally enabled to; many acknowledging that at most perhaps a quarter or third can change). They differ on the appropriate treatment methods for those who seek to change (psychoanalysis, analytic forms of psychotherapy, behavior modification).

Now with regard to one group of homosexuals (and bisexuals), those whose sexual behavior represents deliberate rejection of the Torah's standard and a simple indulgence in the hedonistic ethic of "doing whatever gives me pleasure"—and who, if they chose to, *could* live a heterosexual life—it is clear that from any viewpoint that acknowledges the authority of the Torah the traditional prohibition remains in full force. With regard to another group, those for whom the homosexual way has been, psychologically speaking, the "easier" way—but who, with professional help or with strenuous effort, could manage to change—the Torah's standard also remains in effect. With regard to other homosexuals, however (constituting probably the majority), who are under the constraint of remaining homosexual indefinitely, presumably for life—their only other option being sexual abstinence for life—is there anything less stringent that could, and should, be said by contemporary Torah-interpreters and Torah-observers?

6

For one thing, a truly Torah approach, taking seriously the injunction of the Torah-tradition not to judge another person until one stands in his place,[115] would acknowledge that no human being is able to know the exact degree of another's freedom: that God alone has that knowledge; that God alone, therefore, has the ability and the right to judge a person's culpability; and that none of us humans, therefore, ought presume to judge a homosexual or automatically regard a homosexual as a sinner—since, as already implied, sin involves not only overt action but also intention, decision, and responsibility.[116]

Furthermore, a Torah approach would look with deep compassion *(rahamanut)* upon the plight of many homosexuals in our society. It would share the anguish of a human being who for years—perhaps since early adolescence—has had to live with a growing sense of being different and "queer"; in constant fear of being discovered; knowing that if discovered, one might well be looked down upon as perverted, loathsome, dangerous; with the consequent fear of being mistreated, humiliated and ridiculed,

115. *Avot* 2:5.
116. Even though the tradition does at times refer to sins committed "unknowingly," "under compulsion," or "inadvertently," the sinfulness of such sins consists, presumably, in sinful decisions made previously, when a greater degree of freedom obtained; or in a *culpable* degree of ignorance or negligence; or in a lack of concern for harm inflicted even though inflicted unintentionally.

perhaps blackmailed, excluded or expelled from many types of employment, and denied acceptance and friendship. ("The Lord seeks the pursued,"[117] and we should imitate Him in this regard.)

Not content with withholding judgment and with feeling compassion, a genuinely Jewish approach to homosexuality would require us to *demonstrate* such feelings of compassion by willingly associating with homosexuals and engaging in acts of kindness and friendship—so that the particular individuals whom we meet will not feel grudgingly tolerated but will see that they are included within the circle of our love.

But even more is required, if our Jewish responsibility to homosexuals is to be fulfilled. For it is not enough to attend to our own attitude and behavior; we must be equally concerned with what is felt and done by others, keeping ourselves from falling into the category of those "in whose power it was to protest but did not protest." True, we cannot force a change of heart upon others nor control their actions; we can, however, make a genuine effort to dispel the popular myths and repeal the legal disabilities that have made the life of many homosexuals into a living hell. We now know, for example, that most male homosexuals are not "effeminate" in gait, voice, manner, or dress; that most female homosexuals are not "masculine"; that homosexuality does not mean promiscuity. We should therefore avoid such stereotypes in conversation or in attempts at "humor." We now know that the incidence of crimes such as murder, robbery, rape, molestation, and seduction is no higher among homosexuals than among heterosexuals; we should therefore work for the immediate repeal of laws, rules, and practices that exclude or discriminate against homosexuals on the contrary assumption. Similarly, in acknowledgment of the relative victimlessness of homosexual relations between consenting adults and in opposition to unnecessary government intrusion upon individual privacy, we should, as Jews, vigorously oppose any legal penalties for such homosexual behavior.[118]

---

117. Ecclesiastes 3:15; *Va-Yikra Rabbah*, 27.

118. It is sometimes urged that even though certain laws concerning morality should not be enforced, they should nevertheless not be repealed because a) keeping them on the books serves a moral-pedagogic function; and b) removing them would imply full moral approval of the now decriminalized behavior, thus actually encouraging the young and the "weak" to engage in such acts. Whatever the measure of validity in such an argument, it is outweighed by two considerations: a) the retention of laws that have become recognized as unjust or inappropriate increases disdain for the legal system; and b)

7

If a homosexual, then, is to be considered neither sinner nor criminal, how *shall* he or she be looked upon? As sick, perhaps?

The label "sick" has some obvious advantages over the other two: if considered sick, the homosexual is saved from being religiously damned, morally condemned, or legally doomed to punishment. But "sick" has serious disadvantages too. For the sick we prescribe treatment and therapy; upon the sick we often impose restriction, separation, even isolation; toward the sick we feel superiority and show condescension; in the presence of the sick we feel fear. And if these actions and attitudes are true concerning the *physically* ill, how much more so concerning those who are considered mentally, emotionally, psychologically ill. Realizing that the uniqueness of human beings is related to their mind, psyche, conscience, and "soul," we tend automatically and recklessly to expand and exaggerate the dimensions of their "emotional illness" and to assume that these "sick people" are maladjusted and malfunctioning in almost all regards and all relationships. We tend, therefore, to shudder in their presence, on the cruel assumption that their illness calls into question their actual humanity. (Do we perhaps shudder also from a subconscious fear of becoming like them, or from subconscious horror and guilt at already being at least somewhat like them?)

In the face of these negative connotations of the word "sick" and the negative consequences of applying it to homosexuals, it is quite understandable that hosts of homosexuals bitterly resent and utterly reject such a label, and that even the American Psychiatric Association has removed homosexuality from its list of mental illnesses.

But if the term "sickness" is to be eliminated, what then shall be substituted? Some of the terms that have been used—such as defect or perversion—have so many negative connotations and result in so many negative attitudes that they are hardly an improvement over what they replace. Shall we say then—as urged by many homosexuals, many sexual liberationists and radicals, and some professional experts—that homosexuals should not be singled out at all; that they should receive no special attention, treatment, consideration, description, or label; that their orientation and behavior should be considered equally acceptable with heterosexuality as simply an "alternative life style"?

avoidance of actual harm to known victims must take priority over possible harm to unknown victims.

8

It is tempting to say yes, thus avoiding the accusation of indifference and insensitivity to the anguish that so many homosexuals have undergone, and to the discrimination, deprivation, ostracism, and even persecution that have contributed to that anguish.

And yet—once again—a Jew who seeks to be faithful to the Torah and to the divine word that he affirms to be contained therein, though obliged to guard against the temptation of cruelty and lack of compassion, must also guard against the temptation of reckless relativism and simplistic sentimentality. The most truly Jewish stance would be one that takes with equal seriousness both the authority of traditional standards and the significance of modern knowledge. As already indicated, such a stance would maintain the traditional view of heterosexuality as the God-intended norm and yet would incorporate the contemporary recognition of homosexuality as, clinically speaking, a sexual deviance, malfunctioning, or abnormality—usually unavoidable and often irremediable.

Such an approach has a number of advantages. It remains faithful to the Torah-teaching that heterosexuality is, in principle, not merely recommended but commanded, and that homosexuality is not merely discouraged but forbidden. It places upon men and women who become aware of their homosexual tendencies the responsibility for striving, on their own or with the aid of professional counselors, to develop or strengthen their heterosexual tendencies. It removes from those homosexuals who, after making such efforts, find that they cannot change, all burden of blame and guilt[119]—accepting them as they are. It avoids at least some of the negative connotations of "mental illness." It acknowledges that unalterable homosexuality remains theologically unaccountable. And it warns all of us—both homosexuals and heterosexuals—against self-righteousness.

9

In seeking to do justice to this double claim, the heterosexual majority faces several difficult dilemmas. One is whether homosexuals should *ever* be excluded from any particular roles in society.

---

119. Paradoxically, and yet perhaps understandably, such removal of blame and guilt, and the combination of self-acceptance and acceptance by others, has in some instances been followed by a changeover to heterosexuality!

Granted, as has been indicated earlier, that such exclusion is in most cases unnecessarily cruel and unjustly discriminatory, based on myth or prejudice, and therefore completely unwarranted and indeed intolerable, are there nevertheless a certain few roles—such as teacher, youth leader, or religious guide—that are likely to be so influential upon the lives of young people that when such positions are held by an avowed homosexual those young people whose sexual orientation is not yet set may be influenced toward a homosexual orientation—not through any conscious intention, deliberate effort, or seductive behavior on the part of the homosexual (popular fear of such dangers is based, as we have seen, on myth and prejudice), but simply through functioning as authority figures and role models?

A solution to this dilemma is not easy. Some experts argue that the influence of role models such as teachers or youth leaders is likely to be crucial in a child's life. Others argue that there is little evidence to indicate who are most likely actually to function as role models, and that heroes-at-a-distance, often "present" through the media, can be no less significant as role models than the usual "significant persons" in a child's life. Still others argue that sexual orientation is set at a very early age—according to some, by the age of two!—and is therefore very unlikely to be affected by subsequent contact with any other person, however "significant." In the absence of any clear evidence as to harmful effects upon young people, and in the presence of clear evidence of harmful effects upon homosexuals who have been excluded from a host of jobs, we would advocate that the only roles from which homosexuals should be excluded are those of adoptive or foster parent and of religious leader—since these two roles of parent and rabbi are, by definition, meant to serve as models of what a Jewish woman or man should be. And even the role of rabbi should be open to a homosexual *if* he or she honestly holds the conviction—and would conscientiously seek to convey it to others—that in spite of his or her own homosexuality, the Jewish ideal for man and woman is heterosexuality. (After all, it is accepted that a single or divorced person can legitimately and effectively serve as rabbi provided that he or she holds up marriage as the ideal, and that a childless person may serve as rabbi as long as he or she holds up having children as the ideal.)

10

For the organized Jewish community a further problem arises, in connection with a request—or demand—which, though formerly unheard of and until recently indeed inconceivable, has now been presented by some homosexuals and is likely to be made with increasing frequency and forcefulness: that national synagogue organizations accept congregations of homosexuals as local affiliates. What would be a proper response to this very real dilemma? On the one hand, is not a homosexual synagogue a contradiction in terms? Since Judaism considers heterosexuality to be the norm, how can it accept as legitimate a group that by name and public identification, represents, celebrates, and makes a principle of its deviation from that norm? And yet, does not any group of Jews have a right to form a congregation and the further right to affiliate, on the same basis as others, with a union of congregations?

Our response to this dilemma would be threefold: a) it would be far preferable for homosexuals to be welcome and feel welcome in existing congregations rather than to feel a need to form their own gay synagogues; b) since the present reality, however, is that such a welcome is not assured and is perhaps even unlikely, the formation of gay congregations is legitimate; and c) a gay congregation, to be eligible for affiliation with a union of congregations, however, must not—by rule, name, practice, or implication—restrict its own membership or leadership to homosexuals.

11

There remains one further, far more radical, request—again often couched as a demand—that has been made by some Jewish homosexuals: that rabbis solemnize and all Jews recognize "marriages" between homosexuals, and that congregations admit such couples to "family memberships." Is there any way in which the notion of a homosexual "marriage" could be considered Jewishly valid?

When we speak of "Jewishly valid" with reference to an officially solemnized, publicly recognized pattern of behavior, we must be speaking in terms of traditional Jewish law, the *halakhah*. Now, though the *halakhah* has developed and "changed" over the ages through rabbinic interpretation of biblical law and rabbinic enactment for the public welfare, nevertheless, in the three thousand years of recorded halakhic teaching and practice there is apparently not a single instance of halakhic provision for the legitimization of a homosexual relationship. And even if the flexibility and resourcefulness of the *halakhah* were renewed and increased—as befits the "Torah of Life"—it is hardly conceivable that a homosexual departure from the Torah's heterosexual norm would ever be accepted by halakhically faithful Jews or ever be recognized as *ke-dat moshe ve-yisra'el* (in accordance with the law of Moses and Israel).

12

How will Jewish homosexuals who cherish both Torah-and-*mitzvot* and the community of the people of Israel, but who must live with the reality of their homosexual condition—how will they be likely to respond to such a categorical halakhic "no"?

Some will probably be so embittered that they may turn their backs on the whole Jewish "establishment" or on Judaism itself. But perhaps some may trouble themselves to formulate a response, in the hope of making their position understood, to the "straight" majority of their fellow Jews. And their response might go something like this:

"Granted that marriage in Judaism has always been heterosexual; and granted that one of the major purposes of marriage has been procreation—in order both to populate the world and to pass on the covenant way of life. But is that the sole purpose and meaning of Jewish marriage? What of the legitimacy of sexual pleasure and release—is that not also Jewish? (Long-term abstinence is no more feasible, bearable, or desirable for homosexuals than for heterosexuals.) And does not marriage have other purposes as well: the fostering of mutual affection, care, trust, sacrifice, and support; the encouragement and sustenance of growth—intellectual, aesthetic, moral, and spiritual; the sharing of pain and anxiety; the nurturing of joy and hope; the overcoming of loneliness—all of these on the basis of an enduring commitment of faithfulness? And is not marriage the primary and preferred—and indeed the only fully acceptable—context for furthering these purposes? If it is the Torah-teaching that the fullest possible meaning of personhood is to be found in and through marriage, shall we, because we are homosexuals, be denied the right to seek such meaning and to develop such personhood? If God, in whose image we homosexuals too are created, has directly or indirectly caused or willed or allowed us to be what we cannot help being—men and women unable to function heterosexually—can we believe, and can you heterosexuals believe, that He wants us to be denied the only possible arrangement whereby we can live as deeply a human life as we are capable of?

"If, as you heterosexuals claim, our condition constitutes a deviance and malfunctioning and abnormality, do we not have the God-given right—indeed the obligation—to attempt to live with, adjust to, make the best of, and rise above this "handicap" of ours, just as all of the other handicapped are expected to do?

"If the *halakhah* can provide marriage only for heterosexuals and cannot speak to our condition, then in this one regard we must live nonhalakhically; but we are Jews and we insist on avowing our homosexual condition and our homosexual union, openly and unashamedly, within the covenant community of the people of Israel.[120] In our eyes—and, we feel sure, in God's eyes too—our homosexual bond is worthy, proper, and even holy. We believe that for us, who wish to live as Jews and love as Jews but who, by virtue of our homosexual condition, are not in a position to beget or bear any offspring, God has a word that is no less accepting and no less reassuring than His word to the eunuchs in the Babylonian Exile:

> Let the eunuch not say: 'Behold, I am a withered tree.' For thus says *YHVH:* As for the eunuchs who keep My Sabbaths, who have chosen what I desire and hold fast to My covenant, I will give them, in My house and within My walls, a monument and a name better than sons and daughters,... an everlasting name that shall not perish."[121]

120. When such open and unashamed avowal of homosexuality takes the form of public protest, demonstration, and proclamation, many heterosexuals—even those who have come to grant the validity of such basic gay rights as nondiscrimination in housing, employment, and public office—become resentful, impatient, and angry at what they consider the "constant parading" by gays of their homosexuality. They often fail to realize that such public display is a reflection of the grim reality that denial of these basic rights is still widespread and has only very recently been reduced. When the rights of gays will have been fully accepted and their changed status inwardly assimilated by both straights and gays, both groups will obviously feel less threatened. At that point the need for public demonstration by gays will certainly diminish and perhaps even disappear.

121. Isaiah 56:3-5.

A CALL FOR COMPASSION[122]

Dr. Nathaniel S. Lehrman is surely correct in a number of his observations concerning basic assumptions of traditional Judaism and its attitude toward homosexuality: that the tradition has condemned and forbidden homosexual acts; that it has emphasized free will as a basic dimension of human nature, with the consequent obligation to obey the Torah's commandments; that it has condoned neither the hedonistic philosophy of "pleasure for pleasure's sake" nor the majoritarian rationalization that "everybody's doing it"; and that it has affirmed the ability of human beings often to change from previous patterns of unacceptable behavior. For all these reminders we can be grateful.

The major flaw in Dr. Lehrman's paper, however, is his marked tendency toward overstatement and exaggeration, which results in a failure to make necessary qualifications and distinctions and which thus vitiates much of his argument.

A prime example: the same tradition that affirms human freedom to choose and to change acknowledges significant limitations on that freedom: limitations imposed by heredity, environment, and habituation. The tradition also affirms that God alone knows fully and accurately to what degree human behavior is a result of free choice and to what degree it reflects limitation. The tradition therefore cautions us against the presumptuousness of pretending to such knowledge and against the attempt to judge others until we stand in their place—which we almost never can. (To be sure, actions that clearly endanger life or property require intervention, restraint, and judicial judgment—but this is not at all the same as judging the *person* or assessing *ultimate* responsibility.)

As Dr. Lehrman points out, the traditional prohibition of homosexuality is no doubt related to Judaism's concern for reproduction, sexual fulfillment, and family and societal stability (in traditional terms, "the order of creation"). It is also no doubt related to concern for the survival of humanity and the Jewish people, and to a revulsion against pagan sexual orgy and promiscuity, which thus combined idolatry and immorality. The crucial question, however, is whether homosexuality in contem-

122. In the fall of 1983 *Judaism* magazine published a symposium entitled "Homosexuals and Homosexuality." Hershel Matt's contribution, "A Call for Compassion," responds to that of Nathaniel S. Lehrman, "Homosexuality and Judaism: Are They Compatible?," *Judaism* 32:4 (Fall 1983): 392-404.

porary society is to be identified with what the Torah forbade—whether, that is, the ancient and modern significance and consequences of homosexuality are the same and whether homosexuality today is inherently idolatrous, immoral, and destructive of Jewish existence. The answer to this question involves, once again, the issue of free choice: are homosexuals able to choose and to change? If they are, they should be considered in violation of the Torah's prohibition, which is still binding; if they are not, but except for the sexual identity of their mate, do live faithfully by traditional Jewish standards, they should be fully accepted and respected.

For Dr. Lehrman the answer seems very clear: they are, therefore they should. He sweepingly dismisses the claims of the "biological" school of thought as completely unfounded and lacking all evidence. He categorically denies validity to the psychoanalytic school by attributing any evidence they cite to "retrospective falsification," and dismissing their techniques as useless and their goal of removing all sexual inhibition as unworthy. As for the "new morality," he considers it to be merely the narcissistic glorification of "doing one's own thing," governed by "subjective wishes or even whims," with pleasure as the primary moral standard—all encouraged and sensationalized by the media and supported by the peer community. For Dr. Lehrman the only valid solution is apparently a renewed and vigorous preachment of the traditional condemnation combined with intensive therapy in the behavioral modification mode.

We must leave to the biological scientists and to Dr. Lehrman's psychoanalytic and psychiatric peers the challenge to refute his "refutations." One would have hoped, however, that on an issue that almost all recognized authorities in numerous fields have acknowledged to be complex, multifaceted, multidimensional, and difficult of solution, Dr. Lehrman might be more cautious and less dogmatic. As to the espousers of the "new morality," it is essential to distinguish between those among them who indeed fit Dr. Lehrman's description and thus merit his condemnation and between those who in large measure share the traditional Jewish value system but have performed for all of us a triple service: pointing to the self-righteousness, hypocrisy, and callousness of some defenders of the "old morality"; honestly facing the dilemmas inherent in attempting to apply ancient, absolute standards to new and complex situations; and confronting squarely, and making an effort to assimilate, surprising knowledge very recently attained.

This new knowledge, gained from scientific research and experimentation in various fields and from the personal testimony of numerous homosexuals, indicates (Dr. Lehrman's assertions to the contrary notwithstanding) that for a significant number of gays and lesbians (probably a majority, possibly the vast majority), their homosexuality is established early in life and is for the most part unalterable—except at the cost of the great pain and self-degradation involved in forcing themselves to live a lie. Whether all who become aware of their homosexual inclination should seek counseling in order to resolve whatever inner doubts, anxieties, or conflicts they may have and to clarify their available options, we cannot presume to say. What we can say, however, is a) that most homosexuals evidently do not seek such counseling—whether because they feel no need or desire to change, or see no possibility of changing, or lack the financial means, or for some other reasons; b) that some homosexuals have received such counseling and have thereby been helped to change from their homosexual practice and to live well-adjusted lives as heterosexuals; and c) that others have been helped through counseling to live well-adjusted lives as homosexuals, having come to recognize that the homosexual way of life is for them the only available way to sexual and personal fulfillment. None of us should deny the record or the contribution of the therapists who have helped some people realize that they are not or need not be homosexual; nor should we castigate the therapists who have helped some homosexuals to accept the reality and finality—and the full "legitimacy"—of their homosexual condition. (The decision of the American Psychiatric Association to remove homosexuality as such from its list of illness would not seem to imply, as Dr. Lehrman would have it, an acknowledgment that homosexuals have the freedom to choose their sexual orientation but would rather imply the opposite: an acknowledgment that homosexuality is for many homosexuals their "natural" condition.) Those of us—including presumably Dr. Lehrman—who insist that it is God's "right" to prescribe standards for human behavior in general and for Jewish behavior in particular, and who teach that heterosexual behavior is God's intended norm, must not be so presumptuous as to deny God's "right" to create or permit the "homosexual exceptions." Indeed, with regard to such "exceptions," we must strive to echo and to mediate God's full acceptance and approval.

HOMOSEXUAL RABBIS?

Among the heterosexual majority of Jews, the range of views concerning the minority of Jews who are homosexual runs the whole gamut: from a strict position that homosexuality is an abomination and homosexuals are to be condemned and rejected as sinners, to a moderate position that homosexuality is an illness and homosexuals are to be tolerated and perhaps pitied, to a liberal position that homosexuality is an alternative life style and homosexuals are to be fully accepted and welcomed. In the organized Jewish community there is a correspondingly broad range of response: from those (especially among the Orthodox) who oppose laws that bar discrimination against homosexuals in employment and housing to those (especially among the Reform) who admit gay synagogues into their national congregational union. The vast majority of Jewish organizations remain silent and noncommittal, whether out of confusion or cowardice or a prudent recognition of the sharp division of opinion among their members.

It is only very recently, however, that any consideration has been given, even among liberal Jews, to a far more radical and daring question: is it permissible, perhaps even desirable, for a homosexual to serve as rabbi? That there are avowed homosexuals already serving as rabbis for several of the twenty-to-thirty existing "gay synagogues" is a fact; that a number of "closet" homosexuals now serve as rabbis of (mostly) "straight" synagogues is also a fact. What our question involves, however—and what the Jewish community is only now beginning to consider—is whether avowed gays and lesbians should be admitted to and ordained by rabbinical schools (other than the one school where they already are) and be eligible, upon ordination, to serve as rabbis for any congregation, Hillel Foundation, chaplaincy, or other Jewish communal agency.

Before arriving at an answer to this important—but heretofore unasked, indeed almost inconceivable—question, we must first consider why Jewish tradition has consistently had a negative view of homosexuality.

That its view *has* been negative is clear enough: in Scriptural text, talmudic discussion, and halakhic decision, homosexual behavior has been strongly condemned and categorically prohibited. Among the reasons for this prohibition, explicitly stated or else implied, are the following: the perception of heterosexuality as being in accordance with the "divine order of creation"; the crucially important *mitzvah* of procreation for the perpetuation of humankind; the equally crucial importance of the perpetuation of the people Israel; the central importance of family, both for achieving these purposes and for providing the inherent blessing and satisfaction of human relations at their most intimate, caring, responsive, and responsible. An additional reason, according to some scholars, was the abhorrence of idol worship, which in ancient times often included fertility rites, sometimes homosexual.

In the face of this traditional prohibition and of these reasons for such a prohibition, what grounds could there be, Jewishly speaking, for a more permissive stand?

As to concern for populating the earth, *over*population would today be a greater concern—were it not for our equal concern for perpetuating the Jewish people, a concern shared by all loyal Jews, homosexual no less than heterosexual. There are other ways, however, of contributing to the survival of the Jewish people, aside from physically begetting or bearing children: many Jewish homosexuals support worthy Jewish causes and institutions (some even fill leadership positions); some make their contribution as teachers of Judaism ("whoever teaches Torah to another person's child is as one who has borne or begotten that child").

As to the crucial importance of the family for providing a nurturing, loving, and caring relationship, many homosexuals establish a home in which mutual love, genuine sharing, responsiveness and responsibility, and lifelong faithfulness are a reality; many are prepared, when society allows, to serve as adoptive or foster parents; and some homosexuals lovingly rear children that they themselves have begotten or borne in a previous heterosexual marriage.

Our principal response, however, is to reckon fully and forthrightly with a conclusion reached by a large number of experts, one arrived at existentially by a vast number of homosexuals: that homosexuality, contrary to assumptions that have been widely accepted from biblical times to our very own day, involves not merely a single, overt act, or a series of such acts, but usually reflects a profound inner condition and basic psychic orientation, involving the deepest levels of personality. As to the causes of homosexuality, the experts are divided: some believe that hormonal factors are involved; others stress psychological factors in infancy; still others confess that the reasons are not known or clearly understood. Whatever the etiology, however, there is a significant degree of consensus that, as Dr. Sol Gordon has put it,

> a child's sexual orientation is determined by the time it is five years old. It is not simply a matter of choice. Homosexuality is not a sexual *preference,* though it is commonly referred to as such.... Most of us who have worked in this field and who have considered all the evidence believe very seriously that there is a group of people who are *constitutional* homosexuals.... I know of no therapy that is successful for someone who is a constitutional homosexual.

In other words, for the homosexuals we have been speaking of, the prospects of change to any healthy, satisfying pattern of heterosexuality are almost nil.[123]

For such homosexuals, therefore, their basic choice is not whether to *be* homosexual, but whether to live openly and with integrity what they truly are—men and women who, for reasons not of their own making or choosing, are able to know the blessing of true sexual fulfillment primarily or exclusively through relationship with someone of their own sex—or to suppress and deny their own true nature, thus forcing themselves to live a life of pretense and hypocrisy, involving continuous concealment, constant fear of being discovered and then blackmailed, blackballed, or publicly humiliated. (While the theoretical ideal of the "divine order of creation" may indeed be heterosexual, they, having been created homosexual, are evidently "God's exceptions.") Those who have chosen the former course—openly to acknowledge their homosexuality—and who, after preparing themselves through a long period of Jewish training, observance, and personal commitment, now wish to serve God and the Jewish people through the rabbinate, should not be excluded from consideration for service in that role.

Nevertheless, in spite of all that has been said above, is it fitting for an avowed and practicing homosexual to serve as rabbi when a rabbi must serve as moral guide and example? Our response must be forthright. As

---

123. There are obviously some men and women for whom their homosexuality constitutes or creates a severe psychological problem, stemming in some cases from early upbringing or traumatic experience. Such homosexuals can sometimes be helped, through psychotherapy, to explore the origins of their problem and perhaps be enabled to live a satisfying heterosexual life. Many experts hold the view that such homosexuals are in the minority. In any case, such homosexuals are not the subject of this article.

implied above, we do not consider as at all immoral a relationship between two persons that is responsible, caring, faithful, exclusive, and enduring. As for the Torah's condemnation of homosexuality, we follow those teachers who have taught us that though the Torah *contains* God's word, it is not *identical* with God's word; it is both divine and human. Insofar as the Torah reflects the divine intent, its prohibition of homosexuality could not have had in mind the kind of homosexuality we have been speaking of; insofar as it reflects mere human attempts to grasp the divine intent, it reflects also a human misunderstanding of the kind of homosexuality that is forbidden.[124] (All this is not to deny, of course, that any person whose sexual behavior is exploitative, seductive, promiscuous, adulterous, or otherwise immoral should not be admitted to a rabbinical school and certainly not ordained—since rabbis *are* expected to strive to serve as guides and models of sexual—as well as of all dimensions of—morality. Since there is no basis for assuming that homosexuals as such are guilty of such immoral behavior, we must not ourselves indulge in, nor encourage in others, such stereotyped thinking or prejudiced attitudes.)

As for the concern sometimes expressed that an avowed homosexual would not be a proper model for young people, since such a rabbi might encourage some young people to become homosexuals, our response must once again be forthright. For one thing, since, as already indicated, one does not choose *to be* homosexual, a homosexual rabbi could not influence a person *to become* homosexual. Furthermore, if some men or women are helped, through the ministry of an avowed homosexual rabbi, to "come out of the closet" and live openly as the homosexuals they really are, this should not be deemed a negative but a positive. And as for the effect of a homosexual rabbi upon the heterosexual majority within that rabbi's congregation or community, it is to be hoped that such a rabbi can help deepen their understanding of the true nature of homosexuality, increase their sensitivity, and indeed encourage them to extend a hand of friendship and acceptance to those who are so often made to feel like outcasts.

---

124. This dual approach to Torah as human-yet-divine has clear implications for halakhic decision making on this issue of homosexuality in the contemporary situation. After all, in the development of the halakhic tradition, what had appeared to be clear and absolute Torah-commands sometimes—as social conditions changed or new knowledge became available—came to be interpreted to mean almost the opposite of what they had at first been understood to mean.

Many Jews find the notion—and certainly the existence—of gay-and-lesbian synagogues to be embarrassing and deplorable. They are right—but for the wrong reasons. The existence of such synagogues is embarrassing and deplorable because it reflects the perception of homosexuals—an accurate perception—that they are not welcome in "regular" congregations. Perhaps only when the phenomenon of a gay or lesbian rabbi serving a "straight" congregation has become accepted will the phenomenon of a separate gay-and-lesbian congregation no longer be necessary. For such an eventuality to come about, the Jewish community must engage in some serious and prayerful rethinking and in some bold and courageous action.

For example, the Torah-text clearly states that capital punishment is to be imposed for numerous offenses; in the course of time, however (perhaps because the very notion of capital punishment had become deemed inherently unjust or otherwise offensive), the command was almost "interpreted away." The Torah-text clearly states that debts are to be cancelled in the "seventh year of release"; in the course of time, however, when the new reality was that would-be borrowers could find no lenders, Hillel "found" that the Torah's command did not apply to debts owed to the court; he and his court therefore enacted the *takkanah* ("ordinance") of *prosbul,* through which all personal debts were transferred to the court. The Torah-text clearly states that the brother of a deceased man who left no issue is *obliged* to marry his sister-in-law in order to "raise up seed for his deceased brother," and if he declines to do so he is to be publicly disgraced in the ceremony of *halitzah;* in the Middle Ages this Torah-law was interpreted to mean that the brother-in-law *may not* marry his sister-in-law—but must nevertheless go through the procedure of disgrace-and-release. Numerous other examples could be cited.

Is it not therefore quite conceivable that recognized halakhic authorities may come to "find," concerning homosexual acts forbidden in the Torah, that though they are generally forbidden, for "constitutional" homosexuals they are permitted?

KAVVANOT AND PRAYERS

What does it mean to pray? Hershel Matt reflected often on this question. He described prayer as "the articulation of the awareness that one stands in the presence of the Living God." He lived a life of prayer, and saw prayer as "essential to the full flowering of the human personality, to the full development of the image of God."[125] He once wrote: "Of all the definitions of a human being, perhaps the most significant is that he is a praying animal."

Hershel always emphasized that true prayer requires *kavvanah*. This term has a rich tradition in rabbinic sources, Kabbalah and Hasidism. It is a multivalent word, which literally means "intention" or "direction" but connotes feeling, focused awareness and a meditative state of mind. Prayer with *kavvanah* cannot be rushed. Hershel encouraged whoever was leading the prayers to "pray slowly, distinctly, reverently.... When time is lacking, abbreviate rather than rush.... Better a little with *kavvanah* than much without *kavvanah*."

Gradually, Hershel developed a whole series of *kavvanot*. These are directions for the heart to follow, or what he called "bridges to prayer." They serve to introduce individual prayers in the *siddur*, giving people a sense of what the prayer is really about, helping them focus their attention on the upcoming words. Hershel read the *siddur* as poetry rather than prose.[126] His *kavvanot* sensitize one to the lyrical quality of prayer. They represent a fresh contribution to the resources of Jewish spirituality.

Printed here are two introductory pieces written by Hershel, followed by his *kavvanot* for *Shabbat* and weekday prayers and the High Holy Days, as well as several prayers he composed for various occasions.[127]

125. "The Goals of Teaching Jewish Prayer."
126. Ibid.
127. A number of the *kavvanot* originally appeared in Hershel Matt, *"Kavanot,"* *Rabbinical Assembly Program Notes* 3:1 (January 1967); idem, "Bridges to Prayer," *Pastoral Services* 7:2 (November 1976): 18-21; idem, "Creating *Kavanot," Response* 41-42 (13:1-2) (Fall-Winter 1982): 42-51; in *New Prayers for the High Holy Days* (Bridgeport, Connecticut: Media Judaica, 1971); in *Mahzor Hadash: The New Mahzor for Rosh Hashanah and Yom Kippur,* ed. Sidney Greenberg and Jonathan D. Levine (Bridgeport, Connecticut: The Prayer Book Press, Media Judaica, 1978), pp. 6, 244, 392, 453; in *Liturgy in Reconstructionism,* ed. Sidney H. Schwartz, *Raayonot* 3:2 (Spring 1983): 46; *Reconstructionist* 52:2 (October-November 1986): 18; and 53:1 (September 1987): 29.

CREATING *KAVVANOT*

No external device or series of devices can guarantee *kavvanah* (praying with concentration or intention). Yet certain steps can be taken that are likely to encourage *kavvanah* rather than hinder it. Much attention has been given to such matters (in communal worship) as decorum, responsive reading and chanting, unison reading and chanting, musical background and silent prayer. These are all important; all of them can be dealt with more creatively perhaps than heretofore. Not enough attention, however, has been given to the insertion, at numerous points in the service, of introductory comments to particular prayers. These introductory comments must not be explanatory, historical, didactic, informational—in a word, "adult educational"—or even interpretive in the sense of telling *about* what the prayer contains, for they would then be diversions from prayer, obstacles to prayer ("the rabbi talks too much"). No, these comments should be rather bridges to prayer, prayerful preparations for prayer; not directions to the congregation but directions to the heart.

They should be in the line of traditional *kavvanot* (meditative formulas designed to help people attain *kavvanah*). Needless to add, the comments before a given prayer should be varied from service to service, and there should be variation also in the choice of prayers on which to comment. The advantages of such an approach to leading *tefillah be-tzibbur* (communal prayer) are many. First, a balance is created between *keva* (fixed prayer) and *kavvanah*, between *keva* and *hiddush* (innovation). In fact, *kavvanah* implies *hiddush*. Second, we are forced to pause and let ourselves be confronted by the meaning of the words we know, while each time a different one or two of the countless meanings of a given prayer are brought to the fore. Third, in creating *kavvanot,* the need to be creative, contemporary, and relevant is not stifled, and yet the *matbe'a shel tefillah* (the required order of the prayers) is preserved. Fourth, we are guarded against the temptation of putting our own formulations on a par with the gems of the tradition, and fifth, we are guarded likewise against the risk of letting our fresh insight become routine. Finally, the *sheliah tzibbur* (prayer leader) becomes, in a revitalized sense, the congregation's delegate. He leads *in* prayer and *to* prayer, instead of "conducting a service."

Every leader of a service should try his or her hand at formulating *kavvanot;* and yet there is a genuine need for an anthology of *kavvanot*—a continuing anthology—to be drawn upon, adapted, reworked, and added to by each *sheliah tzibbur.* The following *kavvanot* are intended for use in three ways: 1) as preface to a particular prayer in the traditional order of the service—to aid in nurturing the mood of worship and to direct the worshiper's heart to one of the many faces of that particular prayer; 2) as an alternative version of that particular prayer; and 3) as a vehicle or trigger for moments of private meditation.

SUGGESTIONS FOR USING *KAVVANOT*

1. In any given service, not every prayer should be prefaced with a *kavvanah.*

2. From one service to another there should be variation as to which prayers should be so introduced.

3. Since a number of different *kavvanot* are provided for various prayers, there should be variation (perhaps rotation) among the *kavvanot* used for any given prayer from service to service.

4. *Kavvanot* may be used before either the Hebrew or the English recitation of a prayer.

5. If on occasion a particular *kavvanah* seems too lengthy—abbreviate!

6. If a page number in the *siddur* is to be announced, the announcement should be made *before* the *kavvanah* is read—so that the mood that will (hopefully) have been created through the *kavvanah* will not be broken by the page announcement.

7. *Kavvanot* need not be read by the Rabbi only; they can be read by the Cantor, by a congregational official on the *bimah,* by a worshiper who ascends the *bimah* for this purpose, or (if the sanctuary is not too large) by a worshiper rising at his place in the congregation.

8. Whoever reads the *kavvanah* should examine and rehearse it in advance.

9. *Kavvanot* should be read aloud only by those who can do so effectively, i.e., by those who, in addition to being able to articulate clearly and pronounce correctly, can personally enter into the words and are likely to convey to others at least some of what they have found.

10. If a particular *kavvanah* commends itself in some ways but does not seem quite adequate or "natural," or does not ring true to the one who will be reading it aloud—revise!

11. Some of the *kavvanot* lend themselves to reading by two or three or more persons as a choral reading, unisonal or antiphonal.

12. Some of the *kavvanot* can be chanted in recitative fashion.

13. The Rabbi and any others possessed of religious and aesthetic sensitivity, and of some degree of literary talent, should be encouraged to compose their own *kavvanot.*

KAVVANOT

On Entering the Synagogue

My God and God of my parents,
Purify my heart to worship You in honesty;
Open my lips, teach me what to say.

Let me understand where sinfully I have turned away,
     that I may now turn back to You.
Let me understand where unaware I have been blessed,
     that I may now give thanks to You.
Let me understand where I am still in need,
     that I may now ask help from You.
Hear my prayer, O God.
Send me not away empty from Your presence.

*

Teach me, O Living God, to long for You and look for You
As eagerly as I crave a bit of food, a sip of water.
Teach me to know that
Without You I am hungry, thirsty, poor, and all alone,
Without You life is vanity and confusion;
With You life makes sense and has a purpose,
With You I have plenty, need no more.

*

I have entered Your house, O God,
I who am unworthy to enter.
For who may sojourn in Your tabernacle?
Who may dwell upon Your holy mountain?
He who walks before You in innocence and integrity,
He who acts with perfect righteousness,
And speaks the truth even in his heart.

How then dare I enter?

Yet You are near to all who call to You in truth,
To all whose hearts are broken and contrite.

O cleanse me from all self-righteousness and conceit.
Teach me how in humility to speak to You,
And how to listen.

At the Beginning of *Shabbat* Services

Let all who have come here on this holy Sabbath eve—
For whatever reasons we have come—
Now pray
That He who commanded us to come
May take our rest
And make our rest into a rest of holiness.
May He take our words
And make our words into words of genuine worship.
That we may inherit, in full measure,
The Sabbath heritage of holiness.

Before *Lekhah Dodi*

On the sixth day of the week
When the sun begins to set,
Queen Sabbath, Bride of Israel,
Knocks at the door of every Jewish home,
Of every Jewish heart—
Waiting, hoping to be allowed to enter.

And if we welcome her,
Opening the door of our home and of our heart,
She comes in,
Bringing with her royal gifts:
Regal strength, sparkling gems, richest blessing.
She brings with her bridal gifts:
Joy and warmth, fragrant love, purity,
An extra soul.

Before *Barekhu*

Our Father in Heaven blesses us
In granting us, at every moment,
Benefits beyond count, beyond desert.
But how shall we bless Him?
By acknowledging His blessings.

*

How many blessings come to us
Each week, each day, each hour.
Indeed, at each and every moment of our lives.
Blessings beyond count,
Beyond our desert, they come to us.
Let us bless God
For blessing us so richly.

*

Let all of us who have been blessed
In this past week, in this past day,
Indeed, in this past hour—
And who of us has not been blessed—
Now bless God
From whom alone all blessings come.

*

Bend the knee, bow the head,
Incline the heart—
As we gratefully acknowledge
The countless blessings
That come to us each day,
From the hand
Of our Father-Mother who is in heaven.

*

Since we last gathered here
To praise God for our many blessings,
How many more we have received:
Continual blessings

Of food and drink,
Of family and friends,
Of health and healing;
Of being able to sleep, and dream,
And wake and breathe,
And walk and work,
And tire,
And sleep again, as night returns.

*

"A Jew is duty-bound
To utter a hundred blessings every day."

A hundred is too many, shall we say?
Or shall we rather say, A hundred is too few?

For "if our mouths were filled with song as the sea,
Our tongues with joyful praise as the multitude of its waves,
Our lips with adoration as the spacious firmament;
Were our eyes as radiant as the sun and the moon,
Our hands spread forth to heaven like the wings of eagles,
And our feet swift as hinds—

We would still be unable
To thank and bless Your name sufficiently, O Lord our God,
For even one measure
Of the thousands upon thousands of benefits
That you have granted to our ancestors and to us."

Before *Ha-Ma'ariv Aravim*

Not by mere chance have we lived through another day;
The days do not just pass.
It is God, Creator of the heavenly bodies,
Who causes days and nights and months and years to pass,
And allows us safely to pass through them.

*

The sun has set, and night has come.

Let us praise God
"Who by His mere word created the heavens,
And by the breath of His mouth, their whole array.
Fixed laws and times He set for them,
That they not deviate from their set task.
They rejoice and delight
To do the will of their Creator."

*

How good it is to know,
Each time the sun goes down,
That it will rise again,
And set again, and rise again,
With unfailing regularity,
In accordance with the will of the Creator,
From the very beginning—
Marking our passage
Through the weeks and months,
The seasons and the years.

As Scripture assures and reassures:
"So long as earth endures—
Seedtime and harvest, cold and heat,
Summer and winter, day and night,
Shall never cease."

Before *Ohev Ammo Yisra'el*

God so loved the world—
That He gave His Torah to the people Israel,
That through the Torah we might learn
The whole meaning and purpose of our life.

*

Laws, commandments, statutes, rules.
How burdensome they all would be—

Were it not that all these laws
Are Torah laws:
Signs and tokens of God's abundant love.

Pointing out the way to us,
Guiding us along the way,
Giving direction to our life,
Providing life with depth and meaning.

Burden?
Yes,
But blessed burden,
Burden far outweighed by blessing.

*

Without Torah,
Our wedding gift from God on high—

We would not see with Jewish eyes,
We would not hear with Jewish ears,
We would not think with Jewish mind,
We would not feel with Jewish heart.

Indeed as Jews we would not be.
For "Israel is a people
Only through and by and for—
Torah."

*

Many are the ways of seeking happiness,
And many are the kinds of happiness
That one can find.

Help us, O God, to seek and find
Our deepest happiness, our truest joy,

In Your Torah:

Studying its words,
Fulfilling its commands,
Absorbing its instruction,
Weaving its text into the texture of our lives.

*

Blessed is the One
Who, in the greatness of His love,
Singled out from among the peoples
The people Israel—
Giving us His Torah of truth.

She thus planted within us life everlasting,
And granted us a taste and glimpse of eternity,
Here and now.

*

How great is God's love for Israel!
In giving us Torah:

He has taken note of us,
Has spoken to us,
He has revealed His will for us.

She has expressed Her concern for us,
Shown Her care for us,
Graciously providing us
With guidance and direction,
And with light.

Torah illumines our world,
Disclosing to us the meaning of our life,
The purpose of our existence.

Before the *Shema*

Come now—
In the words of the *Shema*
Let us take upon ourselves anew
The blessed yoke of the Kingship of Heaven.

*

How blessed we are!
How happy is our portion,
How sweet our lot!
How blessed are we who at dawn and twilight,
Twice each day,
Can say in love *Shema Yisra'el*.

*

Touched by God's love for us,
We can love Him in return;
For we love with the love by which we are loved....

*

Oh, the blessed joy of knowing
That God calls to us,
And that we can hear and listen to His call,
Shema Yisra'el....

*

In the handwritten scroll of the Torah
The word *shema* of *Shema Yisra'el* ends with a capital *ayin*.
And the word *ehad* ends with a capital *dalet*.
Taken together
These two letters spell *ed,* meaning "witness."

Whenever we recite the *Shema,*
We bear witness to our awareness of God's presence;
We make acknowledgment of His unity;
We reaffirm His kingship;
We testify that He alone is our Master and our Lord.

*

There are many authorities
To whom we properly give our loyalty and obedience,
And there are many people whom we quite properly love.

But it is God alone, the one-and-only God,
Whom we are to accept as our *absolute* authority;
It is He alone
To whom we owe our *ultimate* loyalty;
And it is He alone
Whom we are bidden to love with *all* our heart,
With *all* our soul, with *all* our might.

*

From our earliest childhood
To the very last moment of our life—
And twice each day
Through all the intervening years—
The words of *Shema Yisra'el*
Are upon our lips:
Declaring that God is One and Only,
Unique,
And mysterious in His Oneness.

*

God is One,
The world He made is one,
And all humanity is intended to be one.

May the one true God
Unite our hearts in love and awe,
So that we band together,
All of us,
To do His will with undivided heart.

*

Why does the first portion of the *Shema*
(Calling us to love God and obey Him utterly)
Precede the second portion

257

(In which the consequences
Of our obedience or disobedience are told?)

It's all quite logical:

First we must take upon ourselves
The yoke of divine kingship,
Acknowledging God's right, in principle,
To bind us with commitment.
Only then can we proceed
To take upon ourselves
The yoke of the actual commands.

*

The second verse of the *Shema Yisra'el* in the *siddur*
(*Barukh shem*—Blessed be His glorious kingdom evermore)
Is not found in the actual Torah text,
Though all the other words of the *Shema* are there.
Why have these words been inserted
Into the *Shema* of the *siddur?*

To remind us—
Lest the very familiarity of the *Shema*
Make us forget—
That every time we say the *Shema*
We renew our allegiance to *Adonai,*
Our only God and Master,
Confirming our acceptance of Him alone as sovereign,
Pledging ourselves anew
To abide by His word and obey His command.

Before *Ga'al Yisra'el*

The same one God, *Ha-Shem,*
Who redeemed us from Egyptian bondage
Has renewed the redemption through the ages.

Ever and again She has delivered us
From the power of the enemy—
The enemy without and the enemy within—
Until this very day.

*

God miraculously redeemed our ancestors
At the Red Sea in days of old
And God renews the miracle of redemption
Each day ever since.

*

How many are the miracles
That You, O God, Have wrought on our behalf,
Through all the ages
Since You first delivered us from Egyptian bondage—
When the sea was split
And we escaped from the pursuing foe.

If enemies arise again,
Deliver us, again.

*

From that first moment of deliverance
At the shores of the Sea, in the days of Moses,
Till this present moment of deliverance,
As children of Israel
We chant the very same song of gratitude and wonderment:
Who is like You, God,
Who performs miracles on our behalf,
That we may be redeemed!

*

Not by mere accident
Have we survived our enemies' attempts
Throughout the ages to destroy us.

Nor by any laws of history

Can our survival
In the face of all the perils
That beset us be explained.
(If there *are* any laws of history,
We are the exceptions.)

Only by the miraculous,
Providential hand of God—
Who wants His people Israel to remain alive—
Can our survival be accounted for.

Who is like you, *Adonai:*
Doing wonders,
Working miracles without number!

Before *Hashkivenu*

Without God's gift of *shalom* we are in turmoil:
We go around in circles,
We don't know where to turn, or what to do.
We are overwhelmed and desperate.
But when we pause,
Allowing ourselves to be opened
To God's peace and grace and strength,
To Her healing presence,
It all seems different:
Now, anything can be borne.

*

When the blessing of *shalom* is lacking,
However much we have of other blessings,
Wealth or power, fame or family,
Even health—
These all appear as nothing.
But when *shalom* is present,
However little else we have
Somehow seems sufficient.

*

The word *shalom*—
How shall we translate it?

Shalom means "peace," of course,
But it means so much more as well:
Wholeness, fullness, and completion;
Integrity and perfection;
Healing, health, and harmony;
Utter tranquility;
Loving and being loved;
Consummation;
Forgiveness and reconciliation;
Totality of well-being.

And even all of these together
Do not spell out sufficiently
The meaning of *shalom*.

But though we cannot accurately translate
Or adequately define *shalom*,
We can experience it.

We can readily taste the sweetness of its presence,
The bitterness of its absence,
And the double blessing of *shalom* regained, restored.

*

Who is this Satan who always tempts us.
And attempts to rob us of *shalom?*

Satan is our evil inclination
That tempts us
To put our ultimate trust in something else
Or someone else than God.

And when that someone else or something else
Proves to be less than fully trustworthy
And not entirely dependable—

As always happens—
Our evil inclination tempts us
To yield to fear and to despair.

But when we put our trust in God
We need not fear, for God is near;
Satan is subdued, *shalom* restored.

*

When fears multiply and danger threatens;
When sickness comes, when death confronts us—
It is God's blessing of *shalom*
That sustains us and upholds us.
Lightening our burden, dispelling our worry,
Restoring our strength, renewing our hope—
Reviving us.

Before or After the *Amidah*

Hear my prayer, O God,
And turn me not away empty from Your presence.

*

Open my lips, O God,
And teach me how to praise You.

*

The needs of Your people, O God, are many;
Their own resources fall short.
May it be Your will to grant to each of us
What seems to be our need,
What seems to be our lack.
But what is good in Your own eyes—this do.

Before *Va-Yekhullu*

Who is it that hallows the Sabbath day
And makes it holy?

Surely it is God;
For He it is
Who from the very beginning (as Scripture says)
"Blessed the seventh day and made it holy."

Yet it is we no less than He
Who can make the Sabbath holy;
For He commanded (as Scripture says)
"Remember, observe, guard the Sabbath day
To keep it holy."

Thus He granted us the blessed, awesome power
To hallow this day or (God forbid) to profane it.

Yes, He waits for us to yield ourselves
To the holiness of the Seventh Day
Which He has hallowed—
And, by resting on it in holiness,
To confirm His original hallowing
And hallow it anew.

                    *

For six days
(Or was it six years or six decades,
Centuries or millennia,
Myriads or even millions of years?)
God worked on His creation
(Though His work was not laborious work;
He had but to command
And each thing came into being).

And then, when all had been completed,
Though not fatigued

(He alone never tires or wearies)
He "rested"—
Perhaps to teach that we must rest.

He blessed the seventh day,
Making it an unfailing fount of blessing
To all who, by observing it,
Open themselves to its blessing.

He declared the Sabbath holy, made it holy,
An endless source of holiness
To all who, by keeping it and guarding it,
Open themselves to its holiness.

*

"On the seventh day God completed the work of Creation."
But had not the work been completed already on the sixth?
No, the created world still lacked one crucial thing:
Shabbat,
The goal and purpose of it all.

Before *Kiddush*

What greater joy and blessing could there be
Than to be marked for holiness among the nations,
As *Shabbat* is marked for holiness among the days?

And yet—
What kind of holy vessels can we claim to be?
The holiness of the Sabbath is greater than we deserve.

Indeed, we don't deserve it, could not bear it,
Were it not for the extra soul
With which the Holy One endows His holy people Israel
On this holy Sabbath day.

In joy and yet in trembling
We ready ourselves for *Kiddush*.

*

Just to think:
God, who redeemed us from Egyptian bondage,
And revealed to us at Sinai His command
To observe the seventh day and keep it holy,

Had long before, so long before—
From the very time of the Creation—
Assigned this self-same seventh day
To be the holy Sabbath, day of rest.

And so
Each seventh day throughout our lives,
When we observe *Shabbat* and chant *Kiddush*,
We call to mind
These three crucial ways of God's involvement,
These three tokens of divine concern,
These three dimensions of God's love:
Creation, Revelation, and Redemption.

*

The cup of wine is our cup of joy:
Joy in the remembrance of Creation;
Joy in the remembrance of the Exodus from Egypt;
Joy in the remembrance of the Revelation at Mount Sinai—
When we were singled out
To receive Torah and *mitzvot,*
Including the command to keep the Sabbath holy.

Yes, the *Kiddush* cup is the cup of holiness
From which we sip in joy and trembling.

Before *Aleinu*

Ha-Shem is One, of course,
Sovereign over all the earth.
And yet—
Of what avail for Her to be the One,
When human beings worship many gods?
Of what avail for Him to be the King,
When human beings don't accept Him?
And yet—
The day will surely come
When all who dwell on earth will at last acknowledge
The sovereignty of the Holy One.
On that day at last
God will be truly One, and His name: One.

*

As Daniel refused to bow
Before King Darius the Mede;
As Mordechai refused to bow
Before the wicked Haman;
As Hannah's seven sons refused
Before the King Antiochus—

So may we be firm in faith,
Refusing to succumb to threat or bribe,
Coercion or temptation,
Of the self-deifying powers
That confront us and surround us.

For not to any human power
Does Israel bow and bend the knee,
But only to the King of Kings,
The Holy One, blessed be He.

Before *Ve-Shameru*

How strange it seems
That on a par with the command
To honor parents,
On a par with the command
To refrain from idolatry,
Murder, theft, and adultery—
Is the command to keep *Shabbat,*
Surprise command among the Ten Commandments.

In the eyes of the Commander, evidently,
Shabbat is as essential,
As crucial and fundamental to our well-being
As are all those others.

*

Shabbat is the recurring sign, weekly reminder,
Of the Creation of the Universe.

Those who observe *Shabbat*—
Pausing from their work, resting on this day
In joy and holiness—
Testify thereby to their belief in the Creator.

*

Just as circumcision is a crucial sign
Of the *berit,* the holy covenant
Between the Creator of the world and His people Israel—

So is *Shabbat* an equally crucial sign
Of that same covenant,
Binding together God and His holy people.

In keeping the *Shabbat*
We confirm the covenant.

*

"The children of Israel shall keep the Sabbath,"
And in keeping it
Shall themselves be kept and sustained.
For, "even more than Israel has observed the Sabbath,
The Sabbath has preserved Israel."

*

How many "sevens" there are in Holy Scripture:
The seventh year of release,
Sabbatical year, *shemittah* year,
In which the slaves went free,
And debts were cancelled, fields lay fallow.

The jubilee year, the fiftieth year,
When after seven cycles of seven years,
All land throughout the land of Israel
Reverted to the original family owners.

Seven branches in the gold menorah,
Seven days preceding circumcision.
Seven days of *Pesah*, season of *matzot*,
Seven weeks from *Pesah* till the feast of *Shavu'ot*,
Seven days to dwell in huts on the festival of *Sukkot*.

And most familiarly, most frequently recurring,
Most precious of all the biblical "sevens": *Shabbat*.

There must be something special about this number seven:
It is the symbol of wholeness and completion,
Fullness and perfection, consummation.
No wonder that in telling the story of Creation
The Torah text declares:
"In six days God made heaven and earth,
But on the seventh day He rested."

FOR THE HIGH HOLY DAYS

A READING FOR *SELIHOT*

If we tonight have once again
Begun to face the depth and vastness of our sin—
Keep us, O God, from sinking into helplessness and hopelessness,
Teach us, O God, to know
That when You granted us the power to sin,
You blessed us also with the power to repent.

We need not continue on in all our sinful ways:
We need not lie and cheat, deceive, pervert,
Slander and ridicule, hate and hurt,
Build ourselves up, tear others down,
(Tear ourselves down, build others up)
Desecrate and profane all that is holy—
Allowing our world, our life, to be a hell.

You have allowed us to share Your goal of righteousness and mercy;
You have allowed us to share Your qualities of justice and compassion.
You have given us the power to do good:
To help the poor, relieve the suffering,
Befriend the lonely, heal the sick,
Raise up the downtrodden, protect the weak,
Comfort the mourner, welcome the stranger,
Calm the troubled and the fearful,
Give hope to the discouraged—
To act, to work, to do that which is holy.

In this season of repentance,
Of confession of sin, of yearning for forgiveness,
Which we in awe of you, O God, this night have ushered in—
Help us, O Father, to turn,
Help us, O Mother, to change,
Help us to learn from You and from Your Torah
How to work and how to wait.
May we not presume to do that which is Yours to do,

May we not neglect to do that which is ours to do,
And may we not despair.

May both our working and our waiting,
Our acting and our trusting,
Serve to speed and not delay
The coming of the day
Of Your messianic deliverance and redemption.

Before *Rosh ha-Shanah* Eve Services

TO SEEK RENEWAL

On this night, O God, we have come into Your house,
To pray with our fellow Jews in Your sanctuary.

But if the heavens are merely Your throne,
If the earth is but Your footstool,

If the heaven of heavens cannot contain You,
How much less this house, built by mere human hands.

Yet, although Your dwelling place is *every* place,
And although You can be sought and found in *any* place,

It is to *this* place that we come most confidently—
To seek renewal in Your purifying presence.

Before *Teki'at ha-Shofar*

The following twenty-four formulations of the meaning of *teki'at ha-shofar* may be used—one each day—on the twenty-four weekdays in *Elul* when the *shofar* is sounded. They may also be used on *Rosh ha-Shanah* or after *Ne'ilah,* either recited (one or more at a time) by the Rabbi (or some other person) or read (after rearrangement) as a responsive reading.

May the sound of the *shofar*

1. shatter our complacency—revealing the corruption of our situation, and summoning us, with God's help, to correct it.
2. penetrate into our inmost being and cause us to turn back to our Father in Heaven.
3. renew our trust in the promise of the *mashiah*—and inspire us to work toward hastening (and not, God forbid, delaying) the day of his coming.
4. alert us to the danger of the enemy, and remind us who the enemy really is.
5. renew our loyalty to the true King, and strengthen us to withhold obedience from all usurpers.
6. break the hold of our evil temptation, and free us to bend our will to the service of the Holy One.
7. summon us to sacrificial service, and stir us to respond, in love and in obedience, with Abraham's response: "Here I am."
8. reveal to us the brokenness of our existence, and open us to the mending power of God's love.
9. awaken us to the enormity of our sin, and to the vastness of God's mercy for those who truly repent.
10. recall to us the moment at Sinai, and enable us again to pledge that "all that God has spoken we will do and obey."
11. summon us to dethrone all false gods, and restore us to the true worship of Heaven.
12. renew our hope for the ingathering of our exiles, when Israel will be restored and all humankind redeemed.
13. remind us that we stand in judgment before the one true Judge, who is mindful of our deeds—and of our needs.

14. make us tremble at the right moment, for the right reason, in the right spirit, before the right one: the righteous Judge.
15. herald the triumph of right over wrong, of good over evil, of peace over war, of love over hate, of blessing over curse, of life over death.
16. teach us what to remember and what to forget, how to work and how to wait.
17. herald the fall of all citadels of evil and the conversion of enemies into friends.
18. shatter the shackles of all human bondage and summon all slaves to go free.
19. teach us when to be afraid and when not to be afraid.
20. awaken us from our lethargy and arouse us to do what must be done.
21. renew our trust in God's promise to resurrect the dead: for judgment and chastisement, for cleansing and refining, and for life eternal.
22. alert us to the shortness of the day, the magnitude of the task, and the abundance of resources that God makes available to us for the performance of His will.
23. strengthen us to make our will accord with God's own will, no matter what the cost.
24. become our jubilant shout of joy and gratitude for the promised redemption.

Blessed are those who know the meaning of the sound of the *shofar!*

THE SOUND OF THE *SHOFAR*

May the sound of the *shofar* shatter our complacency
And make us conscious of the corruptions in our lives.

> May the sound of the *shofar* penetrate our souls,
> And cause us to turn to our Father in Heaven.

May the sound of the *shofar* break the bonds of our enslavement to the evil impulse,
And enable us to serve God with a whole heart.

> May the sound of the *shofar* renew our loyalty to the one true King
> And strengthen our determination to defy the false gods.

May the sound of the *shofar* awaken us to the enormity of our sins,
And the vastness of God's mercy for those who truly repent.

> May the sound of the *shofar* summon us to service
> And stir us to respond, as did Abraham, "Here am I."

May the sound of the *shofar* recall the moment
When we stood at Mount Sinai and uttered the promise:
"All that God has spoken, we will do and obey."

> May the sound of the *shofar* recall the promise of the ingathering
> of the exiles,
> And stir within us renewed devotion to the land of Israel.

May the sound of the *shofar* recall the vision of the prophets,
Of the day when all people will live in peace.

> May the sound of the *shofar* awaken us to the flight of time,
> And summon us to spend our days with purpose.

May the sound of the *shofar* remind us that it is time to
"Proclaim liberty throughout the land
To all the inhabitants thereof."

May the sound of the *shofar* become our jubilant shout of joy
On the day of the promised, long-awaited redemption.

May the sound of the *shofar* enter our hearts:
For blessed is the people that hearkens to its call.

THE PROGRESSION OF TRUE REPENTANCE

What does it mean to repent?
This is what it means to repent:
To make inward acknowledgment of my sin,
To be truly heartbroken over my sin,
To be deeply ashamed of my sin,
To make open confession of my sin,
To make full restitution for my sin,
To seek reconciliation with others for my sin,
To resolve firmly not to duplicate my sin,
To ask divine aid in avoiding such duplication,
To beg God's forgiveness for my sin,
To find the burden of my sin now removed,
To know the comfort of God's pardon and the sweetness of atonement,
To be tempted to repeat the same sin—but to overcome, with God's help,
        such repetition,
To find it now more difficult to sin than not to sin.
That is what it means to repent.

HOW CAN I REPENT?

How many moments of despair we have at the enormity of our sin!

> And how many moments of doubt over the possibility of forgiveness!

But we are not alone in our sin, in our despair, and in our doubt;

> We have this congregation of our fellow Jews, we have each other.

Together let us delve into our Torah tradition, and seek there for some answers to our questionings.

> How can I repent? My deeds are so outrageous. How dare I come into the holy presence of God?

"When Israel says: 'How can I repent? With what face can we come into God's presence? Have we not provoked Him to wrath and outraged Him?'—God replies: 'When you come to Me, is it not to your Father in Heaven that you are coming?'"

> How can I repent? My sins have made me filthy.

"As soiled garments can be cleansed, so Israel—though they have sinned— can turn in repentance to God."

> How can I repent? With what shall I come when I come before God? Can I bring anything worth bringing? I am like damaged goods, defective merchandise.

Rabbi Alexander said: "With mortal humans, to use broken vessels is a disgrace; but with God it is otherwise, for true service to Him *consists* of broken vessels, as it is said: 'God is near to the brokenhearted, and the contrite in spirit He does save.'"

> How can I repent? I am desperately lonely in my sin. No one sees and no one hears.

"If you repent, I will accept you and judge you favorably. The gates of Heaven are open and I am listening; I am looking out the windows, peering through the crevices."

> How can I repent? Who ever sinned as I have sinned and was forgiven?

Adam said: "Master of the World! Remove my sin from me and accept my repentance, so that all generations may learn that there is such a thing as repentance."

> How can I repent? My hatred makes me feel like a murderer.

God says: "I accepted the repentance of Cain; shall I not accept your repentance?"

> How can I repent? My wantonness makes me feel like an adulterer.

"Just as I received David, King of Israel, when he repented after committing such a grievous sin, so—if you repent—will I receive you."

> How can I repent? I have been a worshiper of false gods.

"When the angels say to God: 'Is there repentance for such a wicked one as King Menasseh, who set up an idol in Your holy Temple?' God answers: 'If I am not willing to accept him in repentance, I shall be barring the door in the face of all penitents.'"

> How can I repent? My sins are so vast that I do not know where to begin.

Says the Blessed Holy One: "Make an opening of repentance as narrow as a needle's eye, and I will open gates for you through which even wagons and coaches could pass."

> How can I repent? I am an inveterate sinner who can never change.

God says to Israel: "Repent during these Ten Days—and I will make of you a genuinely new creation."

How can I repent? I have strayed too far. I am too far gone.

"A king had a son who had wandered from his father a distance of one hundred days' journey. His friends said to him: 'Return to your father.' But he said: 'I cannot; it is too far.' Then his father sent a message saying: 'Return as far as you can, and I will come the rest of the way.'"

How can I repent? By now it is too late.

"Even till one's dying day You wait for him—perhaps he will repent; and if he does, immediately You accept him."

HOW GREAT IS REPENTANCE!

How great is the *need* for repentance:

> "When God drew His plan for the world, He saw that it could not endure—until He created repentance!"

How great is the *chance* for repentance:

> "As the sea is always accessible, so is the hand of the Blessed Holy One always open to receive the penitent!"

How great is the *promise* of repentance:

> "Let no one say, 'I have sinned, there is no hope for me.' Let him but put his confidence in the Blessed Holy One, who rejects none of His creatures!"

How great is the *power* of repentance:

> "No matter how many wicked deeds are charged against a person—even if he has piled up a hundred sins—if he repents, God accounts it as if he had not even sinned!"

How great is the *efficacy* of repentance:

> "Though your sins be like scarlet, they shall become white as snow!"

How great is the *force* of repentance:

> "As soon as a person decides in his heart upon repentance, it instantly rises above the seventh heaven to the throne of God!"

How great is the *merit* of repentance:

> "The place which the penitent occupy even the perfectly righteous cannot occupy!"

How great is the *reward* for repentance:

> "If all Israel would repent for but one day, they would be redeemed at once and Messiah, son of David, would come immediately!"

How great is the *value* of repentance:

> "Better is one hour of repentance and good deeds in this world than the whole life of the world-to-come!"

How great is the *blessing* of repentance:

> "There is nothing greater than repentance!"

On *Rosh ha-Shanah*

TASHLIKH

Standing by the water,
Emptying our pockets of the remaining crumbs of sin,
We turn to You, O God,
Creator of heaven and earth, Creator of the water.
We pour out like water the confession of our sin.
Hear our prayer, and
> "*Tashlikh*, cast all our sins
> into the ocean's depths."

As You appeared to grieving, exiled Hagar
(Who, in desperation,
Had cast her thirsting child under the bushes)
And assured her at the well of water
That You, the Living God, look mercifully upon the afflicted—
Look upon us in our affliction, and
> "*Tashlikh*, cast all our sins
> into the ocean's depths."

As Abraham and Isaac, on their way to Mount Moriah,
Confronted by an impassable river
(The guise that Satan took
To deter them from fulfilling the command of Your dread test),
Marched boldly into the water—
So strengthen our faith and trust,
That we may pass whatever test You set for us, and
> "*Tashlikh*, cast all our sins
> into the ocean's depths."

As You sustained our people Israel, Your people Israel,
With the never-failing well of water
That accompanied them (through Miriam's merit)
In their desert wanderings—
So save us and sustain us with your living water, and
> "*Tashlikh*, cast all our sins
> into the ocean's depths."

As fish in water are ever in danger
Of being caught and then devoured,
So are we in peril constantly.
We turn to You, our only sure protection.
Shelter us, and
> "*Tashlikh*, cast all our sins
> into the ocean's depths."

As in days of yore
A king was crowned at river's edge,
So too do we at water's edge renew Your coronation,
O Sovereign of the Universe,
And take upon ourselves anew
The blessed yoke of Your sovereignty.
Accept us as Your loyal servants, and
> "*Tashlikh*, cast all our sins
> into the ocean's depths."

As You promised through Your prophet Ezekiel
To sprinkle upon the people Israel
Your pure and purifying water,
Do so now, we pray,
As we turn our hearts in penitence to You, and
> "*Tashlikh*, cast all our sins
> into the ocean's depths."

Let these waters be a token of Your covenant promise:
"As I swore that Noah's waters
Never again would flood the earth,
So I swear that I will not be angry with you or rebuke you.
For though the mountains may move and the hills be shaken,
My steadfast love shall never move from you,
Nor My covenant of *shalom* be shaken,
Says *Ha-Shem,* your Compassionate One."
So
> "*Tashlikh*, cast all our sins
> into the ocean's depths."

Before *Kol Nidrei*

HOW CAN WE ENTER?

On this sacred night, O God, we have entered Your house—
We who are unworthy to enter.

> For who may sojourn in Your sanctuary?
> Who may dwell upon Your holy mountain?

They who walk before You in innocence and integrity,
Who act with perfect righteousness,
And speak the truth even in their hearts.

> How, then, dare we enter Your house, O God,
> Knowing that our failings are so many?

We come strengthened by the assuring promise:
"God is near to all who call upon Him,
To all who call upon Him in truth."

> O cleanse us of all self-righteousness and conceit;
> Teach us to speak to You in humility and in truth;
> And teach us, O God, to listen.

Before the Thirteen Attributes

Who has ever lived who did not sin?
Is there any mortal untainted by iniquity?

> No one is free of all transgression;
> All, therefore, stand in need of God's forgiveness.

Our ancestors sinned at the very foot of Sinai,
Where the command of God had just been proclaimed.

> Though they had pledged "We will do, we will obey,"
> They soon broke their promise of loyalty to God.

Faithlessly, they broke the commandments of God;
They fashioned and worshiped a calf of gold.

> How wondrous then was God's compassion;
> For He did not destroy the rebellious people.

He subdued His wrath and forgave our ancestors,
Revealing the thirteen aspects of His mercy.

> Now we, O God, come before You in contrition,
> Recalling those same attributes of Your compassion.

As You had mercy upon our ancestors,
Have mercy also upon us, we pray;
For we, O God, have also sinned.

> We too forsake and break our pledge;
> We too worship the work of our own hands;
> We too make of gold a god;
> We too cast off the Torah's yoke.

Show compassion, O God; forgive our sins;
For we, like our ancestors, need Your pardon.

Before *Ashamnu*

When we confess our sins, we confess from *alef* to *tav*, through all the letters of the *alef-bet*.

> For when we call to mind our sinful acts, and add to them our sinful words, and add to them our sinful thoughts—our sins are found to be too numerous to count, too numerous to list.

Accept then, O God, this single alphabetical enumeration of our sins.

> May this *alef-bet* confessional be considered in Your eyes as full and adequate confession of our manifold transgressions.

*

When we confess our sins, we confess them in the plural, not in the singular—concluding each verb of sin with *nu* not *ti,* "we" not "I."

> For we come before You, God, not as isolated individuals, but as the covenant people Israel.

Bound together in a solidarity of sin.

> Bound together in a solidarity of confession.

Often we have sinned together with our fellow Jews:

> Together violating Your commandments, together desecrating the holiness of Your name.

And even when the overt sin committed was our brother's act and not our own, we confess our involvement in his sin.

> For often we have failed to strengthen our brother, sustain our brother, guide our brother on the path of right—or warn or guard him from the path of sin.

Whether by act of commission or by omission, God, we acknowledge our complicity in our brother's sin.

Bound together in confession of our common guilt, may we be bound together in the shared blessing of Your forgiveness.

Before *Al Het*

"Have we not all one Father? Has not one God created us? Why then do we deal treacherously everyone against his brother?"

> O God, united in confession, we acknowledge our solidarity of guilt. Our Father and Creator, we have sinned against You by mistreating Your children—forgetting that though they are of different color or class or status, they are our brothers and sisters.

We have sinned against You by excluding our sisters from our jobs and clubs, from our neighborhoods and homes.

> We have sinned against You by neglecting our brothers' poverty— and thus perpetuating it.

We have sinned against You by shutting our eyes to our sisters' sickness and suffering and pain.

> We have sinned against You by closing our ears to our brothers' cry of anguish.

We have sinned against You by aggrandizing ourselves at our sisters' expense—through deceit and trickery, through lies and subterfuge.

> We have sinned against You by shaming and degrading our own brothers—by remaining untouched by their shame and degradation.

We have sinned against You by enacting unjust laws against our brothers—and administering just laws unjustly.

> We have sinned against You by amassing power for ourselves— and using it to suppress our sisters.

We have sinned against You by taking the law into our own hands— committing violence against our brothers and inciting them to violence.

We have sinned against You by deploring violence while provoking violence.

We have sinned against You by succumbing to the fear within ourselves and by fomenting fear in others.

We have sinned against You by hatred of our sisters—and by fanning the flames of hatred.

We have sinned against You by perverting the truth, spreading false rumors, perpetuating stereotypes.

We have sinned against You by offering to our suffering brothers smooth words, glib promises, crocodile tears, token deeds, and superficial remedies—always too little and too late.

We have sinned against You by separating ourselves from our sisters, separating our brothers from ourselves—thus separating ourselves from You.

For all these sins against our sisters and brothers, we are appalled and ashamed—and we beg Your forgiveness, O God. We share in the common guilt, we share in penitence; may we share in Your forgiveness. Amen.

PRAYER FOR A *BAR* OR *BAT MITZVAH*

O God, here I stand in the presence of the Torah, and in the presence of this congregation in Israel, on the *Shabbat* of my *bat mitzvah*.

Put the desire into my heart, O God, to love Your Torah and to study Your Word which it contains—so that I may always learn from You: what to think, what to say, and what to do.

Let me never forget that I am a Jew, a child of Your covenant, born into the community of Israel, which has been called by You to be a kingdom of priests and a holy nation.

Purify my heart, O God, and grant me strength of will, to serve You faithfully—so that I may ever act toward my fellow human beings in justice and in love. Thus will I bring joy to my dear ones, honor to the people Israel, and glory to Your holy name. Amen.

WORDS OF PRAYER ON A WEDDING ANNIVERSARY

We turn to You, O God, in gratitude for our married love;
      touch our heart, we pray, with Your own.
Teach us to know that on this day and every day
      we stand in Your very presence, fully exposed to Your gaze.
Grant us the faith and strength to remove all tarnish
      from our love, renewing it as of old. Amen.

*

Renew our love this day, O God.
Forgive us for profaning the holiness of love
whether by acts of cruelty done
or acts of tenderness left undone.
Purify our hearts,
that we may become ever more sensitive
to each other's needs
and to Your will.

The following serves as conclusion for each of the above:

Praised are You, O God, Ruler of the Universe,
who has kept us in life, and sustained us
and enabled us to reach this moment.

The preceding "Words of Prayer" were sent by Hershel Matt to couples on their wedding anniversary along with a note of greeting, such as the following:

May God allow your love to grow ever deeper during the months and years to come—and may your love for each other strengthen you also in your love for God.

What's really so special about a wedding anniversary?
What's special is that on this day you pause to remember what on other

days perhaps you forget: the wonder and the privilege, the blessing and the gift, the holiness and awesomeness—of married love.

May this day serve to renew the holy covenant of your marriage—and provide a fresh awareness of the blessings God makes possible through the love of man and woman.

AT THE GRAVE OF A BELOVED

O God of consolation, be with me as I stand in sorrow at this grave.

O You who have taken back what I thought belonged to me, I turn to You now for renewed strength and faith. Help me to be grateful for the life of this beloved ＿＿＿. Help me to live on in (his) (her) absence, making my thoughts and words and deeds into a holy monument to (his) (her) memory.

Let my visit of reverence this day teach me anew that not how long we live but how we live is what You care for. Purify my heart to work and wait for the coming of that day when You will make clear to us the full meaning of our life and death. In You, O Lord, I put my trust.

HOW GOD RESPONDS

Were we the first to call to God in prayer,
We might well despair of receiving any answer—
For who are we
To come before the Sovereign One on high?

But we are not the first to call to God in prayer;
In every generation Jews have called.
They called to God
In time of need, in time of trouble,
In loneliness and bereavement,
In despair and desperation—
And found that they were answered!
Will not the One who answered them
Now answer us?

Whenever we turn to God in prayer
We can count on being answered;
But the response comes in a variety of ways:

Sometimes God responds
By giving us what we ask for,
And sometimes by helping us understand
That our request does not reflect our genuine need.

Sometimes He responds by helping us see
That the fulfillment of our request
Does not depend upon Him alone
But upon us as well;
And sometimes by renewing our will to do
That which is ours to do.

Sometimes She responds by giving us strength
To change what can be changed;
And sometimes by giving us courage
To accept what can't.

Sometimes He responds by enabling us to discover
Ample blessing in what we already have;
And sometimes by enabling us to find
That we even have enough to share with others.

Sometimes She responds to our questions and our doubts
By providing us with answers;
And sometimes by reassuring us that the answers,
Though not revealed to us,
Are known to Her.

Yes, the answers to our prayers come in many different ways;
But always God responds.

BIBLIOGRAPHY OF THE WRITINGS OF RABBI HERSHEL JONAH MATT

"*Siddur Hadash*" (review of Reconstructionist Sabbath Prayer Book), *Niv* 7:4 (May-June 1945): 15-16.

"*Ha-Halutziyyut ve-ha-No'ar ha-'Ivri ba-Amerikah,*" *Niv* 8:1 (September-October 1945): 8-10.

"Politics in the Pulpit," *Hebrew Union College Monthly,* Hanukkah 1946.

"A Life of Principle and Action" (memorial appreciation of Judah L. Magnes), *Tidings* 5:1 (February 1949).

"A Rabbi Looks at Christianity," *The New Hampshire Churchman,* March 1949.

"The Bar Mitzvah Treasury, ed. Azriel Eisenberg" (review), *Synagogue School* 10:4 (April 1953).

"What Shall a Son Say of His Rabbi-Father?" (eulogy for Rabbi C. David Matt), in *The Collected Poems of Rabbi C. David Matt,* ed. Milton Nevins (Philadelphia: The West Philadelphia Jewish Community Center, 1953), pp. 145-49.

"*Apikursut,*" *Approach* 1 (1955).

"*Kashrut* in Conservative Judaism," *Conservative Judaism* 12:1 (Fall 1957): 34-38.

"Synagogue Committees," *Conservative Judaism* 13:4 (Summer 1959): 27-34.

"Service for *Pidyon ha-Ben,*" *Rabbinical Assembly Program Notes* 1:2 (November 1963).

"Circumcision," *Rabbinical Assembly Program Notes* 1:2 (November 1963). (Reprinted under the title "Circumcision: *Brit,*" *Jewish Heritage* 8:3 [Winter 1965-66].)

"Jewish Commitment," *Rabbinical Assembly Program Notes* 1:2 (November 1963).

"Miracle and *Berakhah,*" *Rabbinical Assembly Proceedings* 27 (1963): 205-207.

"Miracle and *Berakhah:* How Shall We Approach the Miracles of the Bible?," *Synagogue School* 22:3 (Spring 1964): 6-13. (Reprinted in *What Is the Answer?,* ed. Stuart A. Gertman [Union of American Hebrew Congregations, 1971], pp. 164-69.)

"Planning Your *Seder,*" *Rabbinical Assembly Program Notes* (February 1964).

"The Fringed Garment: *Tzitzit,*" *Jewish Heritage* 8:3 (Winter 1965-66).

"Why Keep Kosher?," *Women's League Outlook* 36:3 (March 1966).

"The State of Jewish Belief," *Commentary* 42:2 (August 1966): 117-20. (Reprinted in *The Condition of Jewish Belief* [New York: Macmillan, 1967], pp. 146-54; and, in part, under the title "Judaism and Christianity," *The Sign* 46:11 [June 1967].)

"*Kavanot,*" *Rabbinical Assembly Program Notes* 3:1 (January 1967). (Reprinted under the title "Bridges to Prayer," *Pastoral Services* 7:2 [November 1976]: 18-21.)

"*Bat Mitzvah's* Prayer, Prayer for Her Parents," *Rabbinical Assembly Program Notes* 3:1 (January 1967).

"Prayer on Entering the Armed Services," *The Jewish Chaplain* 10 (n.s.) (March 1967).

"Dogmas in Judaism," *The American Rabbi* 2:7 (March 1967): 26-30.

"As Your Son Becomes *Bar Mitzvah,*" *The Torch* 26:4 (Winter 1967-68).

"A Jewish Approach to Sex Education," *Your Child* 1:3 (Spring 1968): 14-22. (Reprinted in *Pedagogic Reporter* 20:1 [September 1968]; under the title "Education sexuelle et Judaisme," *Hamoré* 12/46 [January 1969]; and, in part, under the title "Sex and Sexuality: Introduction," in *The Second Jewish Catalog,* ed. Sharon and Michael Strassfeld [Philadelphia: Jewish Publication Society, 1976], pp. 91-94.)

"An Outline of Jewish Eschatology," *Judaism* 17:2 (Spring 1968): 186-96. (Reprinted under the title "The Two Worlds," *Here and Now* 5:4 [April 1968]: 14-17.)

"Synagogue and Covenant People," *Conservative Judaism* 23:1 (Fall 1968): 1-11.

"Current Experiments in Liturgy," *Rabbinical Assembly Proceedings* 32 (1968): 26-29.

"Call to Redeemed Life," *The Recorder* (Metuchen, New Jersey), April 2, 1969.

"The Sound of the *Shofar,*" in *New Prayers for the High Holy Days,* Bridgeport, Connecticut: Media Judaica, 1971. (Reprinted in several publications of Media Judaica, including *Mahzor Hadash: The New Mahzor for Rosh Hashanah and Yom Kippur,* ed. Sidney Greenberg and Jonathan D. Levine [Bridgeport, Connecticut: The Prayer Book Press, Media Judaica, 1978], p. 244.)

"A Ladder of Observance," in *The Sabbath,* ed. Samuel H. Dresner (New York: Burning Book Press, 1970), pp. 80-84.

"Man's Choice and God's Design," *Judaism* 21:2 (Spring 1972): 211-21.

"Tallit" (portions), in *The Jewish Catalog,* ed. Richard Siegel, Michael Strassfeld and Sharon Strassfeld (Philadelphia: Jewish Publication Society, 1973), pp. 51-57.

"The Goals of Teaching Jewish Prayer," *Synagogue School* 31:3-4 (Summer 1973): 4-11.

"What Does It Mean to Believe in God?," *Theology Today* 30:3 (October 1973): 256-65.

"Should Christmas Mean Anything to Jews?," *Jewish Digest* 19:3 (December 1973): 7-9.

"A Jewish Approach to the Mid-East Conflict," *Peace Action* 13:9 (Princeton, NJ: Fellowship of Reconciliation, December 1973).

"What Will You Have?," *Achshav* 16:3 (Spring 1974). (Reprinted in *Your Child* 8:3 [March 1975]: 2-4.)

"Not Every Mysticism Is a Jewish Mysticism," *Sh'ma* 4/74 (May 17, 1974): 110-11.

"Rite and Ritual," *Rabbinical Assembly Proceedings* 36 (1974): 177-80.

"How Shall a Believing Jew View Christianity?," *Judaism* 24:4 (Fall 1975): 391-405. (Reprinted in *Princeton Seminary Bulletin* 57:3 (Winter 1976.)

"Acknowledging the King: The You and He, the They and We, of *Aleinu,"* *Conservative Judaism* 30:2 (Winter 1976): 68-77.

"The People Israel and the Peoples of the World As Reflected in the Jewish Prayer Book," *Face to Face* 2 (Summer-Fall 1976): 11-13.

"Miracles and Modern Jews," *United Synagogue Review* 29:3 (April 1977): 8-9, 28.

"To Seek Renewal," "The Sound of the *Shofar,"* "How Can We Enter?," "Prelude to the Thirteen Attributes," in *Mahzor Hadash: The New Mahzor for Rosh Hashanah and Yom Kippur,* ed. Sidney Greenberg and Jonathan D. Levine (Bridgeport, Connecticut: The Prayer Book Press, Media Judaica, 1977), pp. 6, 244, 392, 453.

"Will Herberg: A Tribute," *Conservative Judaism* 31:2 (Winter 1977): 5-14.

"Guiding Principles and Basic Policies for the Ideal Congregation," *Beineinu* 8:4 (June 1978): 1-4.

"Sin, Crime, Sickness, or Alternative Life Style?: A Jewish Approach to Homosexuality," *Judaism* 27:1 (Winter 1978): 13-24. (Reprinted in *Homosexuality and Ethics,* ed. Edward Batchelor, Jr. [New York: Pilgrim Press, 1980], pp. 114-124.)

"On Transferring" (Suggestions for *Shabbat* Observance), in *The Third Jewish Catalog,* ed. Sharon and Michael Strassfeld (Philadelphia: Jewish Publication Society, 1980), pp. 129-131.

"Is There—and Should There Be—a Jewish Vote?," *Agenda* 6 (October-November 1980).

"But Others Say about Homosexuality," *Sh'ma* 11/203 (December 10, 1980): 21.

"Talking with Our Children about God," in *The Jewish Family Book,* ed. Sharon Strassfeld and Kathy Green (New York: Bantam Books, 1981), pp. 262-74.

"Covering My Jewish Head," *The Jewish Spectator* 46:4 (Winter 1981): 17-19.

"Creating *Kavanot,*" *Response* 41-42 (13:1-2) (Fall-Winter 1982): 42-51

"A Religious and Moral Approach to War," *Menorah* 3:11-12 (January-February 1983).

"*Kavanot,*" in *Liturgy in Reconstructionism,* ed. Sidney H. Schwartz, *Raayonot* 3:2 (Spring 1983): 46.

"A Call for Compassion," *Judaism* 32:4 (Fall 1983): 430-32.

"Taking the First Step of *Teshuvah,*" *Sh'ma* 14/277 (September 21, 1984): 134-35.

"The Measure of Our Freedom (Hardening of the Heart)," *National Havurah Committee Syndicate,* January 10, 1986. (Reprinted under the title "The Ten Plagues Raises Questions," *The Jewish Star,* January 10, 1986, p. 10.)

"Determining Our Duty despite Differences," *Sh'ma* 16/314 (May 16, 1986): 106-108.

"*Tashlikh,*" *Reconstructionist* 52:2 (October-November 1986): 18.

"Fading Image of God? Theological Reflections of a Nursing-Home Chaplain," *Judaism* 36:1 (Winter 1987): 75-83.

"Homosexual Rabbis?," *Conservative Judaism* 39:3 (Spring 1987): 29-33.

"A Reading for *Selihot,*" *Reconstructionist* 53:1 (September 1987): 29.